MADAM ARBITRATOR

Praise for

Madam Arbitrator

Madam Arbitrator is the engaging and inspiring memoir of a teacher and lawyer who combined compassion, fairmindedness, and a keen sense of what is just and true. The story of her experiences as a child raised by a single parent, her brief career as a teacher of foreign languages, and her remarkable success as a lawyer and arbitrator in a field where the "men's club" reigned supreme is a testament to what wise choices and determination can achieve. Her story is an antidote to the facile cynicism often expressed about lawyers. Read Madame Arbitrator *to be reminded that laws and contracts can indeed protect individuals and create a just society and that one person can make a difference.*

—Brian C. Jones, Professor Emeritus,
Wartburg College

MADAM
ARBITRATOR

Working Toward Social Equality
and Employment Justice

S ANDRA S MITH G ANGLE , J.D.

LUMINARE PRESS
WWW.LUMINAREPRESS.COM

Printed in the United States of America

Cover Design by Melissa K. Thomas

Luminare Press
442 Charnelton St.
Eugene, OR 97401
www.luminarepress.com

LCCN: 2020903812
ISBN: 978-1-64388-334-2

*To my mother, Irene Powers Smith, who taught me to
follow my dreams and never accept second-best;*

*To my uncle, Rev. Dr. Francis J. Powers, CSV,
who guided my spirituality and vision for justice;*

*To my husband and life partner, Gene Gangle,
whose undying faith in me has been my source of stability;*

*To my children, Melanie and Rocco,
who inspired me to carry the torch of social justice; and*

*To my brother, Douglas K. Smith,
whose voice of reality gave me the courage
to overcome all obstacles.*

TABLE OF CONTENTS

Foreword

MADAM ARBITRATOR PROVIDES KEEN INSIGHT INTO the personal and professional life of Sandra Smith Gangle, one of the Pacific Northwest's most accomplished labor arbitrators. Interest in this career retrospective will be predictably high among labor historians, law professors, and social scientists. But advocates for labor and management— anyone responsible for winnowing lists of proposed labor arbitrators—are certain to consider *Madam Arbitrator* as essential reading for its candid review of modern principles of ethical arbitral decision-making for today's workplace.

The signposts of Ms. Gangle's professional life pointed with remarkable clarity from her youngest days in the direction of neutral dispute resolution. Two indicators, in particular, are significant parts of her story.

First, as a young girl, Ms. Gangle admired the legal skills of a talented Massachusetts lawyer who helped her family through a painful dissolution of marriage and, later, with a serious automobile accident tort claim. The accident case involved a jury trial that produced a successful outcome for Ms. Gangle's family. She saw firsthand how a talented lawyer could change lives for the better.

Second, during law school in Oregon, Ms. Gangle was mentored by Professor Carlton J. Snow. Professor Snow was a revered law teacher at Willamette University College of Law; he also enjoyed a national reputation as a labor arbitrator. Snow's lessons—hard work, adherence to ethical principles, and strict neutrality—demonstrated to Ms. Gangle what it would take to pursue a career as a lawyer and labor arbitrator.

Launching a legal career, however, was no simple task. She declined to join a law firm and, against the advice of her brother, a practicing lawyer, she chose instead to open her own law practice. She candidly reports the good and the bad of that choice. Indeed, there were times when a slight shift of fate could have cost her everything.

Ms. Gangle's earliest experiences in the world of labor arbitration opened her eyes to a stark reality: state and federal protections against sex discrimination in the workplace had no practical application to a woman serving as an arbitrator. The familiar but secretive process of striking names from a list of proposed arbitrators could easily result in the removal of a female arbitrator's name for no reason except the hidden factor of her gender. Responding to this workplace reality, she trusted that her adherence to Professor Snow's fundamental teachings—especially the necessity of unbiased objectivity—would help her surmount sex discrimination in her chosen field.

Pulling her audience in, Ms. Gangle reflects on her principal contributions to arbitral decision-making during her career. Labor practitioners will value her effort because, as she notes, many arbitration awards and opinions are confined to the secrecy of the parties' files and, thus, are unavailable for citation, analysis, and application in later cases. She concludes with her own observations on the factors that continue to undermine fairness in the modern workplace. One is the growing effort to replace genuine arbitration with artificial dispute resolution processes, produced by artificial "waivers" of employee rights, leading to proceedings that cannot justly share the name "arbitration." It is these views of Madam Arbitrator Gangle that perhaps carry the greatest weight. These are her opinions of the world of work formed after a lifetime in the trenches of arbitration: her candid assessments on full display here but never to appear in an arbitration award.

Hon. Robert D. Durham
Senior Justice
Oregon Supreme Court
Portland, Oregon

Introduction

WHILE GROWING UP, I BELIEVED EVERY PERSON IN THE United States had an equal opportunity to achieve the American Dream through a combination of ambition and hard work. Long before reaching adulthood, however, I realized the dream was a myth.

The American Dream has been defined as "a social ideal that stresses egalitarianism and especially material prosperity." But sexism, racism, even religious bigotry and a variety of social conventions created obstacles that denied many Americans the same opportunity for social mobility and prosperity that the more privileged were able to achieve.

Until the 1930s, workers without a college education or a skilled trade had little ability to change their meager incomes or their social or economic status. If they worked in urban factories, they were subject to the whims of powerful industrial employers, as well as nepotism policies in hiring, retention, and promotion. They had no bargaining power to achieve fair wages, hours, and working conditions. They had no legal right to strike.

Things began to change in 1932 through Congressional action. First, the Norris-LaGuardia Act allowed workers to engage in nonviolent strikes. "Yellow-dog" agreements, in which workers had to promise they would not join a union, were abolished. In 1935, Congress passed the National Labor Relations Act (NLRA) as part of President Franklin

D. Roosevelt's New Deal. That sweeping legislation not only authorized private-sector workers to join unions and bargain collectively for wages, hours, and working conditions, but also established the National Labor Relations Board to enforce labor organizing and process complaints of alleged refusal to bargain. Qualified impartial labor arbitrators could resolve grievances, protecting workers' negotiated rights once the labor contracts were ratified.

Public employees, including police officers, firefighters, and teachers, lacked the right to bargain collectively until 1959. Eventually, forty-five states and the federal government implemented collective bargaining statutes for public employees.

As a result of unionization, after 1935, working-class white males and some white women were better able to pursue the American Dream. A prosperous white middle class grew. Home ownership and comfortable suburban living were byproducts of higher incomes. Many of these workers enjoyed an array of benefits ranging from medical insurance to retirement pensions, further enhancing their economic status

Not all workers were able to share in the middle-class boom, however. Single women, even if they had a job and a savings account, were routinely denied a home mortgage. Many residential subdivisions that rose up during the 1950s and 1960s incorporated racial exclusions in deeds and homeowner association policies. Women and persons of color faced obstacles in employment that the NLRA and early public-sector collective-bargaining legislation did not prohibit. Hiring notices in the 1930s routinely announced exclusions based on gender, national origin, and race. Although in World War II many women were hired to work in industries manufacturing airplanes and weapons, the days of Rosie the Riveter were short-lived. Those industries quickly closed their doors to women when the war ended. Recruiting notices for many jobs, even some with union contracts, boldly announced, "No Irish or Italians or Negroes Need Apply." Some employers openly refused to hire Catholics or Jews.

A series of hard-won legislative victories for workers began to change all this. In 1964, Congress passed Title VII of the Civil Rights Act, which abolished employment discrimination based on race, color, sex, national origin, and religion. The federal Fair Housing Act of 1968 abolished racial exclusions for sales and rentals of homes and in real estate deeds. The Equal Credit Opportunity Act of 1974 allowed women to obtain mortgages in their sole names.

All this ground-breaking legislation ultimately led to more equitable housing and employment opportunities for most Americans. Title VII initially applied to employers of one hundred or more employees, then to those with at least twenty-five workers beginning in 1967. Enforceable through federal court action, the legislation opened employment opportunities to large segments of the population previously deprived of pursuing the American Dream.

The ethic these laws promoted had a significant impact on reducing discrimination in the legal and medical professions. With few exceptions, before the 1970s the only students who attended law or medical school were wealthy white males. Some colleges in the Southern states served African-American students for law and medicine, but graduates were often limited to working in segregated African-American communities. A few women-only colleges were founded before 1900, including Vassar, Smith, and Wellesley, but they were expensive and attracted mostly wealthy white women. Extremely small numbers of those women went on to study law or medicine; even fewer practiced.

As a result of the Civil Rights Act, women gradually were welcomed into law schools. It still took many years for cracks to appear in the glass ceiling preventing employment in the legal profession, however. Many law firms had fewer than twenty-five employees and were not covered by Title VII. Others contended their clients, especially those handling business-related litigation or financial disputes, would not allow a woman to represent their interests. Some argued maleness was a bona fide occupational qualification for lawyers. Most women law graduates therefore went into government service or opened solo practice offices. Many focused on domestic relations matters and estate planning for women.

It was especially difficult for women to become judges and labor arbitrators, due to biased perceptions that women lacked competency and were persuaded by emotion, not legality. Even today, few women serve actively as labor arbitrators, though many female judges serve in state and federal courts and three women justices are on the United States Supreme Court.

I wrote this book to tell my personal story about life as a woman born eight years after Congress passed the NLRA. My mother always told me I could achieve the American Dream. A practical child, I observed the male-dominated culture of my working-class city, Brockton, Massachusetts and understood I would have to overcome serious obstacles to achieve her expectations.

My mother had wanted to become a lawyer, but her parents refused to help with tuition even though they had helped two sons obtain law degrees. I always thought this was unfair. Once I observed the legal profession in court procedures during my parents' separation and in my own personal injury trial (detailed later in this book), I saw that the legal system needed to be more just and fair, especially for women. I decided I would become a lawyer myself someday.

It was many years before I was able to accomplish my dream. It wasn't until I was thirty-four, married, and the mother of two young children that I entered Willamette University College of Law in Oregon. My journey from my youth in Massachusetts to adulthood in Oregon took many twists and turns along the way, and the passing of the Civil Rights Act of 1964 with its Title VII provision was the final event that made law school possible.

This, then, is the story of my zigzag path to becoming one of the first women labor arbitrators in the Pacific Northwest and California, to achieving my own slice of the American Dream, and to helping others do so as well.

—Sandra Smith Gangle, J.D.

My Stormy Beginning

─⊱⊰─

In 1942, America was still reeling from the shock and fear that gripped the nation after Japanese planes attacked the U.S. fleet at Pearl Harbor one year earlier. Families were tearfully saying good-bye to husbands, fathers, and sons as they rushed to join the Army, Navy, and Marines. Often, the women left behind felt vulnerable as they struggled to deal with family responsibilities by themselves.

My mother, Irene Powers Smith, was one of those women.

Eight months pregnant, she knew she would soon be raising a child alone. My father, Milton Smith, had enlisted in the navy, preferring service in that branch to awaiting a draft notice requiring him to enlist in the army. His deployment date was not yet determined, but Irene was already fearful about coping with her firstborn child alone. Other wives were returning to their hometowns to stay with parents and siblings while their husbands served in the military, but Irene's parents had let her know they did not have room. She would be on her own.

Then, the unexpected happened. Irene slipped and fell on an icy sidewalk as she was boarding a bus on January 10, 1943. A nor'easter blizzard was on the way, and a frigid wind was already howling in Brockton, Massachusetts, where she and Milton lived. She went into labor right away, and medics took her to the emergency room. Twenty hours later, after a long night of painful labor while heavy snow and icy winds pounded on the hospital windows and the electric lights flickered on and off, she gave birth to me—three weeks before my February due date.

Mom had wanted to enroll in Portia Law School for Women in Boston when she graduated from high school in 1936. (At that time, high school graduates could attend law school without first obtaining a bachelor's degree.) Her older brother, Francis Powers, had passed the Massachusetts bar exam and was working as legal counsel for a labor union. He had encouraged his younger sister to pursue high academic goals and had coached her when she was qualifying for her high school debate team.

He told Irene about Portia Law School, a private institution originally established with two women students in 1908. By the 1930s, the school admitted a mixed group of women and men, as well as a few African-American students. Irene wanted to study law like her brothers. She believed the education would open doors to a professional life.

My grandparents, Frank and Mary Powers, however, were first-generation Irish-Americans. They had grown up in Pepperell, Massachusetts, north of Boston, where their immigrant parents had found work in the local paper mill. Frank had four younger brothers, and Mary was the oldest of seven natural children and two younger adoptees from the Catholic orphanage in Boston. Frank and Mary believed the proper role for their only daughter was to choose marriage and motherhood. They adopted the limited and sexist ethic of the time and declined to assist my mother with law school tuition. Higher education, they felt, would not lead to the future she expected. "Only the daughters of lawyers and judges get to practice law," they told her. "If you go to law school, all you'll be able to do is work for a while as a legal secretary, until you get married and have a child."

Unable to pay her own tuition and transportation to and from Boston, Irene attended Brockton Business College for a year, then worked as a bookkeeper and office manager for a local construction company. She paid her way by playing the drums in a women's dance band that performed in social clubs on weekends. Never one to enjoy domestic pursuits like cooking and sewing, Irene did not plan to get married until she reached her twenties.

Milton Smith had other ideas. He had been pursuing Irene from the day he first met her in middle school. Irene had beautiful blue eyes and blonde hair, the most desirable female attributes of the time. She was reluctant to date Milton, however, because his interests were very different from hers. A football player, he was not a good student and had no skills or future ambitions. On the other hand, he did not smoke or drink, and was a Roman Catholic whose father had been an Irish immigrant. Irene gradually began to accept his relentless invitations for dates. When he proposed marriage in 1940, she agreed, though she actually knew very little about him. She was twenty-one; he, twenty-three.

Irene quickly learned Milton adhered to the same sexist—even misogynistic—ethic her own parents had followed. Many years later she told me he had insisted she quit her bookkeeping job right after they got married, so she could "stay home and keep house" for him. He said he wanted "home-cooked meals" like his own mother, Rosanna, used to make, and he constantly criticized Irene's efforts to please him. Irene had no idea what Rosanna's cooking had been like, however—Rosanna died when

Milton was seventeen and Irene had never met her, let alone eaten at her table. Milton also argued it was not ladylike to be playing the drums in social clubs once she was married, so he made her quit her extra job. He said he did not want other men ogling her.

Most couples who entered marriage in the 1940s expected their union to be magically permanent and blissful. I think my mother naively adopted that belief. She and my father did not grow up in the same neighborhood and, although their families were both Roman Catholic, their social/cultural backgrounds were very different. Irene's father Frank worked as a foreman in a leather business, and her mother Mary prided herself as being "lace-curtain Irish," which meant she came from a dignified background. Milton's own father had died a few months before he was born, and Rosanna then married her much-older widowed brother-in-law, Patrick Smith, for financial reasons. She raised baby Milton with his six older siblings and some of Patrick's seven children who were still minors. Patrick worked as a laborer in Brockton's sewer beds, so the family was poverty-stricken and chaotic.

Irene, who already had business acumen and authority at work when she married my father, expected to have more equality in her marriage than other brides envisaged in those years. She soon realized, however, that her values differed greatly from Milton's. He did not consider her skills as marital assets. He demanded that she quit her jobs so she could accommodate his cooking and housekeeping requirements. Unfortunately, they had not discussed such issues during their engagement. She felt she had no choice but to agree to his demands, hoping he would gradually trust her judgment and give her greater latitude.

According to what my mother told me later, from the start of their marriage, Milton's caustic attitude also made it difficult for him to get along with his supervisors at work, leading to frequent lay-offs. Whenever he sought a new job, he became moody and domineering. Their communications were strained and the marriage was already under stress by the time I was born.

Milton received his deployment notice to join the navy in August 1943, when I was seven months old. My mother worried about getting along with only the meager spousal allotment my father would earn while serving. Wartime ration coupons were making food options scarce. Irene considered going back to work to supplement her income, but quickly found there were no realistic options. Area weapons factories like the National Fireworks Company hired women whose husbands were fighting in the war, but most of those women were "war brides" who did not yet have children. Eight-hour shifts were scheduled either daytimes, early evenings, or graveyard, six days every week. No childcare options were available during swing and graveyard shifts, when new employees were most often assigned, so, being somewhat entrepreneurial, Irene decided to operate her own home-based business. She repaired, painted, and reupholstered old furniture pieces that she acquired in thrift shops, then resold the upgraded items.

I always knew Mom was lonely and fearful. I remember hearing her tell my grandmother she had a nightmare about a burglar coming in the window. I asked what a burglar was, and she said, "Someone who wants to steal what we have." She tried to calm my fear by adding, "It was only a dream, and all the windows are locked," but I still was afraid to go to sleep.

During the twenty-seven months my father was in the Pacific theater, though, Mom established a wonderful mother-daughter bond with me. I was a bright child and learned to talk early. Mom read to me, and I loved to listen. I asked her to read favorite stories, such as *Heidi*, over and over. Mom's only companion, I listened as she taught me things few children learned. She told me about Amelia Earhart, for instance, and explained I might fly an airplane someday. I wasn't sure I had what it would take to be another Amelia Earhart, however. Mom had high expectations, and I was afraid I'd never measure up.

Mom told me she respected people of foreign backgrounds, like our landlords, the Stratoti family, who spoke Italian. I remember her saying, "All people in the world are our distant cousins; even the Italian family upstairs and the Japanese people Dad is fighting against in the war. Many of them don't like us Americans, but most are good people. We should respect them all because they are human beings." She even taught me some Spanish words and poems she had learned in high school. She told me people speak many different languages, and I could learn foreign languages to communicate with them.

I remember seeing a black-skinned child with his mother one day, downtown in front of the Brockton Post Office. I blurted out, "Oh look, Mommy, there's little Black Sambo." She acted embarrassed and whispered, "Don't say that, Sandra. He's another child just like you. Little Black Sambo was a character in a book." I was confused because I knew the boy's skin was different from mine. I wondered if he was from a foreign country like the Japanese and the Italians. I asked my mother if he spoke a foreign language and was surprised when she said he probably spoke English like us.

Mom told me I would someday go to college and learn skills so I would have a career and be independent and self-sufficient. "You might even be a lawyer," she said, "like Uncle Fran." She took me to church with her and taught me about Christian love and sacrifice. Though she did not realize it at the time, her early training would have a profound effect on my decisions in later life.

When my father returned from the war in November 1945, I was nearly three years old but quite mature for my age. Mom never talked in childish terms, so my vocabulary and thought processes were well-developed. Mom and I were happy to learn that my father had not been involved in any combat or dangerous assignments—he had served as a pipefitter on a ship and intended to look for similar work at the oil refineries in nearby Quincy, Massachusetts.

He shared some gifts from the interesting places he had visited, like Hawaii and the Philippines. I was disappointed when he gave me a necklace of shells and a pair of straw slippers. I didn't like the necklace and the slippers scratched my feet. I wished he had brought me a doll.

I remember my mother asking my father if any of his fellow sailors were married and had children. He said no, most were younger than he was and few were married. One weekend, a couple of his buddies dropped by for a rather raucous visit. Afterwards, I heard Mom tell Dad she did not like hearing about the fun he had had dancing with women in Hawaii. She said he did not understand how lonely she had been while taking care of me by herself. Although I did not understand everything at the time, I knew my mother was hurt by what she had learned from my father and his buddies, and I tried to console her.

17

While my father had been in the navy, Mom often told me that even though he was far away, he still loved me and missed me. As a result, I believed my father cared about me. I expected he would be a good dad, and we would have fun together when he came home from the war. But much later, Mom told me he had never asked about me in any letter. She said she had made up language to read to me whenever his letters arrived, pretending he was thinking about me and missing me.

Her disclosure helped me to understand why, sadly, after his return, he did not seem to enjoy being my dad. He was distant, unreachable. We never established a warm father-daughter relationship. This was heartbreaking to my young self, and I knew Mom felt mystified and betrayed as well.

Though they had another child, my brother Doug, in December 1947, my parents were essentially stuck in a loveless marriage that was going nowhere. It was obvious there were problems growing between them. My father's moody periods become more frequent. He spent long hours at home listening to music and humming along with the tunes, as if in another world. He always blamed his supervisors for unfairness rather than acknowledging he might have had some personal responsibility for being fired. He objected to my mother's cooking and sometimes went into rages without justification. My mother finally asked him if he might have aggravated an old football injury from high school when he hit his head on a pipe on the navy ship. But he refused to seek medical advice.

I'll never know whether the war experience changed my father in subtle ways that were unknown at the time, or he was simply unprepared to deal with family life and the serious differences between his personality and that of my mother. I remember my mother saying often, "Milton, you're not the same as you were before. What has happened to you?"

The only activity I can remember us sharing was his teaching me how to ride a bicycle when I was five. He wasn't very patient, and he didn't offer comfort when I fell. Meanwhile, my father bonded rather well with my baby brother, calling Doug a "chip off the old block" and saying, "You'll be a football player like your dad." He never said kind things like that to me.

Although I started school in September 1948, I had to attend private first grade until my sixth birthday in January 1949. I was then tested to ensure I was ready for first grade in the public school. I passed the test and was placed in a split first/second grade classroom. My teacher was a lovely older woman with fluffy blue hair named Miss Caplice. She tried to make me feel welcome, but starting in mid-year was still a traumatic experience. I felt different. For one thing, I was tall for my age. I also had special work on the blackboard every day, marked "Sandra's Work," because I was ahead of my first-grade peers but behind the second-graders. I didn't even know the words to the Pledge of Allegiance. The girls in the room had already formed their friendships. They all knew how to play dodge ball and hopscotch, so I constantly felt like a fifth wheel during recess. Although I was a good student, I was a rather lonely and unhappy first grader.

The following summer, 1949, my father's veteran's benefit made it possible for my parents to purchase a two-family house on Goddard Road. I was about to start second grade; Doug was still a toddler. At least the house was in the same general neighborhood as our prior apartment, so I could continue at Lincoln School and have Miss Caplice again.

We moved into the downstairs apartment in August, and the upstairs apartment was rented out to meet the mortgage payments. My parents were happy about having their own home. The house even had modern amenities, like a washing machine. It was delightful to have my own bedroom. Doug's crib was in a tiny office area next to my parents' room.

I remember how proud Dad was to show his older sisters Alice and Evelyn and their husbands what he had been able to accomplish so soon after returning from the war. Uncle Bill and his wife Peg came to see the house, too, with my six cousins, including Rosemary, who was a year older than I, and baby Jean, about Doug's age. This should have been a happy occasion. But Dad's older sisters were not pleased. I overheard Aunt Evelyn saying, "Babe [they always called him Babe because he was the youngest in the family], how can you afford all this? Irene must have talked you into buying this big house. It's too hoity-toity for you. None of us have been able to buy a washing machine."

Dad's eyes drooped sadly when he heard those words. He seemed irritated and confused, offering no defense. The joy he had demonstrated a few moments earlier seemed to evaporate, and I felt bad for him. I also felt bad when I extrapolated from what Evelyn said that Uncle Bill's large family could not afford a washing machine.

That was the first time I understood that my aunts and uncles held a strange power over my father and their values were very different from those of my mother. I knew they were belittling my mother, but my father hadn't spoken up and defended her. Mom was angry after they left, and my father just sat brooding. I realized my parents were not getting along well. I felt anxious, not knowing what would happen next.

Perhaps in response to this humiliation from his family, my father later told my mother he wanted to be free to go out dancing on Friday nights and meet other women, as his brother (my Uncle Bill) liked to do. My mother, of course, would not agree to such a request. I remember hearing her say, "You need to listen to me more. We need to solve our problems together." But my father insisted that Mom would simply have to agree to his terms—otherwise, the marriage was over.

Even still, I was not prepared for the summer of 1950, when I was seven and Doug was a toddler of two. My father put some clothes in the family car and drove off. Mom said he had chosen to walk away.

I knew Mom was very sad about this. I felt sad, too, and worried about how I would take care of Mom and my little brother. Both of them seemed to rely on me, even though I was only seven.

After a while, I heard my father had retained a lawyer and filed for divorce. He could not meet any of the causes for divorce per Massachusetts law, however, because Mom was not guilty of any of the acceptable reasons, i.e., infidelity, desertion, or physical violence. He did allege "mental cruelty" as the basis of his petition, but the facts he relied on were silly things like Mom's failure to cook meals the way his own mother had. I heard Mom tell her own mother, "He just doesn't want to be married anymore." But, that was not an acceptable reason for divorce in Massachusetts.

My uncles and aunts helped him pay his legal expenses. Mom thought that wasn't fair—now she would have to hire a lawyer. "Our family is at war," she said more than once. I knew about the violent war my father had been involved in but I didn't yet understand the concept of metaphor, so those words frightened me.

Although I did not understand the legal issues, I did understand Mom was going to be alone again, as she had been before Dad returned from the war. I knew she would be sad and lonely, and I would have to try to make her life happier. I also knew I had to protect Doug from learning what was happening. I told him, "Dad is just very busy with his work." Meanwhile, I regularly prayed to Mary, the mother of Jesus, asking her to help me deal with everything going on in my life.

It was still many years in the future before "irreconcilable differences" would become a sufficient basis to dissolve a marriage and divorcing parents would be required to respect the best interests of the children. The efforts of my Smith relatives only aggravated my parents' conflict and further isolated our family. Even though Doug and I had warm relationships with our Smith cousins during our early years, we suddenly had no contact with them. This confused us both and caused sadness beyond the loss of our father.

When it appeared he was getting nowhere with his divorce arguments, my father took a curious stand. He went to the parish priest, Father Kenny, and asked him to intervene to "save" the marriage. He argued my mother had deserted him because she wanted to be in control of decision making.

Surprisingly (or not, perhaps, given the patriarchal nature of the Catholic Church), Father Kenny supported my father. He told my mother she had to take my father back and listen to his wishes. My mother spoke up bravely, however, telling the priest, "No, Father, I can't take him back on his terms. He wants freedom to live like a single man, and I cannot accept that. I'll only take him back if he agrees that our marriage is a real marriage and not a fraud."

The priest, having never dealt with a woman like my mother before, continued to defend my father, saying, "He is the man of the family, you know. You agreed to submit to your husband's authority when you married him in the Church. He's responsible before God for his conduct. If he sins, he will have to confess those sins. But, if you refuse to take him back as your husband, then you are rejecting your marriage vows."

Ironically, my mother could have won a divorce, if she had taken that route herself. She could have proven the legal ground of desertion. But, as a devout Roman Catholic, she chose not to pursue such a remedy. She believed she and my father had a sacramental marriage that was meant to continue until death, even though she was unwilling to take him back on his terms (he wanted freedom to be with other women!), as that was not what they had agreed to in their marriage vows. Yet here was a priest of the Church advocating for exactly that, on my father's behalf. He even said my mother would be excommunicated if she did not submit.

But the patriarchy would not have the final say with regards to my mother. In order to defend herself and her marriage vows, my mother retained Attorney Robert Cotter, a sole-practitioner lawyer Mom had known when they were high school students many years before. Mr. Cotter filed a petition with the court, asking for a decree of legal separation as the appropriate remedy. He planned to win sole custody of me and my brother for my mother and a "decree of femme sole" that would give her the right to hold some property separately. The property she and my father owned jointly would be divided if the two of them failed to reconcile.

My father's lawyer contested her petition, counter-arguing that, if they were going to be legally separated, Dad should get custody of my brother but have no further obligation to Mom or me. I overheard my mother telling my grandmother that my father was refusing to pay us any support money. "He wants Doug to go live with him and says Sandra can stay with me. Imagine that," Mom added. "He's willing to hire a babysitter to take care of Doug while he goes to work, but he won't give me any money to keep the children together."

I was eight years old by that time. I understood what was happening in the family, and it wrung my heart with helplessness and loneliness. Each night, as I heard my mother crying in her bedroom, I turned to my faith to get me through the turmoil. I prayed to Jesus and Mary to help my parents listen to each other and solve their problems respectfully. "Please, God," I would pray, turning to the words Jesus said on the cross, "forgive them, for they know not what they are doing to me and Doug. Why are they fighting in court, with separate lawyers? Why does Mom have to fight for custody and support money? Why is my family involved in a feud that looks like war? Why does my father not love me or Mom anymore? Why does he want to take Doug away? None of it makes sense, God. It isn't fair. Please, God, make them listen. Make them do what is right."

As an innocent observer of my parents' conflict, I managed to develop compassion and strength for dealing with the pain. I knew my mother was worried about money and my father did not want to pay child support. I had to be strong enough to help her cope with her depression and anxiety. The result was that I became a perfect daughter, never arguing with Mom or disobeying, so she would have less to worry about. I assured her we would get through this with Mr. Cotter's help. I helped take care of Doug so she could sleep each afternoon when I came home from school.

It was frustrating to listen to Mom's tearful stories about being unable to get a job. She said there was discrimination against women, especially single mothers. What would happen to me and Doug if Mom couldn't get a job and my father didn't pay for support? I remember thinking about how a kitten must feel when it is left outside in the cold overnight. All I could do was pray to God that Mom, Doug, and I would not be left out in the cold.

My Early
Legal Education

—◦◦◦—

M om held my hand as we climbed the steep marble
stairs. It was January 1951. I had just turned eight
years old, and the crunching sounds of our boots in the
packed snow made me giggle. When we finally reached
the pillared portico, Mom pulled the giant bronze door
open. She ushered me inside, saying, "This is the Plymouth
County Courthouse. You'll have to be quiet here."

I followed her to a bulletin board where I could read, in
bold print, "Smith v. Smith, Courtroom B, 9:00 a.m." Mom
then located a door marked "B" and pointed to a sturdy oak
bench nearby. She whispered, "Wait for me here. I'll be back
in a half-hour or so." Then she disappeared.

I climbed onto the bench and looked around the long,
wide hall. Grey-streaked marble covered the floor. Dark
woodwork bordered the ceiling and doors. Photographs of
stern-faced men in black robes hung on the walls between
the doors. One was marked Samuel Stone, Presiding Judge.
I recognized President Harry Truman in another.

Mom had been tense that morning, chatting nervously on
the bus in a tight, high-pitched voice. I knew she was uncomfortable about the hearing. Mom told me what she expected
would happen. Her lawyer, Mr. Cotter, would be there, and my
father would be there with his lawyer, Mr. Reservitz. "We're

going to talk about custody and visitation and child support," she said, adding somberly, "Judge Stone might want to talk to you in chambers, Sandra. If he calls you in, don't be afraid. Just answer his questions. Tell him the truth."

Mom was determined that Doug and I should always live with her. "My children are not a loaf of bread," I heard her say. "They can't be split apart." She had hired Mr. Cotter to fight for custody of both of us along with a support order so she could pay the mortgage and buy groceries.

Mr. Cotter said the judge would probably grant her full custody and give my father visitation rights. I understood what "visitation" meant, and I didn't like it. Doug and I had seen our father only a few times over the five months since he had moved out. On each Sunday visit, he had argued with Mom and called her ugly names. He even went into a violent rage once and hit her face, making her nose bleed. Terrified, I ran outside screaming until Mr. Miller, one of our neighbors, came and helped my mother. The police even came.

The courthouse hallway was cold and drafty. I pulled my tweed coat tightly around my chest and tugged my wool socks up over my knees. While reading the library book I had brought along, I noticed some men wearing dark overcoats and Stetson hats walking briskly down the hall, clicking their shiny shoes on the stone floor and swinging their wide satchels back and forth with each step. *They must be lawyers, like Mr. Cotter*, I thought. *I wonder why there aren't some women lawyers here, too.*

Suddenly, the door to Courtroom B opened. Mom appeared with Mr. Cotter. Her eyes were red; her hands trembled. "Judge Stone wants to talk to you," she said. "Go with Mr. Cotter and answer the judge's questions. Mr. Reservitz will be there, too. Don't be afraid."

Mr. Cotter then motioned for me to walk beside him. He took long strides, but I managed to keep up with him by walking fast. Our footsteps echoed in the long hallway as we walked together on the marble floor.

The door to the judge's chambers was open. I immediately recognized Judge Stone as one of the men whose portraits hung in the main hallway. He greeted me brusquely, with, "Come on in, little girl." Then, a bit more gently, "I hope you didn't catch cold out there in the hall."

Mr. Cotter introduced me to the judge, then to Mr. Reservitz. The three of us sat down in the big oak chairs in front of the judge's desk. Uncomfortable with these stern-faced men all around me, I wished the judge had called me by my name, Sandra, instead of "little girl." I wondered how he could possibly understand what Mom was going through and what she needed from my father. *There should be women lawyers and judges,* I thought. *They would understand Mom and me better. I think these men will just pay attention to my father.*

Judge Stone asked me to tell him how things had been during my father's Sunday visits. I told him Dad didn't talk to me very much and I didn't like it when he said mean things to Mom. That made me feel scared. The judge replied, "Well, maybe he wouldn't say those things if your mother left him alone to play with you and your brother." His remark bothered me because I knew it was not accurate. My father always started the arguments, not my mother. I thought the judge wasn't listening to me and must be on my father's side. I knew I should be polite, though, so I did not argue with him. I just decided to speak up for my mother as best I could when he asked me other questions.

Judge Stone then asked how I would feel if my brother went to live with Dad and I stayed with Mom. "I would miss Doug a lot," I said, "and I know Doug will be lonely for me and Mom. Dad doesn't know how to dress Doug or give him his bath, and he doesn't like to read to him or put him to bed. He won't have time to take Doug out to play. I think he will just leave Doug with a babysitter while he goes to work. Doug needs Mom, just like I do." I then looked up at Mr. Cotter and asked, "Didn't you tell the judge these things already? Isn't that what a lawyer is supposed to do?"

Mr. Cotter mumbled something about wanting me to tell the judge my story in my own words. So I turned to Judge Stone and blurted, "What Mom needs is support money, so she can pay the mortgage and buy food for us. Dad has been mean to Mom. He doesn't care if we will be out in the cold. I don't think he really wants Doug to live with him. He just wants to hurt Mom and keep his money for himself. That is not fair."

The judge thanked me for my "helpful comments" and said, "I'll think this over carefully, young lady. I'll make a decision soon." Mr. Cotter then led me out of the judge's chambers and back down the hall to the bench where my mother was sitting.

She looked calmer and more refreshed than before. The first thing I said was, "Mom, I told the judge what he should do for us." Then, when we were out of earshot of Mr. Cotter, I added, "I think I did a better job sticking up for you than Mr. Cotter did."

A few days later my mother received a letter from the court. The judge had granted her full custody of me and Doug. My father was ordered to pay child support as long as Mom allowed him to visit us on Sundays from 2:00 to

4:00 p.m. Mom would have to stay away from my father during the visits. The judge also ordered Dad to collect the rent from the people in the upstairs apartment in our house and pay the mortgage payments with the rent money, so Mom, Doug, and I could afford to stay in the family house. When I learned about the judge's order, I felt proud because I knew he had followed my recommendations during the interview in his office. I thought at that moment that maybe I would become a lawyer myself some day and help other women like Mom achieve justice.

No doubt Judge Stone expected his reciprocal order of support and visitation to end my parents' marital conflict. It did not. My father only paid child support occasionally. Whenever he failed to send it, my mother would refuse to permit him to visit me and Doug until he paid up. My father would then retaliate by withholding support money the following month. Mom would then call Mr. Cotter, who would then talk to Mr. Reservitz, and eventually another check would arrive. And so it went.

The net result was Mom had little money to buy food and pay household bills, and Doug and I hardly ever saw our father. Eventually, the visitations ceased altogether—my father really did not care to spend time with us. He preferred to keep his money and enjoy his freedom. Doug and I hadn't been enjoying the visits with him anyway, because he didn't know how to relate to us. We often visited with Nana and Grampa Powers, Mom's parents, instead of seeing our father on weekends, and we enjoyed those visits more. Nana always gave Mom a big bag of groceries to take home after our visit, and that took care of most of our meals.

The judge's plan for a fair solution failed on another level as well. My parents had only sought a legal separation, not a divorce, so the judge did not order a permanent division of their property. He allowed them to remain joint owners of the house and its contents during their separation. He granted my mother possession of those assets for an indefinite period, on the assumption that they would eventually reconcile. At such time as Mom might decide to move elsewhere, however, the house would be sold and the proceeds divided between her and my father. My father could buy out Mom's half of the equity, if he wanted to take over the house, and they would remain separated.

It seemed like a fair order at the time. However, there were immediate problems with implementation and long-term problems with enforcement. During the first few months, Mom observed my father visiting the tenants to pick up the rent money, so she believed my father was meeting his obligation to pay the mortgage and utilities. He wasn't. After about nine months, the bank notified Mom that the mortgage was in arrears and foreclosure was imminent. Dad had been pocketing the rent money. Also, the electric company and the City began threatening to cancel our electric service, as well as water and sewer, for nonpayment. Those notices caused Mom great concern. If she lost the house, not only would we have no home but her share of the equity would evaporate. She immediately called Mr. Cotter with the bad news.

Mr. Cotter requested an emergency court hearing, and I went to court with Mom again. This time I sat in the courtroom and listened.

Judge Stone was visibly annoyed when he learned of my father's irresponsible behavior. The judge told him sternly, "You must make up those mortgage and utility payments immediately, or I'll issue a charge of contempt-of-court and put you in jail." He told Mom, "Mrs. Smith, you will collect the rent from the tenants from now on and pay the mortgage and utility bills yourself." Then he increased my father's support order so Mom could afford the extra expense she would be incurring for utilities.

This outcome was reassuring, but I was still concerned about Mom. I knew she was exhausted from all the stress and worry. I heard her mumble to Mr. Cotter, "Please contact the bank right away. I hope they agree to go along with the judge's order."

My father complied with the order, paying the bank and taking care of the outstanding bills. The bank then stayed the foreclosure, and my mother became the landlord. We were able to stay in our home for the next four years. By that time it was 1955, and I was in seventh grade. Those intervening years were not without turmoil, however.

Mom and I had to go back to court more than once over medical and dental expenses. The judge had ordered my father to cover me and my brother under his medical insurance at work. When I was admitted to the hospital for a tonsillectomy at age ten, however, we learned he had cancelled our medical coverage. Judge Stone was furious when he learned the facts and promptly held my father in contempt. He allowed him to avoid jail, though, if he immediately restored the insurance coverage, which he did.

Dad's behavior made me angry. I knew he was the one who had decided to leave my mother, but he still had an obligation to support me and Doug. Why did he want to hurt us? It was so unfair. It made no sense to me whatsoever.

In the meantime, by watching the succession of court proceedings, I learned a great deal about domestic relations issues and court procedures—and the power of lawyers and judges. I heard Mr. Cotter speak calmly to Mom about real estate issues, mortgages, bank procedures, and medical insurance. At each hearing, I thought to myself, *I could do what Mr. Cotter does. I'm a good student, and I could learn what he knows. I could be calm like him, and I could talk like a lawyer. I think I would be a good judge, because I would listen to women and men—all people.*

As time passed and I matured, I could see Mom becoming worn down from facing the constant court procedures. She grew more depressed and lonely. She was often sleeping during the day when I came home from school and Doug was taking his afternoon nap, and I knew she stayed up late into the night reading sad novels from the library. She was also writing sad, depressing poetry. I remember reading a handwritten poem I found on her bedside table. It frightened me because I knew Mom had written it, and it sounded like she might be dying. That would make Doug and me have neither a father nor a mother to depend on. *How can I take care of Doug by myself?* I wondered. *Nana and Grampa are old. They can't take care of us.*

Here are the beginning lines of the poem that worried me so:

> *How long are the nights? Eight hours you say?*
> *Or seven, or five?*
> *Long enough to know you're still alive...*
> *If you are...*

Although I tried to appear strong, the situation affected me in many ways. Feeling helpless, I grew sad and lonely. I withdrew from social activity at school. I was too embarrassed to tell my friends what was going on at home. I knew there was a stigma to single-parent households at that time, so I tried to hide my situation as much as possible. When people asked me about my father, I sometimes said he never came back from the war. I knew it wasn't exactly true, but in my mind I justified it because I had heard Mom say he had changed while he was in the navy and came back like a different person.

I became a bookworm, walking to Brockton Public Library several afternoons a week to hide out and read by myself. I knew Mom could not handle any more problems than she already had, so I devoted myself to getting good grades in school and to being the perfect daughter. I also tried to help Doug maintain a normal childhood. He did not understand the situation the way I did because he was only four and I was nine. I wanted to protect him from feeling the deep sadness that I felt. I tried hard to engage in childish play activities with him as often as possible when he came home from preschool.

Meanwhile, my only contact with any extended family was with my maternal grandparents. Since my father had taken the family car, we were unable to visit anyone else. Mom's brother Uncle Robert was married and had seven children, but they lived far away, first in Texas, then later in Spokane, Washington. Some Powers and McGrath relatives lived fifty miles away in East Pepperell, near the New Hampshire border. We only saw them once a year, when they visited my grandparents at Thanksgiving. Uncle Fran, who had been ordained a Catholic priest when I was a toddler, worked as a college professor at Catholic University in Washington, D.C., and only visited Brockton for one week every summer and at Christmas. One winter, he took me and Doug to see the Ice Capades in Boston, a special treat.

I was in the fourth grade by the time Mom finally learned how I was suffering. My teacher, Miss Faircloth, asked Mom's permission to have her sister, a school psychologist, evaluate me by asking questions about my feelings and my worries. Mom agreed, and later Miss Faircloth said her sister recommended that Mom take appropriate steps to alleviate my emotional pain. I needed to spend more time with other girls in recreational activities having fun and not focusing on the problems that were occurring at home.

Mom was surprised to hear the professional advice, as she had not been aware of my depression. She did know, however, that I needed to learn how to swim. She had never permitted me to go swimming with friends because she feared I would contract the dreaded disease of polio if I swam in public pools. She also kept me from going to kids' movies on Saturdays, because she felt polio germs could easily be transmitted there.

But, after hearing Miss Faircloth's advice, Mom decided to send me to a two-week summer day camp at Brockton's YWCA. She apparently thought the danger of contracting polio was less at the "Y" than elsewhere and I would meet other girls my age while I was learning to swim.

This almost inconsequential decision was a serendipitous turning point for me—perhaps even a miracle.

In those two weeks of that summer between fourth and fifth grade, I felt free to develop new friendships with girls who knew nothing about my family's troubles. I enjoyed learning basic swimming skills. I also attended the art, music, and drama classes every day—and thrived. I now had a way to express my feelings in creative ways. I could set aside all thoughts of my problems at home and develop my imagination. I could paint colorful pictures and play dramatic roles in skits. Most significantly, I learned to play some basic tunes on the piano. The teachers all gave me positive feedback and encouraged me to continue working with art and music on my own after the day camp period ended.

My music teacher, Miss Reilly, taught me the rudiments of playing piano during the "Y" program. She also gave me new self-confidence and inspiration. She told me I had a lovely alto voice and selected me to sing a solo, "Alice Blue Gown," at the end-of-session performance for parents. Most significantly, she told Mom I was "starved for music" and should have a piano at home. "Nine years of age is the latest that a child can develop the physical dexterity to play classical piano," she explained, "so if she doesn't build her skill at the piano now, her finger muscles will stiffen and she'll never play well."

There was no way we could afford to buy a piano and pay for lessons, but Miss Reilly was undeterred. Within a few weeks, she had located an old upright piano on sale. The owners were only charging ten dollars but the piano was musically sound. Miss Reilly even located someone who would move the piano to our house without charging a fee. Even though she had retired from private teaching, she also offered to give me lessons for a reduced rate of one dollar, faithfully coming every week from then on.

I believed Miss Reilly was a gift sent by God. I loved practicing my scales and chords and playing the pieces in the John Thompson books. I practiced for hours every day and progressed rapidly. I loved the classical etudes and sonatas. I enjoyed performing in programs to which Miss Reilly referred me. I became her protégée, and she was proud of my progress. Best of all, I no longer felt alone and sad because of my parents' separation. I had new self-esteem. I experienced joy through music.

Doug, who was four years old, begged me to show him how to play piano. He did surprisingly well, and, when he was five, Miss Reilly began giving him a lesson each time she came to teach me. Doug's feet could not even reach the floor when he sat on the piano bench and practiced his lesson. His tiny hands could hardly stretch to play the songs in his beginner's book. But sibling rivalry led him to want to do whatever his big sister could do.

My brother Doug, age 5, sitting with me, age 10,
at our piano (1953)

Another new relationship opened my mind still further. When I was ten years old, our next-door neighbors adopted a Greek war orphan named Tina, who spoke no English. Tina became my friend. I helped her learn English words, and she taught me some Greek words.

It was a rewarding experience to communicate with someone my own age who came from a foreign culture. My sixth-grade teacher, Miss Marks, asked me to mentor Tina with her studies and help her get to know the other girls. She asked me to write a special story for Tina about America, and I chose to write about Abraham Lincoln. Like Tina, Lincoln had lost his mother when he was a young child, then grew up poor, learning to read in a cabin by candlelight.

When I was twelve, Mom decided it was time to sell our Goddard Road house. It needed repairs that she could not afford. According to the judge's order in my parent's separation case, my father could buy out Mom's one-half share of the net equity if he chose to keep the house for himself. Dad did not wish to keep the house, but he was willing to work out a deal with Mom regarding his share of the proceeds. He offered to let her keep all the proceeds from the sale if she would ask the judge to relieve him of having to pay any further child support.

The judge tried to explain to Mom that this was not a good deal. She would not be getting any more support from my father for the entire eleven-year period before Doug would graduate from high school. Mom agreed to the arrangement, however, because she was tired of all the conflict over support issues. I remember her saying to Mr. Cotter, "A bird in the hand is worth two in the bush. I know I can manage." So, when the judge heard Mr. Cotter say, "My client has been fully advised, your Honor," the judge reluctantly signed the order.

The house was sold, and Mom put the net proceeds in a savings account. It was the first bank deposit she had made since separating from my father. I knew this made her feel happier and more secure, and I hoped things would be better from then on.

The third-floor apartment we rented in a three-decker tenement building was quite a change from our Victorian house, however. It was cold and drafty, and the toilet leaked. The mentally-ill lady in the apartment beneath ours banged on her ceiling and yelled obscenities every time we walked around on the creaky wood floors. I didn't have to change schools, but I did have to walk nearly two miles each way to get there. Grampa picked Doug up and drove him to and from his school, as there were no school buses in Brockton. Sadly, I was unable to move my piano to the apartment. We sold it, and I walked to my grandparents' house every day after school to continue practicing.

At the same time, there were positive things happening in our family. I was now in seventh grade in a large, sprawling junior high school, where I participated in advanced classes in English, math, history, and science. Doug was in a gifted class at his elementary school. Mom was feeling more positive about her life because she was free of the stress of renters, mortgage payments, and paying for home repairs. She also had money in the bank, which allowed her to think about the future instead of worrying about everyday expenses.

She began talking about buying a car. And she talked more and more frequently about getting out of Brockton and seeking a better life. Her dream, based on the Zane Grey novels she had read many years before, was that we would go "out West, where the purple sage blows and we can be free."

My First Jury Trial

⸺⸎⸺

E ven before we sold the Goddard Road house, Mom began to save money to buy a car. Each month she carefully sorted the cash from my father and the renters, as well as from various odd jobs she was able to find. Since she did not have a checking account, she would deposit cash in separate envelopes for food and bills—mortgage payment, telephone, and utilities. She always put any leftover dollars in the tall cardboard Quaker Oatmeal canister that sat on a pantry shelf. She said that was our "car savings fund." As soon as we collected five hundred dollars, she intended to buy a decent used car.

Mom stuffed more cash in the oatmeal canister after we sold the house and moved to the apartment. Then one day in early August 1956, when I was thirteen, Mom made an announcement.

"Kids, I have great news," she said. "There's five hundred dollars in the oatmeal box. We can go shopping for a car this weekend. And, there's still enough time left this month for us to take a couple of trips to Plymouth Beach before school starts."

We could hardly wait for Saturday to arrive. My grandfather drove us to several used car lots so Mom could search for the best vehicle for our five hundred dollars. We found a 1951 Chevrolet coupe that met Mom's requirement for quality and value. Its original dark red paint had dulled to a faded, dusty maroon, but Grampa assured Mom the vehicle was mechanically sound and its tires and brakes were in good condition. Mom signed the papers and turned over her precious cash to buy the Chevy. On our way home, Doug and I affectionately named the car "Ruby."

Monday morning, we made a lunch, packed swimsuits and towels into a satchel, and climbed into Ruby's front seat for our first trip to the beach. Doug slid to the middle, I relaxed on the passenger side, and Mom, of course, was behind the wheel. Like most vehicles at that time, the Chevy was not equipped with seat belts. I happened to be wearing a plaster cast on my right arm, because I had broken my wrist a month earlier.

Before we started out, Mom placed a small statuette of St. Christopher on the dashboard, in keeping with the Roman Catholic custom of the time. "He's the protector of travelers," she told us.

It was a warm, sunny morning. We enjoyed seeing the old New England homes along the curvy two-lane road as we drove through the East Bridgewater countryside on the way to Plymouth. We could smell fruit and vegetables growing in the farms and orchards. Traffic was light, so the drive was peaceful and pleasant.

Suddenly, as we rounded a left-facing curve, the huge front end of a blue and silver Hudson Hornet sedan came rushing toward us in our lane of travel. I remember it seemed like a giant alien beetle—the chrome-paneled radiator looked like the beetle's wide tooth-filled mouth.

Mom slammed her feet on the brake and clutch pedals simultaneously and instinctively turned the wheel to the right to escape hitting the oncoming vehicle head-on. With no shoulder to our right, though, there was no way she could get off the road. Ruby skidded directly toward a telephone pole in front of a residence. Mom did what she could to reduce the car's speed by braking hard, but it was still moving fast when we crashed into the pole and came to an abrupt halt. At the same moment, the left front fender of the blue Hornet collided with the left rear fender of our Chevy, leaving its big blue body in our lane of the road.

The force of hitting the pole caused the three of us to lurch forward violently in our seats. I instinctively leaned toward the left and stretched my left arm in front of Doug to protect him before we hit the pole. My body slid forward in front of Doug's knees, and my forehead hit the rear-view mirror, which in turn, smashed against the windshield. Tiny shards of glass from the mirror sliced through my hair and into my forehead and scalp, but the windshield thankfully only developed a sunburst of cracks. Meanwhile my right leg slid along the metal frame of the ashtray that hung beneath the dashboard, leaving a long, bloody gash in my thigh. At the same time, my right arm, reinforced by its hard plaster cast, slammed into the glove box door. Like an anchor, it stabilized my body in front of my brother's and probably protected me from exiting through the windshield.

Mom was gripping the steering wheel so tightly with both hands that it broke under her forearms, leaving her with ugly contusions and lacerations. At the same time, her face slammed down onto the steering post, injuring her nose and mouth and sending her eyeglasses onto the floor, breaking them. Mom's right ankle also suffered a sprain as the result of stomping on the brake pedal.

We were all stunned by the collision and Mom and I were bleeding, but we quickly concluded that St. Christopher had been looking out for us, as none of us were ejected from the vehicle or rendered unconscious. Our injuries were considerably less serious than they could have been.

Several neighbors came out of their homes and stood by as we dealt with our emergency. Someone brought us towels to mop the blood on my head and leg and my mother's face and arms. Another person comforted Doug, who was crying loudly from the terror he was feeling. A third helped my mother get out from behind the crushed steering wheel and assisted her as she bent to pick up her glasses. Someone called the police and asked for an ambulance.

The driver of the Hornet was a middle-aged woman who lived in the local area. She was not injured in the crash, and her car suffered only minor front-fender damage when it hit the rear fender of our car. She came to comfort my mother right away, saying her name was Ellen Archibald and she worked as a visiting nurse. Tearfully, she explained she was running late on appointments that morning and decided to pass a slow-moving vehicle on the curve in order to turn left at the intersection just beyond the telephone pole we had hit. She said she did not expect any cars to be traveling in the lane she used. Looking right at me, she said she was terribly sorry we had been injured in the collision.

A few minutes later, the East Bridgewater police chief arrived in his blue and white cruiser. He quickly began directing traffic around our car and the Hornet, which was still connected to our rear fender on the edge of the road-way. The medics arrived and gave me first aid, then placed me on a gurney beside the ambulance. They put Doug in a wheelchair because he convinced them he had injured his leg during the collision and was unable to walk. My mother declined the medics' efforts to assess her injuries as she was more interested in talking to the police chief.

Something about the chief made me uncomfortable. I had the impression, as I heard him talking to Mom and Mrs. Archibald, that he was more concerned for Mrs. Archibald's welfare than ours. I heard Mrs. Archibald tell him something different than she had told Mom right after the collision and that puzzled me. She said she had been traveling properly in her lane of travel, but had to veer to her left to avoid hitting us, because our car was "rounding the curve at a high speed" in her lane. Then at the last minute, she said, we veered in front of her car and hit the pole.

Although Mom tried to respond by telling the chief the true story of what had happened, he interrupted gruffly, saying, "You must have been driving carelessly and speeding, Mrs. Smith, because nothing like this has ever happened before in this safe, quiet neighborhood."

My mother denied she had been speeding or that she had driven in the wrong lane and stated that Mrs. Archibald had admitted she was responsible for the collision in their earlier conversation. The chief, taking notes, said he had to take care of moving the cars and would write up his accident report later. He then told us to get to the hospital in the ambulance as soon as possible.

The medics were worried about my injuries and were anxious to get going, so we prepared to leave. One of them told me, "You'll keep the doctors busy removing all those shards of glass from your scalp and stitching up your leg, young lady, but the good news is those cuts look superficial." As we drove off with the siren blaring, we took one last look at Ruby in her ugly position against the pole. The chief was continuing to talk to Mrs. Archibald.

When my mother eventually received the chief's accident report, she was shocked. Relying on Mrs. Archibald's story, he had determined that Mom was negligent and was liable for all of our injuries and the total loss of our Chevy. Once again, Mom had to retain Attorney Cotter to represent her. This time he would be filing a personal-injury lawsuit against Mrs. Archibald.

Mom's arm and facial scars had been superficial, so they healed within a few weeks; my injuries were much more serious. I underwent extensive emergency treatment for my forehead, scalp, and thigh lacerations at Brockton Hospital right after the accident. Plastic surgery was needed for the facial scars from my forehead lacerations the following year. Meanwhile the doctors restricted me from all physical education and sports activity at school, due to my leg lacerations. Doug sometimes woke up crying during the night from nightmares about car crashes and telephone poles. Although his physical injuries turned out to be minimal, the doctor said he had probably suffered shock, which could affect him for many years.

Mom went into a deep depression after the auto accident. She didn't sleep well and gained weight from eating lots of snack food. Her eyes lost the look of determination I had seen during the many months she had been saving money in the oatmeal box to buy the car. Her dreams of getting out of Brockton and moving to the West Coast were now dashed. Even worse, we were faced with extensive medical bills, as the insurance companies for both Mrs. Archibald and my mother refused to pay. Since liability for the accident was in dispute, both insurers were allowed to rely on the false and unfair police report concluding my mother was the liable driver.

Despite my injuries, I became Mom's caregiver, in that odd role-reversal that tends to occur between parents and children when families are under severe stress. My grandmother recommended that Mom go to see a psychiatrist, but Mom insisted the medical profession could do nothing to help her. I heard her say, "They just push pills; they can't cure my problems." She also confided in me that she felt her mother was not sympathetic and had let her down. Nana had told her to "get on with life." I believed Nana was trying to be supportive but used the wrong words, so Mom was not hearing the real message. I turned to prayer once again to help me cope with the painful family relationships and to give me the strength to make Mom feel better.

It was heartbreaking that we had only owned Ruby for a few days. The last time we saw her, she was wrapped around that telephone pole. Mom told us we would not be able to get another car unless we won our lawsuit. Meanwhile, we were in worse shape financially than we had been before we bought the car and, of course, we had no car. Mom's insurance company paid for our emergency treatment, but my plastic surgery a year later had not been paid. The unfairness of it all weighed heavily on Mom—and me as well.

I was fifteen and Doug was ten when the jury trial at the Plymouth County Court finally began in the spring of 1958. I had grown four or five inches since the accident and gone through a stage of extreme self-consciousness. I felt conspicuous and embarrassed because I had to wear a scarf over my head for many weeks after the accident to hide the giant white bandage on my forehead. My self-esteem suffered whenever I looked in the mirror and saw my war-refugee appearance. I had to sit in the bleachers, fully dressed, during PE classes, because the doctor said I could not do any physical activity. I couldn't wear the era's fashionable Bermuda shorts because some ugly keloid scar tissue had developed on my thigh's ten-inch-long laceration. My worst fear was that the keloid scar would continue to grow. I had seen photos of keloids that had grown to massive proportions, and I sometimes had dreams of being covered head to foot by ugly purple scars.

Mr. Cotter investigated the case by interviewing witnesses and gathering medical records. He took the depositions of Mrs. Archibald and the East Bridgewater police chief, and Mrs. Archibald's attorney took depositions of Mom and me. Mr. Cotter was not able to find any eyewitnesses to the crash, however. He told us that several of the neighbors had heard the screeching of brakes and the crash of steel against the telephone pole, but no one observed the two vehicles before they stopped in their ultimate locations.

Mom and I were the only people who had heard Mrs. Archibald admit she crossed the center line, intending to pass a slow-moving vehicle so she could make a quick left turn at the intersection. She had apologized to Mom for causing the collision, then changed her story by the time the police chief arrived at the scene. At her deposition she insisted that Mom was driving erratically in the wrong direction, then swerved into the pole for no reason, just as she had reported to the chief.

The critical issue to be decided at trial was whether the chief had mistakenly accepted her version as truthful or whether he should have investigated more closely at the scene to determine if Mrs. Archibald's story or Mom's made more sense. After all, her Hudson had ended up in our lane, its driver's side fender touching Ruby's rear fender, and Mom and I both had told the chief Mrs. Archibald admitted she was in our lane before Mom swerved into the pole.

Mom and I went to Mr. Cotter's office a week before the trial was to begin. He explained that the case would go before a jury of twelve men and women.

"The jury will decide the issues of liability and damages," he said. "We must convince them Mrs. Archibald is liable. If the jury finds that you, Irene, were the negligent driver, her insurance company will not have to pay for any of your medical treatment and will not owe any damages for your pain and suffering or for any permanent injuries Sandra and Doug have suffered."

Mr. Cotter explained his task would be to convince the jury that the police chief's conclusion was wrong. "Mrs. Archibald apparently created her story while you were all waiting for the ambulance and the chief to arrive at the scene. She was pretty clever, telling the chief your car was speeding and crossed the center line, causing her to take evasive action. She apparently realized once she was out of her car that there were no eyewitnesses to the accident. You were the only people who heard her admit she had been in your lane. The jury could find both of you biased. They could disbelieve your testimony. This will be an uphill battle for us."

Mr. Cotter then explained, for my benefit especially, how the lawsuit would proceed. "First, we lawyers will interview the potential jurors. I will have the right to strike a few of them, if I have reason to believe they are biased against us. The other attorney can strike any he believes might be biased in our favor. The judge will swear in the first twelve who remain after we make those strikes. The other lawyer and I will then give our opening statements, explaining what we each believe the evidence will show, to give the jurors a thumbnail sketch of our respective views of what happened. I will explain the extent of Sandra's permanent injuries and Doug's emotional scars."

Mr. Cotter was looking mostly at me as he spoke, probably assuming Mom understood the process. "You and your mom will be my first witnesses," he explained. "Before you each testify, the clerk will tell you to raise your right hand, and then ask if you 'solemnly swear to tell the truth.' All you need to say in response is, 'I do.' Then I will ask you a series of questions. Just listen carefully and answer each one truthfully, based on your recollection. When you answer, look right at the jury, not at me. It is those twelve people who must believe your story. Do you have any questions so far? Am I going too fast?"

"I do have a question," I said. "Can I tell the jury that Mrs. Archibald's version of the facts is false and that they should not believe her or the findings in the police report?"

"No, you cannot do that," said Mr. Cotter. "The jury has to make up its own mind about who is telling the true story. Their job is to weigh the evidence and decide what is accurate and what is not. The judge will give instructions on the law that applies to the case, then the jurors will adjourn to the jury room to deliberate. They will discuss the evidence and decide which witnesses were credible and which were not. They will then apply the law that the judge explained to them and reach a verdict."

"I see," I replied. "But you can ask Mrs. Archibald the tough questions when she testifies, can't you? You can make it clear to the jury that her story is ridiculous and untrue, can't you? You can emphasize the true facts." I felt anger rushing through my veins as I spoke. This would be our only opportunity to get justice, and I knew Mr. Cotter was the person who would have to make that happen. "In her version, our car was speeding on the wrong side of the road, so she swerved into our lane to avoid a collision and then we suddenly swerved back, crossing the entire road and driving into the pole—without ever hitting her car head-on. That sequence is ridiculous and impossible. The accident couldn't possibly have happened that way."

"Your analysis is very good," said Mr. Cotter. "We lawyers have a strategy for poking holes in someone's testimony and demonstrating the truth to the jury. That strategy is called cross-examination. When I cross-examine Mrs. Archibald, I will ask her some very specific questions that she will have to answer with 'yes' or 'no.' I will ask her about her speed and direction of travel. I will have her pinpoint on a map the location where she was when she first saw your vehicle approaching and exactly how both cars moved from that time on. I will ask her to estimate how fast your car was going. Then later, I will use her answers, along with the demonstrative exhibit showing her markings, to convince the jury that the accident couldn't possibly have happened the way she says it did. Also, of course, I will ask you to testify about the conversation you overheard between Mrs. Archibald and your mother after the collision. Your testimony on what she said, word for word, will be critical. By the way, in my investigation, I have recently discovered one additional piece of information that will surprise everyone, including you folks, and I think it will help our case. But I'll wait to let you find out about that at the trial. It will be rebuttal evidence, so according to the rules of court, I do not need to disclose it in advance."

Attorney Robert J. Cotter at his office desk (photo taken in 1972)

When we left Mr. Cotter's office that day, I realized how patient and thorough a trial lawyer must be in investigating a case and preparing for trial. Once again, I wondered why there were no women lawyers. I knew many women who were patient and effective at gathering details. The thought crossed my mind once again that maybe I would be a lawyer myself someday.

A week later, as I walked into the Plymouth County Courthouse with Mom and Doug for the trial, the memories of being there seven years earlier for the custody hearing came back to me clearly. The marble floor and the carved woodwork in the hallway all looked just as elegant as they had the last time I was there, but they seemed less intimidating than before. I breathed a sigh of relief when I saw that Judge Stone would not be our trial judge, as I had not felt he was fair when he spoke with me in his chambers in the custody matter. I said a quick prayer to St. Christopher that he would help Attorney Cotter persuade the jurors to believe our version—the true version—of the facts in our case. I also was very curious to learn what the "surprise" evidence would be that Mr. Cotter said he had found.

The trial proceeded as Mr. Cotter had explained. Mom, Doug, and I all sat at the plaintiff's counsel table. Mrs. Archibald sat with her lawyer at the defendant's table. The jury was a mix of nine men and three women, most as old as my grandparents. They listened intently as the lawyers gave opening statements. Mom was the first witness. Dignified and composed, she did an excellent job of describing, step by step, exactly what had happened. Then she explained her own injuries and mine and talked about Doug's temporary paralysis and subsequent nightmares.

Mr. Cotter had Mom tell the jury more about Doug's fears as Doug was still too young to be called as a witness. She explained he had not been able to see over the dashboard as the Hornet approached our car because he was short. He did observe the pole rapidly approaching the windshield above him, however, and heard the screeching of brakes, then the crash. Those sights and sounds had terrorized him. Then when I moved my body in front of his, he was scared, but protected from hitting the dashboard or windshield. (Not only was this explanation true, but it was a smart tactic to vividly point out Doug's childish vulnerability and my responsible action in guarding him.)

Mr. Cotter then called me to the witness stand. I felt nervous, of course, but confident as the clerk swore me in. I looked at each juror intently as I answered Mr. Cotter's questions. I explained in detail what I remembered seeing from the very moment we rounded the curve and the Hornet headed toward our car. I told the jury what I had heard Mrs. Archibald tell my mother after the collision. When Mr. Cotter asked me about my injuries, I described how my forehead and leg had felt at the accident scene and the fear I experienced during the many hours I spent on the operating room table at Brockton Hospital. I talked about the long period I had worn the bandage on my head and explained the plastic surgery procedure I had undergone in Boston, with its subsequent turban. Then, when Mr. Cotter asked me how things were going presently, I explained that I missed roller-skating and bike-riding in my neighborhood and I missed playing tennis and basketball at school. I also explained how embarrassed I felt about the scar on my leg and how afraid I was that it would continue to worsen.

At that point, Mr. Cotter asked me to do something he had not told me about in advance. He said, "Now I would like you to leave the witness box and walk along in front of the jury. Please lift up your hair so the jurors can see the scars on your forehead. Then lift up your skirt so they can see the scar on your right thigh."

His words came as a shock. I was totally unprepared for a public viewing of my scars, especially the one on my thigh. But I did not feel I could refuse. Slowly I exited the witness box and complied with Mr. Cotter's directions. I'm sure the jury could see my embarrassment, especially as I lifted my skirt in front of the men. My heart was pumping so loudly I was sure the jurors could hear every beat. My face felt flushed and my hands shook. Inside, I felt angry that Mr. Cotter had required me to make this undignified display in order to prove my eligibility for damages. Several of the jurors grimaced as they looked at the purple scar, though most of them did not register any emotion. Years later, I learned that lawyers sometimes use tactics that surprise their own clients, because they know the shock effect will be powerfully persuasive to the jury and will help them remember the details vividly during their deliberations.

The defendant's attorney did not ask me any questions, which I thought was curious. I had expected him to try to poke holes in my story through cross-examination, but he simply said, "No questions," when the judge invited him to cross-examine.

When Mrs. Archibald testified, she told the same story she had told at her deposition. She vehemently asserted that our car had been in the wrong lane and she had taken evasive action to avoid a head-on collision. Then, she said, our car swerved in front of hers and hit the telephone pole, and her car had hit the rear fender of our car. On cross-examination, Mr. Cotter showed her a sketch of the scene and asked her to mark where she had been when she first saw our car approaching. He asked her to place similar marks at each of the relevant places as the events had played out, according to her version of the facts.

Then he asked her a question I had not expected. "Where were you going when you first saw the maroon car coming toward you?"

Mrs. Archibald replied confidently, "I was headed home. I had just completed my last Monday nursing visits and was going home for lunch."

Mr. Cotter asked for her address and told her to mark the location on the sketch. He then asked her who was the last patient she had visited that morning, and she gave a man's name. He did not ask for the man's address.

After Mrs. Archibald testified, the defense attorney called the police chief as his only other witness. The chief reiterated the findings he had written down in the police report. Then the attorney told the judge, "The defense rests, your Honor."

The judge then asked Mr. Cotter if he had any rebuttal. Mr. Cotter replied, "Yes." He called out the name of a woman I hadn't heard about in all of our dealings about the case, asking her to come to the witness stand.

This new witness was sworn in and took her place in the witness box, telling the jury she was the supervisor in the visiting nurse department of the County Health Department. Mr. Cotter asked whether she had brought to court the schedule of Mrs. Archibald's nursing appointments for the day of our auto accident, and she responded, "Yes."

My eyes widened. What could this be about?

The witness pulled a tan file folder out of her purse and held it up for the jury to see. Mr. Cotter then asked her to read the schedule of Mrs. Archibald's appointments for the day in question. The witness read the names of the three patients who were scheduled at nine o'clock, ten o'clock, and eleven o'clock respectively. The eleven o'clock name was that of the man Mrs. Archibald had identified in her testimony as her last appointment. Then the witness added, "But Mrs. Archibald never got to the third appointment because she was running late and had a car wreck on the way there."

Mr. Cotter then asked for the address of the third patient and the witness provided it. After getting the judge's permission to approach the witness, Mr. Cotter gave her a pen and asked her to mark the location of the patient's address on the sketch he had previously used during Mrs. Archibald's testimony. Clearly, the home of the third patient was on the street that turned off the main road, just beyond the telephone pole where the accident had happened.

Looking at the scene from the perspective of Mrs. Archibald's direction of travel, I quickly realized she would have had to turn left onto that street in order to get to her eleven o'clock appointment. I remembered that the collision had occurred at 11:15 a.m. *So that was why she had been in such a hurry that morning! She wasn't headed home for lunch after all.*

The new witness had given credibility to Mom's testimony and mine. I was sure the jury would now conclude that Mrs. Archibald's initial conversation with Mom was the truth—she had admitted guilt and apologized. The jury would realize that by the time the chief arrived on scene, she had created a new story, and the chief believed her lie. Inside I felt elated and hopeful that the jury would see it that way.

After the lawyers gave their final arguments, the judge instructed the jury on their obligation to reach a verdict. "You must first determine whether Mrs. Archibald, the defendant, was negligent in causing the accident. You may only award damages for the injuries the plaintiffs suffered if you find, by a preponderance of the evidence, that Mrs. Archibald was liable. If she was not liable, you may not award plaintiffs any damages, regardless of how sorry you may feel about their losses."

It seemed an eternity before the jury returned its verdict, although it was probably only a few hours—we didn't even leave the courthouse. Finally, the twelve jurors returned to the courtroom and made their pronouncement.

"We find in favor of the plaintiffs," the foreman reported. "The defendant was negligent in that she crossed the center line and caused Mrs. Smith to move her car to the right to avoid a head-on collision. We award the overall sum of twenty-five thousand dollars in damages for Mrs. Smith's loss of property and the combined injuries and treatment to Mrs. Smith and her two children."

We were ecstatic. The jury had reached a fair verdict. The largest portion of the award, fifteen thousand dollars, was for the permanent nature of my injuries, including disfigurement, and the anticipated cost of future treatment for my keloid scar. The remaining ten thousand dollars was for the vehicle loss, the uninsured plastic surgery that I had already received, and the injuries Mom and Doug had suffered.

Mr. Cotter had warned us not to show any emotion, however, regardless of what the outcome might be, so we followed his advice while we were still in the courtroom. We waited until we were outside in the hallway to hug each other. With tears in her eyes, Mom thanked Mr. Cotter for his excellent work in representing us. "Justice has prevailed," she said, joyfully.

New Hope After the Verdict

⁂

A few weeks after the jury announced its verdict, my mother received several checks in the mail. The net amount we recovered, after all attorney fees, court costs, and outstanding medical expenses, was approximately nine thousand dollars. My share of the recovery was the largest—about six thousand dollars.

Mom took me aside and asked if I would agree to combine my share of the proceeds with her share and Doug's. After promising to manage the combined funds to benefit all three of us, she reminded me that we had been deprived of many things since my father had left the family eight years before. The settlement money, if spent wisely, could improve all our lives in many ways.

"We still don't have a car," she said. "We've always dreamed of going out West and living a better life. If we pool our settlement money from the auto accident, we'll be able to afford a decent car and take that trip. We may be able to put a down payment on a house out there. I'll get a nice job. All three of us will have new opportunities."

I thought long and hard about the options. At fifteen, I was a mature thinker for my age, and I already had experience balancing pros and cons to help Mom make financial decisions. My father had agreed to let Mom keep the net proceeds of the Goddard Road house in exchange for cancelling his child support obligation. My parents remained legally married, but my father had taken up residence with another woman and wanted to marry her.

Frankly, to me the laws applying to my parents' situation made no sense. Neither of them wanted to stay married, but because of the law and Mom's refusal to allow my father to get a divorce for his reasons, they remained legally married though permanently separated. In my heart I believed the law, as well as the rules of the Catholic Church, needed to change. (Many years later, the law did change to permit divorce based on irreconcilable differences, and the Church recognized that some marriage partners' vows should be annulled because one party had never intended to make a permanent commitment to the other.)

Now Mom was promising to make wise decisions with the settlement money from the jury trial. She was not coercing me to put my share into a common pool—she was only asking for my permission, and I knew I could say no. If I said no, I knew she would keep my money separate, in accordance with her obligation as my legal guardian.

I thought she was optimistic about how dramatically our lives would change if we went out West and started over. But I knew Mom was trustworthy, and she could definitely stretch a dollar. I believed the financial nest egg, if pooled, would achieve benefits for the three of us that we could not otherwise afford.

On the other hand, my six thousand dollars would probably provide sufficient funds to finance most, if not all, my future college expenses if I said no. But, did I want to see Mom and Doug continue to struggle in Brockton while I kept my own resources separate, then used it for my own tuition? No, I did not want that. I also believed I could earn scholarships for college, as I was a top student in high school and active in music.

So, I decided I would tell Mom yes. This would give her the opportunity to take us on her dream journey out West and to attempt to better our lives.

We began making arrangements to leave Brockton at the end of the school year. We found a classy-looking two-year-old black-and-white Chevrolet Bel Air with low miles and a clean interior for nine hundred fifty dollars. We didn't give this car a special name because it had been so sad to lose Ruby two years earlier—it was like losing a family member. We just called this car "the Chevy."

Next we looked at a map of the United States and talked about where we might settle. Our goal was to breathe fresh mountain air and experience the peaceful open-range territory we had seen in movie westerns. Doug wanted to fish in mountain streams. I wanted to hike on mountain trails and learn to ride a horse. So Denver, Colorado, became our destination.

After a flurry of preparation and research, on the last day of June 1958, we set out on our cross-country journey, feeling like three pioneers on a modern wagon-train expedition.

Each of us had a job to do *en route*. Doug, ten years old, was the navigator. I was responsible for keeping to our budget with a daily journal recording payments for gas and oil, tolls, motel costs, food, and miscellaneous expenses, like fixing flat tires. Mom had converted two thousand dollars into traveler's cheques, in five-, ten- and twenty-dollar denominations. (Back then there were no credit cards or ATMs; traveler's cheques, which functioned as cash, were the safest way to carry funds with you.)

We estimated it would take eight or nine days to complete the trip to Denver. We planned to spend thirty-five dollars a day for the basics. We allocated some money for entrance fees at historic sites and museums as well. "If you keep us within our budget," she told me, "we'll have $1,650 left when we reach Denver, enough for a deposit and first month's rent on a nice apartment, even a TV set."

The trip was a wonderful experience. Except for one terrible thunderstorm in Nebraska, where the hailstones were as big as golf balls, we had beautiful weather. Most important to me, however, was seeing Mom enjoy herself for the first time in years. She laughed, sang, and told funny stories we had never heard about her childhood and young adulthood. We played license plate games whenever the roads got boring or the landscape was monotonous.

In Chicago, we visited Uncle Fran, who was teaching political science and pre-law at Loyola University. He took us to the Chicago Art Institute and the Museum of Science and Industry. In Nebraska, a small airport was featuring passenger flights in a Piper Cub for five dollars per adult and no fee for children under twelve, so we splurged on our first plane ride together.

There were no interstate highways in most of America, so we drove on two-lane roads that connected one town to the next. Traffic was nearly always light, except in large cities. We never had difficulty finding a comfortable motel room or roadside cabin. We had pancakes or bacon and eggs for breakfast and picnic lunches in public parks. Dinner was usually a hot dog or burger at a roadside stand.

Finally, we caught a glimpse of the snow-covered Rockies far ahead. Mom was excited when she saw the purple sagebrush rolling across the desert plains and cowboys riding the open range—that was how she always thought Colorado would look. We rented a motel room outside Denver for three nights. Our plan was to explore the city, look at various neighborhoods, and decide where to live. Mom would look for a job. We studied the classified ads Mom had saved and mapped out the apartment locations and businesses that looked like good choices.

We were bitterly disappointed with what we found. The "affordable" apartments tended to be in poor condition and in run-down neighborhoods. One after another, the owners and managers told Mom, "Sorry, we require an employer's reference, but you are unemployed here," or simply, "We don't rent to single women with children." Even more disappointing, Mom could not get a job because she lacked local references. Although she could pass typing speed tests and was a whiz at math and spelling, she was unfamiliar with the new billing and accounting equipment in most offices. Doug and I could see Mom grow more and more depressed as she concluded Denver did not offer the opportunities she had expected.

We did not give up. We drove south to Colorado Springs, where the Air Force Academy had recently opened. The community was growing rapidly and Mom expected better opportunities there. Unfortunately, our apartment-hunting and Mom's job search there obtained similar results to those in Denver.

After spending three long, hot days in a motel, we put our heads together to decide what to do next. I don't remember who proposed it, but we all agreed, after thoughtful discussion, it would be best to go back to Brockton.

My Winding Path
through High School

—∞∞∞—

Our return was bittersweet. A month had passed since we initially departed on our cross-country adventure. While I was glad to return to Brockton High for my junior year, I was disappointed our expectations about living out West had fizzled. I was especially worried about how Mom would adjust to resuming her life in the city she had desperately wanted to leave. Would she dive into paralyzing depression again? Would she be able to cope with the immediate needs of starting over—finding a place to live, a new job?

Initially, Mom demonstrated a positive attitude. She found us a first-floor apartment in a good neighborhood. We spent a few nights sleeping on mats, calling the experience a "camp-out," then bought some basic furniture, even a small black-and-white television.

I was still fifteen, but I applied for a cashiering job at Coats Field, a department store. I did so well on their aptitude and skills tests that Mr. Kopelman, the manager, hired me with the admonition I was not to mention my age to anyone. He said I looked sixteen and he needed someone who was good at math and willing to work weekends as well as full-time during Christmas and summer vacations.

A few weeks later I learned Mr. Kopelman was seeking a reliable salesclerk for women's sportswear. The job would likely progress to department manager or buyer. *That would be perfect for Mom*, I thought.

When I told her about the job, however, she raised many objections. "I've never worked in a retail store. I don't have the right clothes. I wouldn't be good at dealing with the public."

"Mr. Kopelman is helpful and courteous," I told her. "You don't need fancy clothes; you already have a decent wardrobe. You just need to build up your confidence, Mom, and get over your fear. I know you can do it." I knew she was painfully shy and fearful of meeting strangers. *If I can just convince her to apply,* I thought, *she'll get the job. Then she'll prove to herself that she's competent. She just needs to take that first step.*

Then one day I saw Mom come into the store and go directly to the manager's office. She got the job and started working in the sales position right away.

That was the start of a very positive phase for Mom. Her self-esteem blossomed. After years of isolation and untreated depression, she was becoming the confident person I once knew. There were hills and valleys, of course, because she had deep-set anxieties. But I was grateful to see her feeling worthwhile and competent.

Day by day through my junior and senior years, I watched Mom emerge from her shell of fear and self-doubt. She became more relaxed and less obsessed with the gloom of past events. Even her poetry reflected more colorful images and hopeful thoughts. Our circumstances had led Mom to become dependent on me emotionally, and I had become, in many respects, the parent figure. Now, happily, she was the parent again. I felt more free to be a teenager. The new experience was refreshing.

I went to CYO sock hops at my new parish church. I enjoyed the attention of a couple of the boys at school. My chemistry lab partner liked to play pranks on others and persuaded me to participate in his foolishness, something I never would have done when I was younger. I even bought an evening gown and went to the junior prom.

Meanwhile, Doug was maturing and enjoying early teen life as well. Now eleven, he was able to caddy at Thorny Lea Country Club. I'll never forget Mother's Day 1959, the first day he carried double bags. He spent his entire day's earnings on a huge bouquet of flowers for Mom. It was the first time I had ever seen her cry for joy instead of sadness.

One day, Mom showed us an ad she had torn out of the real estate section of the Brockton *Enterprise-Times*. It featured a new development of ranch-style homes on Carl Avenue in Brockton's far south end. Each of the 1,100 square-foot, inexpensive concrete-block houses had three bedrooms and one bath. There was a fireplace in the living room, but no dining room or garage. The price was $10,500 for each house and lot, including a concrete driveway, but without landscaping.

"What do you think of this?" she asked me. "Wouldn't it be nice if we lived in a brand-new house? These 'tract homes' are simple and cheap, but I could fix one up real cute. We could have our own backyard, and we could play badminton together. No more rented apartments in three-decker tenement buildings."

"That looks like a great price," I said. "But how can we buy a house? We don't have that much money, and you've always told me a woman who is separated from her husband can't get a mortgage."

"Yes, that's true," Mom replied. "But I think I can afford

one of these houses on my own credit now. If we use half of the four thousand left in the bank, we can meet the twenty percent required down payment. I should qualify. I've figured it all out according to the details in the ad."

"Okay," I said. "Let's go see the neighborhood."

Things happened quickly after that. We fell in love with one of the available houses. Mom said she would ask Grampa to help her put in a lawn and a rock garden in the back yard. She told Doug there would be space in his room to set up the ham radio she had promised him.

There were a couple of drawbacks. The street was not yet paved and there were no sidewalks. On rainy days, Mom might have to leave the car a quarter-mile away and walk through the mud to get home. Also, Doug and I would have to take city buses to our schools, and on rainy days, we would be walking in the mud to the bus stop. In spite of the drawbacks, we agreed the house would be an excellent choice. Mom asked the real estate agent to draw up the purchase offer.

Then she applied for a mortgage.

At first the bank turned down Mom's loan application. They said it was "bank policy to lend only to married couples with good credit histories."

Mom called Mr. Cotter.

Mr. Cotter not only agreed to talk to the loan officer, but said he would file a lawsuit if the bank refused to grant Mom the mortgage. He told the loan officer he would sue the bank for misrepresentation because Mom clearly met all the bank's posted requirements for conventional financing and she had a steady job. There was no reason to doubt her creditworthiness, even though she was a single woman. He believed he could even win attorney fees if he prevailed.

A few days later, Mr. Cotter called with good news. The

bank had agreed to give Mom the mortgage.

"They didn't want to get involved in a lawsuit with you, Irene," he said with a laugh. "You've been winning in court rather often these past few years."

A month later, we moved into our own house, which Mom affectionately named "The San-Doug Ranch," in honor of me (Sandra) and Doug. We all appreciated Attorney Cotter's good legal work. Congress would not pass fair-lending and fair-housing legislation that would help women like Mom for six more years, but Mr. Cotter had gotten us there first, with good legal work. Awareness of this fact reminded me of my earlier commitment to become a lawyer.

My senior year was the happiest of my high school years. I had three part-time jobs, but still found time to play the snare drum in the marching band and be piano soloist with the Galloneers glee club.

I am wearing my high school band uniform,
ready to march in a parade (1957).

We took a three-day excursion to New York City, where we climbed the Statue of Liberty and Empire State Building, attended a concert at Radio City Music Hall, took a ferry ride to Staten Island and ate meals at Automat restaurants.

Meanwhile, I had a new academic focus: foreign languages. After two years of Latin, I started French, then German. Now a senior, I was studying third-year French and second-year German. I enjoyed the challenge of memorizing vocabulary, practicing conversations and verb conjugations, and translating literary passages.

As the year wore on, I took the SAT exam and began applying to colleges. Mom had always encouraged me to get a college education and get out of Brockton. She often said a degree would be my "ticket to freedom" and would guarantee an independent and secure future. She encouraged me to choose a college out of state, to benefit from a broader mix of people and cultures.

I knew college outside Massachusetts would be expensive, so I saved most of my employment earnings. I was frugal, resisting the expensive Pendleton pleated skirts and Capezio flats my girlfriends all wore. By the time graduation arrived, I had saved two thousand dollars. That was not enough to finance a four-year college education, however. I would need scholarship assistance.

I identified several small liberal-arts colleges where I could specialize in foreign languages and fit in socially. One of them was the College of New Rochelle, a Catholic women's college Uncle Fran had recommended to me. A priest and university professor, he had long been my mentor on issues of religion and education—and he was my favorite uncle as well. He always listened patiently when I needed a kind ear after my father left.

Uncle Fran had taught many women graduate students who had obtained their bachelors' degrees at New Rochelle. He said they were bright, well-trained in traditional classical studies, and down-to-earth, good people. New Rochelle tended to attract students from middle-class families, rather than wealthy ones, he added. This impressed me as I felt I would not measure up socially to the wealthy students from well-connected families at other women's colleges, like Manhattanville or Smith or Wellesley.

My uncle, Rev. Dr. Francis J. Powers, C.S.V., often spent his vacation time at the Plymouth beach with us (photo taken in 1991).

When I received notice of admittance from the College of New Rochelle, it confirmed a partial scholarship and work-study job in the library as well. I could wait on table in the dining room on weekends to earn money for books and incidental expenses.

I was thrilled and promptly accepted. The New Haven Railroad made regular runs between Boston, New Rochelle and Grand Central Station in New York City, so I would be able to travel home by train for Christmas and I could access the Big Apple on free weekends during the school year. I was excited about the possibility of seeing Broadway plays and perhaps attending an opera at the Met.

I gave serious thought to pursuing a pre-law program. However, my high school guidance counselor gave me advice about the "real problems" associated with becoming a woman attorney. She maintained that the only achievable careers for women were teaching, nursing, executive secretarial and government service.

"Women who get hired as lawyers are usually the daughters of lawyers or judges," she warned. "Other women with law degrees work as legal secretaries or court clerks."

I was bitterly disappointed with her advice because it just reinforced my growing disgust with gender discrimination. But I gritted my teeth and decided what I really wanted to do was improve the lives of women and people who looked and talked differently than I did. So I told my counselor I enjoyed foreign languages and cultures, adding I would like to consider options like working for the United Nations as a translator or the U.S. State Department as diplomat. I also was considering journalism, to become an international news correspondent for the *New York Times* or *TIME Magazine*. My counselor seemed to think those goals were more achievable than becoming a lawyer. She reminded me, however, "You could always teach in high school as a back-up plan."

So, having balanced all the issues, I decided to major in foreign languages, emphasizing French and German, at the College of New Rochelle, and minor in journalism. The rest of my program, which was prescribed for freshmen, would include philosophy, theology, English literature, Western civilization, and biology.

A month before graduation, all college-bound seniors were notified to submit applications for local scholarships. I promptly applied for several. One required an essay on how world peace could be achieved. Since my goal was to study foreign languages, I argued I would help reduce the fear and distrust that people experience when they do not understand another person's language. I also explained my mother, a single parent, had to struggle to make ends meet and could not help with my college expenses.

The Brockton School Board was the screening body for local scholarships, so I was invited to meet with them to respond to their questions. Superintendent Ralph Frellick surprised me by asking: "Sandra, in view of your family's difficult financial position, why have you decided to go away to college? Why don't you stay home, get a good job with the telephone company, and help your mother and your brother? He'll be wanting to go to college in a few years."

I was shocked and dismayed, because his question reminded me once again that males counted more than females in the eyes of most adults. I had a hard time gathering my thoughts to answer. However, I explained that my mother had always wanted to go to college herself, but her family had only supported such education for her brothers.

It was my mother's wish, as well as my own, I told him, that I pursue an education. My mother did not want me to stay in Brockton and work as a telephone operator.

Dr. Frellick's body language and the reactions of some other board members revealed they perceived my response as impertinent. I wondered, as I left the room, whether I had any chance of winning any local award.

Graduation took place on a warm, sunny afternoon in June 1960. Mom and Doug were there, as well as Grampa. I was proud to march into the football stadium wearing my traditional white cap and gown. I sat with the band members and played the national anthem for the large gathering of graduates and our families.

Then, I was especially proud and surprised to hear Dr. Frellick announce that (despite my apparent impertinence) I had been awarded two local scholarships. The Soroptomists had selected my essay on world peace as its winner. The Brockton *Enterprise-Times* had recognized me for skill in writing.

After lining up with my class, all 669 students, I received my diploma from Dr. Frellick's hand, then shook hands with the chairman of the Brockton School Board.

College Years

From my first day on campus at the College of New Rochelle, I knew I had made the right choice. My dormitory, St. Anne's Hall, was a cozy red-brick Colonial-style house that had been converted to a sorority-like residence. It accommodated thirteen freshmen in five doubles and one triple. Most of us became close friends and kept our same roommates throughout all four years.

My roommate, Mary Jane McGovern, was a public-high-school graduate like me, also on scholarship with a work-study job. We shared the wood-paneled dining room, which had been decorated by Bloomingdale's Department Store as the model dorm room for freshman. What a delight it was to have bright red bedspreads and matching drapes.

*I am sitting (left-front) with ten freshmen "sisters"
in St. Anne's Hall. My roommate, Mary Jane McGovern,
is at right-front (1960).*

Ursuline nuns, semi-cloistered members of the Order
of St. Ursula, ran the college. They were dedicated to the
dual goal of educating women and serving the poor and
sick. They had founded the college in 1904, when women
were generally excluded from higher education. The institution was chartered in 1910 and became the first women's
Catholic college in New York State.

By the time I entered in 1960, several thousand women
had earned Bachelor of Arts degrees and the college had
earned a reputation for educational excellence. The nuns
were dedicated to pursuing the motto, "*Serviam*," meaning
"I Serve," and they combined rigorous academic training
with career preparation in a values-driven community.

Although they were our religious role models, most had advanced degrees in literature, science, mathematics, and the arts, so they were role models of scholarship and careers as well. Even the college president was a woman. In an era when men were leading every institution in America except Catholic women's colleges and hospitals, we had the privilege of seeing women acting with respected authority and intellectual accomplishment.

Though we didn't realize it at the time, those nuns were the earliest "liberated women" of the twentieth century. They offered hope to those of us in the post-1950s generation who were grappling with the reality of sex discrimination in employment, business, government, even in social organizations and Church leadership. Most of us students wanted to establish a successful life and career upon graduation—without having to wear a nun's habit.

Most CNR students came from Catholic high schools with strong academic credentials. Many had been high school valedictorians with high SAT scores. I knew I would face stiff competition. Most of us were of the Catholic faith, and we were expected to live in accordance with Christian principles and behavioral rules. Although I could follow those standards, I felt different from other students. They all had grown up in nuclear families with loving fathers. It seemed their lives had been problem-free, while my parents were legally separated and I knew my mother suffered from mental issues. To protect my privacy, I always avoided talking about my family. However, my roommate knew my story. She asked her father to take me to the freshman Father-Daughter Dance along with her, a kindness I have never forgotten.

I loved everything about the campus, not only the buildings and landscape, but the course work, faculty, and my fellow students. I was well-trained in Catholic teachings and had developed a strong sense of spirituality. Although my mother had been excommunicated by her parish priest, she always supported my sacramental trainings and encouraged me to be confirmed by the Archbishop of Boston at age thirteen. I knew she had not lost her faith, although she never went to church. Her excommunication remained confusing and troubling to me.

My grandfather, Frank Powers, escorted me to church on Confirmation Day (1956).

Uncle Fran helped me understand that Mom was conflicted about her faith. He said I could help her by praying for her and by succeeding in my own life. My closest spiritual confidant, he explained the Scriptures in down-to-earth ways, telling me about the majesty of the law and justice as well. He said law and religion have a lot in common, as they are both grounded in respect for the common good and the Golden Rule. He also listened patiently to whatever I shared with him about my mother's mental health issues. He expressed compassion toward Mom for refusing to stay with my father after their marital commitment had been broken. I got the impression that Uncle Fran believed, as I did, that the Church needed to revise its attitudes about women and marriage and that Church leaders needed to be more sensitive to the needs of women in general. I also knew he hoped things would change and women would be able to pursue law careers in the future.

I dove into my new life as a college freshman with enthusiasm. I developed good study habits and did not mind our strict curfew. I learned to play bridge in the lounge beneath the dining hall (and took up smoking as a result). I appreciated the charitable activities we engaged in, such as visiting patients with mental illness at Belleview Hospital and tutoring students at a girls' reform school. I enjoyed my work-study job as a desk clerk in the college library, and I appreciated having the opportunity to earn extra money waitressing on weekends.

Socializing with the male students from nearby schools was also fun, although I never had a regular boyfriend. Whenever I managed to save enough money to spend a Saturday in New York City, I took the train with a few friends, grabbed a Reuben sandwich at Hector's Cafeteria in Times Square, then purchased a standing-room-only ticket for a Broadway play. Sometimes we rode the Staten Island Ferry, a round-trip lasting nearly two hours but only costing fifty cents. Sometimes we pretended we were rich and went window shopping for elegant jewelry at Tiffany's or tried on expensive designer clothes that were modeled for us personally at Bergdorf-Goodman's. We wandered through Central Park and visited the Metropolitan, Guggenheim, and Cloisters museums. Most years we watched the St. Patrick's Day parade on Fifth Avenue. All those wonderful features of New York City enhanced my education at CNR.

Meanwhile, Mom and Doug kept me updated on what was happening back in Brockton. In the spring of 1961, at the end of Doug's eighth-grade year, I suggested that Mom encourage Doug to take the entrance and scholarship test for Thayer Academy, an elite prep school in Braintree. Doug scored a very high grade on the exam and, because of Mom's financial status, was awarded a four-year scholarship.

However, there was no public transportation between Brockton and Braintree. Doug would not be able to attend unless Mom drove him to and from Thayer each day, a 35-mile round trip. So, Mom applied for jobs in Braintree. She landed an excellent office job where she worked for three years, then found an even better job when Doug was a senior. Mom's success at her jobs in Braintree and her joy at seeing Doug thrive at Thayer Academy helped to relieve her occasional bouts of depression.

Mom never became fully stable emotionally, however. Doug told me when I returned from CNR each summer that he was glad to have me home because he needed some relief. Mom had not outgrown her anxieties and paranoia. She still had ups and downs with fears and irrational beliefs of impending disaster, which she shared with him frequently. This was an ongoing problem I could see we both would have to live with well into our adult years.

Even though I worked hard at my studies, I was disappointed in my grades. I rarely earned an "A." The Ursulines theorized that "C" was a good solid grade. To get a "B," one had to show a spark of excellence and, to earn a rare "A," the work had to exhibit a unique genius quality. Topping off the problem was the college's unique GPA system, which had a maximum of 3.5 instead of 4.0. My GPA was somewhere in the middle of my class, with an overall average of B- and a GPA of about 2.7 at graduation. I was not alone in being concerned that our GPAs might be a hindrance in the future if we applied to graduate schools. Students had no ability to change the system, however.

I did well in my major, which was French language and literature. I even earned a few "A"s in advanced French courses and was elected president of the German Club. I felt confident my successes would lead to eligibility for a career in the foreign service or at the United Nations.

However, every French major was expected to spend the summer before junior year at the Sorbonne or the University of Grenoble, living with a French-speaking family and speaking French. The cost of either program was more than I could possibly afford. For students like me, a six-week total-immersion program at Laval University in Quebec was an acceptable alternative. Even that recommmendation presented a dilemma, as I counted on my summer earnings to fund part of my college expenses for each subsequent year.

Our college president, Mother Mary Robert, often told us during convocation speeches, "If you ever have a problem you cannot solve by yourself, come to my office and talk to me. My door is always open to you." My problem seemed unsolvable, so I went to her office one day to ask her advice.

Somewhat hesitatingly, I explained my situation and asked if it might be possible to increase my scholarship and work-study package for junior year. The president graciously replied, "Yes, Sandra, I think we can do that for you." She then went on to suggest I apply for a new position that would open in the fall, as foreign language laboratory assistant. If selected, I could replace my library job with the new one and the compensation would be greater. "Also, that job might open doors for you if you decide to teach French after graduation," she said with a smile. I have never forgotten that nun's kindness in meeting my needs.

The Quebec program in 1962 was enriching on many levels. Not only did we learn Parisian French pronunciation from the distinguished professors who came from the University of Paris to teach us, but we were immersed in the historic and cultural features of Quebec's old city every day.

While I was in Quebec, I heard news of a horrific event in New York City involving one of my classmates. Barbara had been a day student, so I didn't know her well. Shockingly, her body had been found in a shabby area of New York City after she underwent an abortion.

All abortions were illegal in 1962, so Barbara had obtained her procedure at a back-alley "clinic." Something had gone terribly wrong, and she hemorrhaged and died. The abortionist had dismembered her body to cover up the crime, then disposed of the body parts in the City sewer.

The story shook all of us CNR students to the core. The Catholic teaching that abortion was not only sinful but legally and morally reprehensible for all women regardless of religion was generally accepted by all of us. We had been taught that abortion constituted the murder of the fetus. Therefore, our initial reaction to Barbara's story was to be horrified and judgmental at the same time. Barbara had made the wrong choice. It was hard to feel any mercy or compassion for her.

Once we learned the reasons why Barbara had obtained the abortion, however, we had to think again. Barbara was nineteen when she became pregnant. Her boyfriend wanted to marry her and she had agreed to his proposal, but her parents did not like him and were furious about the pregnancy. They reminded her that if she married or had a baby out of wedlock, CNR's attendance policies would prohibit her from returning and graduating. She was willing to accept that fate, but she needed her parents' consent to get married under New York law. Her parents had never been able to go to college themselves. The children of Italian immigrants, they had worked hard with the goal of seeing their daughter graduate from CNR. They also feared the relationship would not last and Barbara would be left a single parent. So they denied their consent to the marriage and initiated the trip to the abortionist to arrange an abortion against their daughter's will.

Once we learned the full story, it became clear that abortion was a complex issue. We had never discussed it that way before. We had believed the full responsibility for taking such awful action always fell on the pregnant woman herself. We were suddenly faced with the fact that Barbara might not have been the most guilty party, and some of us began to ask questions.

Could ugly outcomes like what had happened to Barbara be prevented if women had more control over their own lives and bodies? Why did CNR prohibit married students from completing their degrees, when other colleges did not? Why did Barbara's parents have such power that they could prevent her from marrying her boyfriend and force her to have an illegal abortion, since she was considered an adult for most other purposes in New York? Why did *anyone* who sought an abortion, even a victim of rape or incest, have to go to an unsafe, unsanitary place and be treated by an unlicensed criminal instead of by a competent medical professional? Why did the law not recognize that male abuse and coercion sometimes caused the unwanted pregnancies in the first place?

Some of us even began to question the public policy regarding abortion as a crime and our initial belief that our fellow student had committed an unforgiveable mortal sin. While we did not all agree that Barbara was a victim of her parents' powerful intervention, many of us ultimately became advocates for giving women the right to make their own reproductive choices, even if we remained personally opposed to the choice of abortion based on our moral compass as Catholics. We felt the Church and the government were both being unreasonable in forcing all women, including victims of date rape (fairly common at that time although not yet called that), to have babies conceived against their will.

Most of us finally concluded we should never judge the motivation of another woman who chose to have an abortion. She might be acting under coercion that stripped her of freedom of choice. We should only judge ourselves on the morality of our own decisions. We further came to believe that women's reproductive rights should be protected by law and enforced through proper medical care by licensed physicians. And, many of us became advocates for safe methods of birth control, which was still prohibited by the Church. We knew many Catholic families had large numbers of children. Most of us at CNR, on the other hand, privately wished to limit our families to two or three children. Safe methods of contraception, like the birth control pill and the intrauterine device, were now available to women. We thought these methods were morally appropriate, in that they allowed women to be good parents for a reasonable number of children who were welcome and wanted, not just accidental results of their marriage.

It was eleven years later, in 1973, that the United States Supreme Court decided in *Roe v. Wade*[1] that a woman's right to an abortion was implicit in the right to privacy protected by the 14th Amendment to the Constitution. The Catholic Church has never agreed that abortion is morally permissible, however, even if the pregnancy resulted from rape or incest or if the mother's life is at risk. Nor has the Church agreed that contraceptives are morally permissible, though individual priests often counsel women to make their own judgments in such matters. Because of these facts, coupled with my mother's excommunication by her parish priest, I began to question whether I wanted to remain a Roman Catholic.

I did not leave right away, but years later, after I learned many priests had themselves abused both girls and boys of all ages, I joined the more welcoming Episcopal faith. By that time, women were acting as clergies in many Protestant churches including the Episcopalian. I appreciated the fact that the Episcopal church retained the Mass structure and the Eucharist, as well as the Scriptures and rituals I was familiar with, so I adopted that setting for my faith participation.

During my final year at CNR, I had to give serious consideration to my career options. My dream of going to law school remained impractical, as there were still no employment opportunities for women lawyers. Although Congress was debating a civil rights law that would protect black-skinned men from racial discrimination in employment, there was still no discussion about protections for women of any race.

Ironically, the Civil Rights Act of 1964 was passed within months of my college graduation. Surprisingly, that law included the words "on the basis of sex," which prohibited discrimination based on gender as well as race (the original purpose of the legislation). The addition resulted from one Congressman's last-minute effort to kill the bill. I have thanked God many times for the Congressional acceptance of the bill with that last-minute addition. Although motivated by a mean-spirited desire to perpetuate racism, the added words opened the door to all women's equality in employment. When I heard about this, I knew becoming a lawyer might be possible in the future, so I kept the dream alive.

I had thought studying French would enable me to become a translator at the United Nations, a diplomat, or foreign correspondent. However, I learned there was a quota system at the U.N. whereby native speakers and persons from member nations were preferred as translators. Most European hires were fluent in three, even four languages. Additionally, the State Department usually hired people with political connections as diplomats, and nearly all were men. Most American newspapers only retained one foreign correspondent at a time, almost always a male.

In spite of those disappointing realities, I took the Foreign Service exam and the federal service exam. The only position I was offered as a result of those tests was in the debt-collection office of the Internal Revenue Service in New York City. I respectfully declined.

Teaching remained my only viable option. When I went home for spring break, I checked with the Brockton School Department. They were seeking French teachers for a new conversation course at each junior high. Three of the positions were already filled, but North Junior High was still seeking applicants. I interviewed and within forty-eight hours, I was hired for the position, to begin in September at the excellent salary of $5,200 per year.

I was thrilled to have a job ready for me upon graduation, but immediately became concerned about how I would approach teaching conversational skills to twelve- and thirteen-year-olds. I had no student-teaching experience. Also, there was no budget for books, so I would have to create my own materials.

When I went back to CNR to finish the semester, I happened to see an announcement that some universities offered summer institutes for foreign language teachers. The National Defense Education Act (NDEA), a comprehensive law supporting humanities and sciences as a way of preventing war, funded the institutes. Their purpose was to instruct teachers on how to use the new audio-lingual method (ALM), so students would become fluent in the spoken language, not just able to read and write. One of the French institutes would be offered at Notre Dame University in Indiana. I immediately applied—I urgently needed to learn the new audio-lingual techniques. Within a few weeks I received notice that I had been admitted to the Notre Dame institute that would be held during the summer, right after my graduation.

Uncle Fran attended my graduation in June along with Mom and Doug, who was a teen-ager of sixteen. They were all proud of me, and I was proud that my family was there to celebrate with me. I received my Bachelor of Arts degree from the hand of Cardinal John Spellman, Archbishop of New York. As I knelt down to kiss the Cardinal's ring, my heel caught in the hem of my academic gown and I nearly fell onto the stage, but the Cardinal managed to grab my hand and steady me to an upright position. Then he teetered a bit, nearly losing his balance. The near-accident was apparently visible to the audience, as Doug later said, "Tomorrow's newspapers will probably carry the headline, 'Cardinal Falls for CNR Graduate.'"

As I packed my things to leave New Rochelle later that same day, I realized I had grown and matured in many ways. I had acquired a broad academic foundation. I became familiar with the cultural features of the Big Apple. I spent a summer in historic Quebec and became fluent in French. I made life-long friends and dealt with financial issues in mature ways. I dealt with a moral and legal issue I had never questioned before, abortion, and reached some surprising conclusions about my faith and my religious beliefs. Most importantly, I was about to participate in an NDEA Institute at Notre Dame University where I would train for a new career as a French teacher, one I had not expected to enter when my college education began four years earlier.

LIFE AS A TEACHER

⸻⸺⸻

There were 54 French teachers in the 1964 NDEA Summer Institute at University of Notre Dame. Fifty-three were experienced teachers, some for decades. I was the only participant who had never taught French in a secondary classroom.

I quickly learned, however, my conversational ability in French was better than that of most of my colleagues. As for ALM, the new pedagogy we were there to learn, we were all in the same boat. We had all been taught French the old-fashioned way, by memorizing vocabulary, grammar rules, and verb tenses and writing out translation exercises. ALM emphasized oral conversation from day one, with the goal of having students become fluent before reading or writing. This approach was new, for even the most experienced teachers at the best public and private schools in the country.

Our classroom was an indoor amphitheater. We watched a master teacher instruct twenty volunteer students with no previous foreign language instruction to speak French through listening to and repeating what she said. She asked questions, which the students attempted to answer to show they understood. She used gestures and encouraged the students to figure out what her words meant, avoiding English translation unless absolutely necessary. She taught them to mimic French sounds by watching her mouth and observing her tongue as it moved against her teeth. They learned to conjugate verbs through oral drills. For relief, they sang French songs and played an occasional game by moving around, following the teacher's instructions. There was no reading or writing, only active, verbal language usage.

Watching day after day, we gradually learned the process. During afternoon sessions, we practiced what we had learned that morning on each other. Additional professors gave supplemental information on theory and how to develop lesson plans and tests. By the end of the ten-week program, I was just as trained and experienced in ALM as any of the other participating French teachers.

I went home from Notre Dame, ready to begin my new job, with about seven hundred dollars in my pocket. The NDEA legislation included a weekly financial stipend in addition to our free tuition and living expenses. I soon found a 1959 Chrysler Windsor sedan with fins and double headlights that I managed to afford by borrowing three hundred dollars to supplement my savings. Although getting a loan as a single woman was still difficult, the loan officer at the bank approved it—however, he warned me he would come right over and pick the car up if I missed any payment. Meanwhile the dealer put new tires on the car and painted it the color I wanted, metallic blue. My beautiful car looked practically new.

Doug was a senior at Thayer Academy by that time. Mom was still working in Braintree and driving Doug to and from school each day. Doug worked part-time as a stock boy at a super market after school. The three of us shared the Carl Avenue house but led totally separate lives. My teaching assignment demanded my full attention.

Mr. Ford, the principal at my school, assigned me eight sections of Conversational French, each meeting twice a week. My students were the most proficient seventh and eighth graders. They learned quickly, and I was challenged to prepare new dialogs and drills every week. I did lots of xeroxing during my free period every day. I also taught one traditional first-year French class five days every week to the best and brightest ninth graders. In addition to all that, I was assigned two sections of seventh-grade remedial-level health, each meeting twice a week. My combined student load was about two hundred and fifty—double the load a typical teacher carried. I still did not know all my students' names by the end of the first six-week grading period. Also, I was totally unprepared for the difference in capacity between the high achievers in French and the slow learners in health. Keeping up with the various classes was a constant struggle.

I soon learned that teaching was not my only task. A staff person came to my classroom one day and said, "You need to change the monthly exhibit in the lobby display case." I was also responsible for collecting a quarter from every teacher every month, then buying cards and flowers for those who were sick or hospitalized. The staff person also added, seemingly as an afterthought, "Oh, and by the way, our music teacher can't plan the Christmas program this year, so Mr. Ford wants you to come up with something for that assembly."

These extra jobs came as a complete surprise and were overwhelming, especially the Christmas program. There were no teachers' unions in Brockton schools. No collective-bargaining law existed yet in Massachusetts that would allow unions to organize public-sector employees. Even though my job description had not referenced any extra duties, I had no right to object. No extra-duty pay was available to compensate me. Only male coaches of boys' sports teams received extra-duty pay.

My job became my whole life, twelve to eighteen hours every day. Luckily, I was still single and lived at home. Mom prepared my dinners and did my laundry. I could not have done what my job demanded if I were obliged to help out at home also.

The Christmas program was my most difficult challenge. Pageants depicting the Nativity had been standard in public schools when I was growing up, but were declared unconstitutional by the United States Supreme Court two years earlier, based on the First Amendment, in *Engel v. Vitale*.[2] So I had to come up with a non-religious holiday theme. The school librarian showed me a play, based on Charles Dickens's novel, *A Christmas Carol*, written at middle-school level. I decided to use the play to fulfill my extra job for December. Since I had no access to drama students, I asked my ninth-grade French class if they would like to participate for extra credit, and they eagerly agreed. Their parents made costumes and sets and coached the children at home. The production came together well during our after-school rehearsals and was a big success. Whew!

Meanwhile my newly acquired audio-lingual techniques for teaching French were working in my seventh- and eighth-grade classes. The students especially enjoyed singing French folk songs. The parents were thrilled to hear their children speaking French. The Latin teacher, however, whose classroom was next to mine, was not so happy. Miss Reddy was nearing retirement and her approach to language learning was the old-fashioned one. She complained to me several times, saying "I don't know what you are doing in your classes, but in my classes we work. We don't play act and sing songs!"

In January 1965, Mr. Ford came to me with a new proposal. "Would you be willing to take on a student teacher for the rest of the year? A professor from Stonehill College has asked me to place one of her French students in your classroom, and I understand she is well-qualified."

I reminded him I was not even certified yet as a secondary teacher. I was unsure of how I could supervise and train a student. I had never had student-teaching experience myself.

Mr. Ford said he thought I'd do a good job anyway. "She just needs to watch you and copy what you do. You're doing a great job getting your kids to speak French."

Carolyn Murphy then became my protégée. She had excellent French pronunciation and was a serious worker. I told her I was a brand-new teacher myself, but would do my best to explain the audio-lingual techniques I used in my classes.

"I've only been teaching a few months, so I'm not an expert," I admitted. "We'll be more like partners in the classroom; we'll be learning together."

Carolyn understood the challenge. Fortunately, she was a quick learner and a cooperative partner. We were only one year apart in age.

In May, Stonehill College's Education Department held a special dinner for student teachers and their supervising teachers. After the meal, Carolyn walked to the podium. I had no idea she was going to speak. She focused on thanking me for her "wonderful experience" working at North Junior High. She said I had treated her more as an equal than as a trainee and she had thrived under my supervision. She especially appreciated the effective way I demonstrated the new audio-lingual teaching method. She said she now felt qualified to accept a teaching job for the coming year.

After Carolyn finished, the head of the student-teaching program asked if I would be willing to teach the course in Methods of Teaching Foreign Languages at Stonehill College the following year. I explained I had only been teaching for one year, and the instructor said she was already aware of that.

"You really know what you're doing," she said, "and you're the best person to teach these students how to use the audio-lingual method. So we want you for this job." I taught the Methods course at Stonehill the following year, 1965–66.

Later that spring of 1965, I learned a second-level NDEA Institute would be offered during the summer. The program, arranged by the University of Oregon, would be conducted in Tours, France, in the heart of the Loire River Valley. I promptly sent in my transcript and requested a letter of recommendation from the director of the Notre Dame program. Within a few weeks I received notice I had been accepted for the Tours program.

Right after the school year ended in June, I took a Greyhound bus to New York City and met my new colleagues at the French Embassy. We soon began with a week-long visit in Paris before proceeding to Tours.

The Institute allowed me and my colleagues the opportunity to experience true French culture and everyday French language, as spoken by ordinary people in the city most famous for using "the most perfect French pronunciation." We were each assigned to live in a French family and take breakfast and dinner there every day. I was housed with the Berbonde family, which included a married couple, their five-year-old daughter Isabel and a house guest from South Africa. Dinner was a three-hour event with multiple courses and wine every evening.

There was an interesting side benefit to my stay at the Berbondes' home. I learned about an issue of which I had little previous knowledge, South African Apartheid, from the family's house guest, a young white man from Johannesburg who had just spent a year studying in London. He was preparing to return to his native country. While in England, he had reached the conclusion that the views of his white community were wrong. He now believed black people were equal to whites, and he intended to demonstrate his commitment upon returning to Johannesburg.

His views made me think about the Supreme Court's decision in *Brown vs. Board of Education*,[3] which had abolished segregated schools in my own country. I recalled that the Freedom Riders had courageously helped black people ride buses and eat at lunch counters beside white persons in the American South. Their conduct had led Congress to pass the Civil Rights Act of 1964, abolishing discrimination in employment and public accommodations. I also recalled singing "We Shall Overcome," along with my fellow French teachers and a large contingent of Peace Corps volunteers at a hootenanny in the Notre Dame University stadium while I attended the NDEA Institute the year before.

Although some progress had been made in abolishing both race and sex discrimination in my own country, I knew that, somewhat similarly to the situation in South Africa, we still had a long way to go.

When I returned to the United States after my summer in France, I thought more and more about my future. Did I want to stay in Brockton forever? Could I pursue other options? I gradually decided to pursue teaching at the college level and began looking at universities offering Master's degrees in foreign languages. I kept my long-term goal of becoming a lawyer alive as a possible future option, but I knew women were still not welcome in the legal profession, in spite of Title VII.

Mr. Ford added a new extra job to my North Junior High teaching schedule in the spring of 1966. He asked me to play the piano during rehearsals of the school's theater production, a Gilbert and Sullivan operetta, "Trial By Jury." I was not familiar with that operetta and was charmed by the farcical British story and music. I enjoyed helping to make the production a success, though I received no extra compensation for the work. The story was somewhat silly, but it reminded me of the sexism of the legal profession. The characters—a judge, two barristers and several jury members—were all male. According to the operetta's plot, Defendant Edwin was on trial for abandoning his fiancée, Plaintiff Angelina, because he loved another woman. Unfortunately for Edwin, the jury members and the judge all swooned over Angelina, so Edwin proposed to marry both women as a way to stay out of jail. The judge then chose a better solution—he decided to marry Angelina himself!

In the late spring, I applied to several graduate schools, including the University of Oregon, which offered me a teaching assistantship, including free tuition and fees plus a monthly stipend for living expenses. I promptly began planning my move to Eugene, Oregon, on the West Coast.

In many ways, I had become a new person. At age twenty-three, I was more self-assured and confident. I had achieved success as a college student and foreign-language teacher, then supervised a student-teacher and taught a course at Stonehill College. I had spoken French in Quebec and made friends with interesting people at Notre Dame University and in Tours, France. I had thought deeply about serious moral and social issues of my time. At home in Brockton, I had watched my mother gain self-confidence through owning her own home and succeeding at her work experiences. My brother Doug had graduated from Thayer Academy one year earlier and was a freshman at Cornell University in Ithaca, New York. For all these reasons, I felt confident that moving on to graduate school in Eugene, Oregon, would be a further positive and liberating experience.

ON TO OREGON

―❈―

O nce I decided to move to Oregon in 1966, I invited my mother to go with me. I knew it was her chance to do what she had wanted so much to do: get away from Brockton.

"Come out West with me, Mom," I said. "We can share an apartment. You'll be able to get a job in Eugene. We'll visit Uncle Rob in Spokane and get to know his kids and grandkids. You'll finally live in the Far West, as you've always wanted."

Mom was hesitant at first. She was afraid to pull up stakes again. Eight years older than when we went to Colorado, she realized it would be more difficult to go back to Brockton and start over now. She would have no family to return to. Both of her parents—my grandparents—had passed away, and Doug was now a college freshman at Cornell University in Ithaca, New York.

Critical to her ultimate decision, however, was a comment her boss at Grass Instrument Company made when Mom told her about my invitation. "Irene, go to Oregon with your daughter. If things don't work out for you there, you'll always have a job here." Mom realized she would have nothing to lose if she took a leave of absence from her job and traveled with me to Oregon. So she agreed to make the trip.

We invited Doug to accompany us on the trek. We needed his help in sharing the driving and helping us get established in Eugene. We assured him he could find a summer job there, then return to Cornell in September. He agreed and was helpful as we packed.

By the end of June the three of us were on our way westward, by a different route this time. After visiting Uncle Fran in Chicago, we drove into South Dakota, passing through the Badlands and visiting Mount Rushmore. We dropped down to Omaha, Nebraska, to visit an eleven-year-old cousin, Bruce Powers, who had recently begun living at Boys Town, a well-known Catholic orphanage.

Bruce had been tragically orphaned the previous year in 1965 and was happy to see us. In the years that followed, we invited him to visit us in Oregon during school vacations. Then, after graduation from Boys Town, he came to Oregon, enrolled at University of Oregon and spent his adult life as part of our extended family.

Continuing on our trip to Oregon, we visited Yellowstone National Park, the Grand Tetons, and the Buffalo Bill Museum in Cody, Wyoming. Finally, we arrived in eastern Oregon. We were thrilled to see the Painted Hills of the John Day area and the Old West towns along the route, some of which were ghost towns. Seeing the forests of Douglas fir trees, I remember thinking I would spend the rest of my life in the beautiful Pacific Northwest.

The next few weeks were busy and exciting. We rented a brand-new furnished apartment that accommodated the three of us comfortably. Doug and I scoured the employment ads in the *Register-Guard,* looking for summer jobs. Unfortunately, it was too late to apply for the most lucrative opportunities at the canneries. I applied to work in the dining room of the Country Squire Motel, but learned only men were eligible for those positions. I thought about reminding the interviewer of the Civil Rights legislation that was passed two years earlier, but decided against it as the interviewer offered me a lower-paid job in the coffee shop. I just wanted a summer job, not a lawsuit. Doug also quickly found employment making patio tents and awnings (still advertised as "men's work").

I couldn't wait to start hiking the wilderness trails of the Cascade Mountains, so I joined the Sierra Club on the U of O campus, bought a pair of sturdy hiking boots and participated in the club's weekend expeditions. I also joined the Newman Center, the Catholic parish for U of O students, as I knew I would make new friends among the graduate students at weekly Mass.

Mom had a harder time adjusting to the new environment than Doug or I had. She held onto her Massachusetts driver's license and declined to register to vote in Oregon. Reluctant to sever her ties back East, where she had spent her entire forty-seven years, she kept open her option to return.

Mom did enjoy visiting her brother and sister-in-law, Rob and Ann Powers, and their family in Spokane. Mom and Ann had been friends back in their teen years, so, when we visited their Hayden Lake retreat in Idaho, the two would stay up until the wee hours renewing their friendship. Mom also tried waterskiing behind Uncle Rob's boat, something I never expected she would do. And she enjoyed talking with her many nephews and nieces, most of whom she had not seen since they were young children. Renewing her relationships with family members made Mom realize she might enjoy living in Oregon after all.

Over the following months, several things happened. Doug went back to Cornell for his sophomore year. I started teaching and taking graduate courses at the University of Oregon. Then, Mom landed a job with the Eugene School District as property records clerk. In that position, she was responsible for tracking millions of dollars' worth of furniture, equipment, and musical instruments in forty schools and eight administrative buildings. She even learned to operate state-of-the-art computer equipment. The job was more than a step up from her previous position. She felt valued and respected. She also had fair compensation and was even a participant in a retirement program.

Doug's life took some major leaps during the following year. When he returned to Ithaca in September 1966, he declared political science as his major field of study and planned to go to law school upon graduation. Then one day he noticed a bulletin-board announcement addressed to "Oregon Residents." The office of Oregon's senior Senator Wayne Morse in Washington, D.C., was inviting political science students who lived in Oregon to apply for internships for the following summer. Doug filled out an application and was selected for one of the internships. The following summer, Doug worked in Washington and we didn't see him at all. Meanwhile, he met and fell in love with a fellow student at Cornell, Pamela Gales. A year later, in September 1968, Doug and Pam eloped to New Hampshire and got married, as parental permission would have been required in New York State. They were both just twenty years old and juniors in college.

My life took some big leaps in 1967 as well. In June I traveled cross-country by train to New York City to meet fellow participants in a third-level NDEA Institute course before flying to Paris once again and spending a wonderful summer in the city of Arcachon on the Atlantic coast of southern France.

A week after returning from France, I met a young man at the Newman Center named Gene Gangle.

Gene was quiet and studious, and I liked him from the start. He had also been in France during the summer, so we had a lot to talk about over coffee. He had studied at Mt. Angel Seminary for three years after high school in Eugene, then graduated from Gonzaga University in Spokane in 1965. He had intended to enlist in the Marines (rather than default to the Army, as he had a low draft number for Vietnam), but the recruiters denied him due to knee injuries he had incurred over years of playing football and throwing the discus. Subsequently trained as a teacher, Gene had decided to take a few months off to drive around Europe. Since returning, he had been working long hours on the night shift at the Eugene Fruit Growers cannery, uncertain about what he would do next.

He invited me to go crabbing on the Alsea Bay at the Oregon Coast. Little did I know, as I pulled his pots out of the water that afternoon and learned how to hold angry Dungeness crabs so they couldn't pinch my fingers, that sixteen months later I would marry this interesting man, who was so different from any of my previous boyfriends, and that we would eventually build a retirement home on a cliff overlooking the Pacific Ocean about one mile north of that very bay.

Gene had grown up on the Oregon coast as the third of eight children in a dysfunctional family, so he was a bit rough around the edges. He impressed me, however, because he talked about many of the same issues that interested me. He was deeply religious and intellectual, but, like me, had concerns about the power and wealth of the Catholic Church, as well as its sexist attitudes.

We both believed the Church should acknowledge that women were competent equals to men in running Catholic colleges and hospitals and should be allowed to study for the priesthood and be ordained to serve the faithful in parishes. We both had read the philosophical writings of Teilhard de Chardin, and we had faith in that theologian's broad-minded approach to the evolution of the human race. We theorized that, if he had lived longer, Chardin would have broadened his views to propose the equality of women and men. We also were both excited about Pope John XXIII's views on bringing together people of different Christian faiths. We had watched the Second Ecumenical Council unfold and believed the Church was moving toward a universal form of Christianity that would treat all people of the world equally. (Later, we were disappointed that the bold teachings of Chardin and Pope John failed to produce meaningful change.)

Gene was physically strong and loved to explore the outdoors, especially the Oregon Cascade mountains and the Pacific coast. He also liked to read and write poetry and study philosophy. He lived frugally, often eating just one meal a day, but had splurged his savings on a bright lemon-orange "Bahama-yellow" Porsche 912 sports car while he traveled in Europe. I certainly enjoyed riding in that car, although I was never able to master its five-speed standard transmission.

In April 1968, Gene and I became engaged. He bought me a lovely opal ring. We were invited to attend the first Mass of Gene's former seminary roommate, Father Ed Haasl, in North Bend, Oregon. After the ceremony, we asked Ed to bless our engagement, and he was happy to accept.

The engagement caused emotional upheaval for my mother. She did not share my level of trust in Gene and was terrified he might have some undisclosed faults and expectations, like my father's. Gene, for his part, always demonstrated respect for Mom when she showed hostile reluctance to accept him as a son-in-law. He patiently assured her we would never move far away from her, reminding her often that we would always care for her.

I had earned my Master's degree in March and was applying for college teaching jobs by the time of our engagement, while Gene applied for high-school teaching jobs. There was a good chance I would be hired by a community college in northern California and Gene would find an opening somewhere in Oregon. Since we did not expect to be hired in the same city for the coming school year, we did not set a wedding date right away. Our plan was to work for a year at whatever jobs we found, then select an appropriate wedding date based on where we would decide to live and work from then on.

I was fortunate to be hired to teach advanced French courses at Oregon State University in Corvallis. Assigned to teach Composition and Conversation, Twentieth-Century French Literature, Linguistics and French Civilization and Culture, I was thrilled to have such challenging work and jumped in with both feet.

I moved into an apartment in Corvallis in May 1968, as my assignment was to begin with summer school classes in June. Meanwhile, Gene stayed in Eugene and traveled throughout Oregon for job interviews. The teaching field was very competitive that year, so Gene was disappointed to learn time and again that he had come in second for a position. Meanwhile, he continued to work at the Eugene cannery during the week and visited me in Corvallis on weekends.

Then, in late August, a miracle happened. The Corvallis school district announced a last-minute opening for an English teacher and invited Gene for an interview. He was promptly hired for the position and told he would start immediately. He quickly rented his own tiny apartment in Corvallis, just a few blocks from mine.

We could now set a wedding date much earlier than we had expected. We chose December 21, because that would be the first day of the Christmas vacation for both of us.

We were married at the Cathedral of the Immaculate Conception in Portland, Oregon. Father Ed Haasl, who had blessed our engagement, was now serving as a curate at the Portland cathedral and had arranged the tiny wedding for us there. My friends Lynae and Kathy attended, along with Mom, who was still nervous about my marrying Gene, but attended the service and even signed the wedding certificate as the groom's witness. Kathy, who had gone hiking with us frequently, was my witness. Lynae had made my beautiful knee-length silk wedding dress and veil, adorned with marabou feathers resembling white fur, as her wedding gift to me.

My brother was unable to attend because he was still a busy student at Cornell University and had recently told us about his elopement with Pam. We chose not to tell Gene's parents about our plans, because there was no way we could arrange a wedding that would accommodate them, as well as Gene's seven siblings and his many aunts, uncles, and cousins. We had wanted a ceremony that would be as close to an elopement as possible.

After the ceremony, which involved a full Mass with holy communion of both bread and wine (a very new option in that era), the six of us enjoyed a festive wedding dinner at the Trees Restaurant in the Hilton Hotel. Then Gene and I headed for the Empress Hotel in Victoria, British Columbia.

An early winter snow was already falling when we left Portland after the wedding dinner and continued throughout most of our week-long Canadian honeymoon. We finally arrived back in Corvallis on New Year's Day 1969.

Gene and I pose for a wedding photo in the cathedral courtyard (December 21, 1968).

WE'RE A FAMILY NOW

W hen we called Gene's parents and siblings in Sacramento on Christmas Eve 1968 while in Victoria and told them we were married, they were not surprised. They said they had expected such a call. Gene had a habit of keeping his life decisions private until after he had made all the arrangements. They had realized, when we visited them the previous spring, that he must be serious about our relationship, so they fully expected a wedding might be imminent and that they would probably be notified after the fact.

In a very real way, it was better to share our news after the wedding than it would have been to deal with our extended family and friends in the context of a church ceremony. We were able to talk individually with each person or couple and share our happiness in a unique and personal way with everyone. We frequently heard the comment, "Oh, so you eloped. How romantic!" I cannot remember anyone saying, "I really wish I had been invited to the marriage ceremony."

We both started back to work during the first week of January. My French language and literature courses at Oregon State University were challenging but a real honor for a twenty-five-year-old with a brand-new master's degree and just four years of prior teaching experience. My course load included some classes I had myself just taken for my master's degree.

Gene had moved into my apartment as soon as we returned from Victoria. It was a one-bedroom, second-floor unit of a private home within walking distance of my university office. We each carried a briefcase home each afternoon and spent several hours after dinner in our tiny living room preparing for our next day's classes. We talked a lot about our long-term goals and dreams: traveling and seeing the world, having a family with two or three children.

Most of all, we agreed we would work to avoid the mistakes our parents had made. We knew we would make our own mistakes, but were committed to solving them peacefully and cooperatively. During our pre-marriage counseling, which was required of all Catholic couples at the time, Father Ed had told us, "Never go to sleep without solving an argument, even if you have to stay up all night talking things out." We never forgot his advice.

In the spring of 1970, a little more than a year after the wedding, we applied to teach in the Military Dependents' Schools abroad. Mom was feeling more secure by that time and encouraged us to apply. She agreed it would be a great way to combine our teaching careers with our goal of seeing the world and a foreign appointment would only last two years. We were thrilled to be accepted to teach on the island of Guam, to start in the fall.

However, shortly after applying, I had discovered I was pregnant. In my acceptance letter from the Military Department, I was required to affirm that I knew of no reason why I would not be able to teach throughout the entire one-year term. Gene was not asked to sign the document, so I knew the requirement only applied to women who might become pregnant. I felt it was sexist and unfair, but the Civil Rights Act of 1964 did not cover pregnancy or parenting issues. Pregnancy leave would not be protected until 1978. I had to announce my pregnancy.

I admitted that I would have a baby the following December or January and would need to take maternity leave of several weeks. Soon after, the administrators sent me a letter withdrawing our invitation to serve on Guam.

We started looking for a house to buy, so we would have a home of our own by the time the baby arrived. Property values were high in Corvallis, so even with our good incomes and some savings in the bank, we could not afford a house there. However, houses were less expensive in Salem, about an hour north. Gene could qualify for a better paying position there and could coach track as well. I would have to commute the forty miles, but that was doable as my work schedule was only three days a week. Gene applied and was hired at McNary High School in Salem, and we put a down payment on a comfortable albeit dated house. We were ready to become parents.

My mid-section proceeded to grow from a bump to a balloon. I bought a portable sewing machine at a garage sale and made some maternity smocks and jumpers. At first I wore a belt around my middle, but eventually I let the smock hang freely over maternity slacks. Yes, slacks. I had already been one of the first women to wear a pants suit when teaching in 1969. Once I became pregnant, I was clearly the first French instructor to wear a maternity pants suit into a classroom at Oregon State University—and I continued teaching until the day before my daughter was born. Times were changing.

*My close friends Kathy Woodley (center) and Lynae Edwards
(right) celebrate with me upon learning that I will
become a mother (summer, 1970).*

The biggest problem I dealt with during my pregnancy was
Mom worrying about me. She had two bouts of depression
during the fall of 1970. I spent the weekend with her in Eugene
each time. I think she feared I was distancing myself from her
and we would be totally separated once the baby arrived. I had
to constantly reassure her I would never abandon her and she
would soon have a grandchild to cuddle and love.

Fortunately, she was doing well at her job and felt valued
and competent there. Weekends were the difficult times. I
hoped she would be strong during the Thanksgiving and
Christmas holidays, while waiting for the baby to arrive.
That season had always been difficult for her. It was harder
for me to console her now as I had concerns for my own

physical and emotional health.

We invited her to stay with us as much as possible over the holidays and things went fairly well. Gene brought home a giant Christmas tree, and Mom helped decorate it. She made us her special Granny Smith apple pies, and Gene lavished her with praise and gratitude for those. On Christmas morning Mom surprised us with a huge box of baby clothes and blankets. She was starting to look forward to the big day.

Melanie was born on January 7, 1971, two weeks after her due date. Gene was the first parent to hold her, as medical professionals were encouraging new fathers to bond immediately with their babies at the time. It was a joy to see him melt as he cuddled her. I remember seeing tears in his eyes as he watched me nurse her. He said, "Women are so lucky to be able to be mothers."

As I had promised, I went back to work when Melanie was two weeks old. Other professors in the department had been covering my classes during my absence, so I could not wait any longer. There was no maternity leave or sick leave for college instructors. We were fortunate to enlist Gene's aunt Agnes Rowley, a retired widow living in a town just twenty miles from Salem, to be our babysitter when I returned to work. She came and stayed with us for several days each week while Melanie was a tiny infant. After a few months, I felt comfortable bringing Melanie along with me to Corvallis and leaving her with a former student whose own baby was the same age as Melanie. It was an effective arrangement, as it permitted me to continue nursing Melanie longer than I could have otherwise.

We visited Mom in Eugene regularly on weekends after Melanie was born. Mom was thrilled to be a grandmother, and she always cried when we returned to Salem. Although she liked her job, had made friends, and had even bought herself a bicycle to ride on the trails throughout Eugene, Mom still had frequent bouts of depression. We were always concerned for her well-being. She continued to write poetry, however, and took a writing course for seniors at the university. I felt she was doing as well as she possibly could. I think she understood she was better off in Eugene than she would have been back in Brockton, and that encouraged her.

Meanwhile Gene suggested we buy a piano, after I told him babies respond well to music and I used to play piano well. It had been about six years, however, since I accompanied the "Trial by Jury" performance, so I was worried my fingers might not permit me to play anymore. I was wrong to worry. The piano became a new source of joy for me as well as for Melanie and Gene. I had emphasized classical music of Chopin, Beethoven, and Bach during my teen years, but now I played show tunes from *My Fair Lady* and *Phantom of the Opera* as well as Christmas carols, children's tunes, and Irish music for Mom. We even enjoyed singing along.

A year later, when Melanie was eighteen months old, Gene and I took her on a cross-country trip in our new Volvo station wagon, visiting various relatives and friends from Nebraska to Massachusetts, where I visited Attorney Cotter to update him on Mom's move to Oregon and to thank him for his wonderful legal help during my childhood. We continued on to Quebec, then returned across Canada. By the time we arrived back in Oregon, I knew I was pregnant again. Melanie was twenty months old and learning to talk in full sentences. We were thrilled that our family would soon include a sibling for her.

School was starting, and we returned to our respective jobs. On January 17, 1973, our son was born. We had not decided on his name before his birth, and the nurse told us we had to choose it before he could leave the hospital.

Gene wanted to name him Rocky, but I preferred something more traditional, like Jonathan. Gene reminded me that my home-town hero was Rocky Marciano and I replied, "Yes, but he was a prize fighter! Our son might be an intellectual like you. Kids might punch him in the face if his name is Rocky. Besides, Rocky Marciano's real name was Rocco, a nice Italian name, not Rocky."

With that, we both realized we could reach a compromise. I would agree to accept Rocco as our son's middle name if Gene would agree to Jonathan as his first name. We would both call him Rocky until such time as he might prefer to be called Jon or JR or Rocco. Gene agreed. With that, the nurse prepared the birth certificate and we went on home.

We loved our cozy little home with the two little ones. In April 1974, however, while we were eating oatmeal in the breakfast nook, a City of Salem truck parked in front of our house, behind our Volvo, and workmen tacked a "No Parking" sign on the telephone pole. When Gene went out to ask what was going on, the men greeted him brusquely, explaining, "Sir, you have to move your car. You can't park here anymore. The City Council has designated this street a major four-lane arterial connecting downtown to the freeway. We'll be painting lane markings in the street this afternoon."

We were shocked by the news. There had been no advance notice, and we had no way to object. It was a done deal. We realized we would have to move, to protect our children from the dangerous traffic conditions we expected.

We were fortunate to find a buyer quickly—a piano teacher who would benefit from having her home and music studio face the busy arterial street. We found a split-level house in a quiet cul-de-sac with two bathrooms and a basement playroom, as well as a treed backyard. That became our family home for the next seven years.

From the day the city workers arrived, I became politically alert and active. I would not be caught unawares again. I read the local news, stayed informed about zoning and construction projects and joined the neighborhood association. Later I became a member of the League of Women Voters and studied the issues and candidates carefully before voting in every election. I followed the progress of the Watergate hearings and the impeachment of President Nixon. I was concerned about what was happening in Vietnam and was glad when a Peace Accord was finally negotiated. But I was worried about the corruption in Washington, D.C. First, Vice President Agnew resigned in disgrace, then President Nixon resigned and Vice President Ford became our president. What would the future hold for our children? Once again, I wished there were wise women in government leadership and law, so corruption and war would give way to justice and peace.

Being the mom of two little ones became my major role. I did not want to quit my French teaching entirely, but I thought about a part-time position so I could spend more time with the children. As luck would have it, a French professor at Willamette University in Salem announced her retirement that spring and recommended that her department hire me to fill her course assignment on a part-time basis. Willamette was a perfect fit, as the campus was only four miles from my home. Beginning in September 1974, I brought Melanie and Rocky to drop-in day care at the YWCA near campus whenever my classes were scheduled.

Then one day in the spring of 1975, while walking through the Willamette campus pushing two-year-old Rocky's stroller and holding four-year-old Melanie's hand, I noticed a number of women students entering the law school building. I realized legal challenges had worked their way through the courts. Title VII of the Civil Rights Act of 1964 was finally being enforced. Women were finally becoming lawyers.

Memories of accompanying my mother to court at age eight and testifying in my jury trial at fifteen came flooding back to me. I realized the time had come to make my dream of law school come true. It was what I had always wanted to do. It was what my mother had wanted to do back in 1936. It was what my uncles Fran and Robert had done and what my brother Doug had done. Now, it was my turn.

A Law Student at Last

I told Gene that evening what I had seen at the law school, then asked, "What would you think if I applied to be one of those women, with the intention of becoming a lawyer?"

He didn't miss a beat. "The first thing you should do is go down to the Book Bin and pick up a copy of the review book for the LSAT exam. Then order your college transcripts and get an application packet so you can start the process."

From that response, I knew right away he was on my side and we would be able to make it happen. I wasn't surprised to have his encouragement, as he had demonstrated his belief in gender equality in the past. He had urged his younger sister Rose to attend his own alma mater, Gonzaga University, and was proud of her feminist leadership activities there. In 1972, Rose was elected the first female student body president, then was appointed to the male-only Board of Trustees.

She had attended Georgetown University Law School for one semester after Gonzaga but had left because she had felt unwelcome as one of only six women students. She intended to enter politics and was already planning her first campaign for election as a representative in Congress. We had hosted her many times on visits to Salem and shared her enthusiasm for social justice issues, especially feminism. Rose was outspoken and confident in expressing her opinions.

I followed Gene's advice and took the LSAT. Ordering transcripts was quite a challenge, as I had to send requests to five institutions: College of New Rochelle, Laval University, Notre Dame, University of Massachusetts, and University of Oregon. I applied to Willamette University and received a letter of acceptance within a couple of months. Then, reality set in.

Law school would demand my full daily commitment, not only during class hours, but evenings and weekends as well. My children were only four and two years old. They still needed me at home part of every day. While they enjoyed the YWCA's day care and Gene could handle their bedtime procedures, I knew I still needed to give them quality mothering until they started attending school. I decided to wait a couple of years before starting law school.

I made an appointment to speak to the Law School Dean, Carlton Snow, and asked him if I could delay my entrance for two years. He agreed, saying the administration would recognize my LSAT result for up to five years and would keep my file open until I reapplied. My future acceptance, however, would depend on the comparability of my record with the records of the applicants in that particular year.

Dean Snow also told me the admissions officers had been concerned about my college GPA, but resolved the problem in my favor. "While I have you here," he said, "I would appreciate it if you could explain why your GPA at College of New Rochelle was so disappointing. Your grades were much better at every other institution you attended."

The Ursulines' unusual GPA system had shown up to haunt me. I explained CNR's policy regarding issuing few grades above "C," hoping it didn't sound like an unbelievable excuse.

Dean Snow understood. He said, "You'll be happy to know our admitting committee adjusted your college GPA figure upward by one full point anyway, because grade inflation has been occurring in higher education generally over the past ten years. We figured your average would be higher if you were earning your bachelor's degree today. Also, of course, you are teaching French right here on our own campus, and we would not have hired you if you weren't competent. We are looking forward to having you as one of our law students."

I was proud to share the news with my family, but unsure of what their reactions would be to my new ambition. Mom, of course, was supportive. Uncle Fran was glad I was following my dream. He told me my French-teaching experience would be beneficial in legal studies, explaining, "Law is like a foreign language in many ways. It's verbal and based on logic. Lawyers have to communicate clearly in speaking and writing. You have those skills, Sandra. I think you will do well as a lawyer."

Gene's sister Rose, who was now working in Portland as an advocate for women of color and victims of sexual abuse, warned me, "Sandra, you'll need thick skin to attend law school, but at least you have white skin." I realized what she meant. I was aware that I benefited from what is now called "white privilege" in being admitted, as none of the law students I had observed were persons of color.

My brother Doug had earned his J.D. in 1972, had already served as a JAG officer, and had opened his own solo practice in Tacoma, Washington, by the time I was admitted to the law school. During those years, Gene and I visited Doug and Pam frequently. Our children formed wonderful relationships with them and later, their cousin Tracy whom Doug and Pam adopted. I envied Doug whenever he talked about helping clients with legal problems. Knowing my younger brother could appear in court and fight for justice had been a constant reminder of what I would be doing with my life.

But when I told Doug I was finally accepted in law school and would start in two years, he was far from encouraging. He tried hard to convince me to stay in foreign-language teaching.

"You're not tough enough to be a lawyer, Sandra," he said. "You have no idea what impossible challenges you'll face. It's no career for a woman."

I reminded Doug I had been thinking about a legal career since I was eight years old. And, I did not intend to practice criminal law, only civil matters, especially civil rights issues like employment discrimination and land use.

Doug was not convinced. When I told him my ultimate goal was to be a judge, his response was even more negative.

"Don't you know how political that road is and to what extent a judge's work involves criminal law? You've said you want to practice employment discrimination and land use. To get elected as a judge, you would have to have criminal law experience, representing defendants and prosecuting criminal cases. It's an ugly world out there, Sandra. You have no idea. You'd have to raise money to run a political campaign to get elected. And you'd have to hear lots of divorce cases, which you've said you don't like." His arguments came at me one after the other. His summary? "You could never do it, Sandra! Stay home with your kids. Be a teacher. That's the best role for you."

I was disappointed in what I thought was a misplaced lack of confidence in my ability (or perhaps unfair sibling rivalry). Not to be dissuaded, though, I argued my case right back. "You've done it, Doug. You went to Cornell Law School, and now you're a successful lawyer. I'm your sister. We grew up in the same family, dealt with the same struggles along with Mom. I'm just as tough as you. Why can't I do what you've done? Maybe I'll never be able to run for a judgeship, but I believe I can help people solve legal problems. There will be many options for me once I pass the bar exam. I believe I can do it, and Gene is firmly behind me."

Many years later, Doug confided his real reason for his objections. He had become disheartened with his practice for many reasons and wanted out, right at the time I was deciding to get in. He tried to protect me from the disillusionment he felt after dealing with a few unethical lawyers and irrational judges, and even clients who had unreasonable expectations of his role as their attorney. He chose not to disclose his unhappiness to me because he had not yet decided what he was going to do. Instead, he tried to warn me that it was not a perfect career and I should be wary of its shortcomings. Eventually, Doug did close his practice and become a commercial real estate broker.

In any case, Doug did not dissuade me from my goal. I still intended to enter law school in 1977.

I returned to my part-time teaching assignment at Willamette and spending half-days with my children. But administrative changes at the college led enrollment in foreign language courses to drop by fifty percent. My position, as well as that of one other language instructor, was eliminated, effective at the end of fall semester 1975. There were no appeals, no exit benefits. My employment was at-will, meaning I could legally be terminated at any time and for any reason. The memory of union picket-lines from my childhood came back to me, but I had no such recourse.

During that same year, Vietnamese and Cambodian refugees, many of whom spoke some French, were being welcomed to Salem. Instructors were needed to teach English as a Second Language (ESL) at Chemeketa Community College. I applied and was promptly hired to teach an evening advanced adult class, beginning in January 1976.

The position was a perfect switch from my Willamette teaching position. Not only did it allow me to spend my daytime hours with my children, but I was able to undertake a new challenge, one that brought back memories of my friendship with Tina, the ten-year-old refugee from Greece who lived next door in Brockton. I looked forward to working with an entirely new group of immigrants from a different culture who, like Tina, had survived a bitter war experience and needed to learn "survival English" to live and work in their new country.

Teaching ESL went beyond the basic audio-lingual French conversation I had once taught at the middle-school level. I now taught American culture and adult-level phrases for purposes of employment, apartment-seeking, and shopping. I coped with a wide range of learning abilities. Some students were well-educated, including a former diplomat from Phnom Penh and several ex-military officers of the Vietnamese and Cambodian armies. Others were simple folk with limited education—merchants, farmers. A few Laotian women had never been to school.

Complicating the situation even further were the social and political divides. Distrust issues were evident among the students from the three countries. My job was as much that of a diplomat and conflict-resolver as one of English teacher. Most of the students worked all day at Salem's mushroom factory before coming to my three-hour class every evening. They were looking forward to being qualified for better employment, where they would have to speak English, so they were highly motivated. I taught them as much as humanly possible in a very limited amount of time. Fortunately, they worked hard and made rapid progress.

The best part of the experience was the intense respect I received from my students; I was their "Madam Teacher." They were deeply grateful for their warm reception in America and the opportunity they now had to live in a safe and secure community where they could raise their families. My best memory is of the day my women students came to my home to learn how to make American sandwiches, salads, and desserts. They brought me a tray of Vietnamese *cha gio,* or spring rolls, a big bowl of noodles, and a beautiful Asian tea pot. We enjoyed a wonderful international party together.

The time finally came in September 1977 to begin my studies at Willamette University College of Law. My starting day was also the first day of school for six-year-old Melanie in her first-grade class at Queen of Peace Catholic School. Rocky attended the four-year-old pre-kindergarten class at South Salem Baptist Church. Gene was a counselor and driver's education instructor at Sprague High School. All four of us went off to school at the same time that morning and most school days for the next three years.

I was thrilled to be back in the role of student, after twelve years of teaching. My class included 120 future lawyers, one hundred of whom were males under twenty-five. I was one of the three oldest students, at thirty-four. Most women were above thirty. Five of us were mothers of school-age children.

It was a new time in the history of law school education, thanks to the Civil Rights Act of 1964 (although I do not recall any students of color in the class). We women were acting on the faith that law firms and government agencies would overcome their past beliefs that we were less competent and less competitive than men and would hire us once we graduated. Our future careers were still highly uncertain.

My first-year courses were Contracts, Torts, Property Law, Constitutional Law, Legal Research and Writing, and Criminal Law. Each textbook weighed about five pounds and consisted of hundreds of multi-page opinions in cases decided by the United States Supreme Court, interpreting and applying the laws that the relevant course covered. Together, the books filled an entire shelf of my bookcase at home.

I eagerly read every case assigned for every class session and prepared for the inevitable questioning that would come from the professors the following day. Classes were held in a large amphitheater. Professors used the Socratic method, calling on us to answer questions without warning, debating with us, making us defend our answers. I found the experience stimulating, though it was sometimes humiliating if I couldn't give an adequate answer.

My best course was Research and Writing, where I had to write briefs in which I argued specific legal questions as if I were representing a party in litigation. My end-of-year brief earned the highest grade in my class, a real honor and source of encouragement. I knew persuasive writing was the most important skill for a successful lawyer to master.

In my second year, I studied Criminal Procedure, Commercial Law, and Legal Ethics. As electives, I chose courses that would be important for areas I planned to emphasize in my future legal work—Labor Law, Arbitration, and Land Use. I was elected to an editorship on Willamette's *Law Review*, an honorary position that involved regular writing assignments. My article about Oregon's Land Use Goal 10 analyzed the need to include affordable housing in all neighborhoods, particularly new residential developments.[4] I was passionate about the subject, based on my earlier involvement in my neighborhood association.

Rocky became ill with chicken pox that year, so my role of mother took precedence over my law student role for a couple of weeks. Kindergartens do not accept children with contagious diseases, for good reason. I certainly had no objection to their policy. I had never contracted chicken pox myself as a child, however, so I caught the disease while caring for Rocky and was still contagious when he returned to school. I therefore missed nearly a month of classes in all. My fellow students tape recorded all the class sessions and my good friend Ellen Johnson brought the tapes to me each day. I was able to keep up with the lectures and readings at home while recuperating.

During that same year, Dean Snow, who had a private practice handling labor arbitration cases, called me to his office. Noting I had merited the distinction of "high paper" in Research and Writing, he asked if I might be interested in a clerkship working for him. I accepted enthusiastically, as I knew it would give me excellent hands-on experience in real-life labor arbitration matters, not just textbook research.

When Dean Snow asked why I was interested in labor relations, I told him about growing up in Brockton, where I had observed union workers from the shoe factories picketing for better wages and benefits. Additionally, my mother and I had both experienced discrimination based on our gender in several different circumstances. Not only had I been denied some jobs that were designated "men's work," but I had to wait until the age of thirty-four before I could attend law school.

He asked me if I would favor unions or management in collective bargaining disputes. I replied, "Neither. I believe the process is based on reasonable negotiations between equally represented parties. Their resulting contract is actually a 'private' law, which the parties established between themselves through mutual agreement. I would respect the parties' agreement in the same way that I respect our public laws enacted by elected representatives in our national and state legislatures. If either party violates some provision of the contract, that party should lose the dispute in arbitration, just as someone who violates a public law would incur a penalty of some kind." Dean Snow seemed to like my response.

One of the goals of every law student is to find a clerkship that provides professional training and experience beyond book learning and classroom instruction. I was concerned it might be difficult to find the kind of supplemental work that would prepare me for the particular areas of law I intended to emphasize. Professor Snow was both an expert in one of my chosen fields and appeared interested in my career. As it turned out, I was able to do most of his research and writing during evenings and weekends at home. I was even able to listen to tapes of his arbitration hearings, in order to synthesize the testimony of witnesses, while sitting in the bleachers watching one of my children play soccer or softball.

While I served as his clerk, Dean Snow was willing to dialog with me about the labor-relations profession. He always discussed the issues in his cases from a broader perspective than the specifics of the grievance at hand, and he often challenged my views. He asked important "what-if" questions to make me think about nuanced hypothetical differences that would produce alternative solutions. Since he was an expert in contract law, he refined my understanding of contract theory beyond what was explained in my textbooks.

After I had worked for Dean Snow for a year, he recommended I visit the Oregon Employment Relations Board (ERB) to observe actual hearings. I would learn the procedural structure and see how union and management advocates represented their clients. I followed this advice. Board Chairman Cleveland permitted me to observe hearings, then offered me an unpaid clerkship at ERB the following summer. I assisted with legal research on scope of bargaining, refusal to bargain, and issues in litigation pursuant to Oregon's Public Employment Collective Bargaining Act (PECBA). The experience was invaluable for a law student who intended to become involved as a neutral in labor relations.

Later during my internship, I asked Dean Snow point-blank, "How can I become a labor arbitrator? How can I achieve a reputation like yours?" I knew he was highly trusted by the labor-relations community and had been selected for hundreds of cases.

He explained that an arbitrator earns a reputation for

"acceptability" when an increasing number of labor and management advocates accept the arbitrator as trustworthy, fair, and impartial, never favoring either party. An arbitrator earns that reputation by always listening without bias and making strong decisions based on the applicable collective bargaining agreement and the evidence. "It's all about building trust over time," he said. "There is no other way to ensure job security as an arbitrator."

Then, having paused a moment, he added, "Keep in mind that I'm a white-haired male. You would have a fundamental obstacle, Sandra. You're a woman. Some parties will strike your name because of stereotypes about women being emotional, unable to focus on facts. Some think women are illogical, not analytical. The civil rights law does not apply to arbitrator selection. Only one woman has achieved acceptability in Washington, none in Oregon."

In arbitration matters, unlike judicial appointments, there is no job security. Except for permanent rosters in a few labor contracts, where the union and management have agreed on a specific list of arbitrators to decide cases on a rotating basis during the term of their contract (usually two or three years), the parties' regular practice is to obtain a new list of arbitrators for each individual case that arises. The agencies that provide such lists are the Federal Mediation and Conciliation Service, American Arbitration Association, and the Employment Relations Boards in various states. The advocates normally recognize some names on a particular list that they receive, because they already worked with those arbitrators. Other names are unknown because the referring agency just recently approved the individuals. One by one, the parties strike the names of the arbitrators they reject. The remaining arbitrator will decide their case.

A party's representative can reject an arbitrator for any reason or no reason. They may be unfamiliar with the arbitrator's record. They may have disagreed with the outcome of a prior case before that arbitrator. Dean Snow told me, "In reality, the decision to become a labor arbitrator involves a huge risk. Every case appointment is a one-time event. Eighty percent of the cases are heard by twenty percent of the approved arbitrators. Arbitrators' awards are usually final and binding, only challengeable in court for evident partiality or corruption or reliance on evidence outside the record. Lacking such proof, a challenger's remedy is to reject that arbitrator in future cases."

I told him that despite all this, I was confident I could be successful and would appreciate his guidance on how to build a foundation for my career. His response was complicated.

"First of all," he said, shaking his head, "most arbitrators are at least fifty before achieving acceptability. You are looking at a long-term project."

He went on, thoughtfully, "If you really want to set arbitration as your goal, there are two basic routes to follow. One, you could apply for a position as legal counsel for a union, work hard for several years, then quit and apply for an advocacy position with a management firm. After proving yourself competent representing parties on each side, you could declare yourself neutral, let it be known you will decline to represent either party in any labor or employment dispute from then on, and apply for approval by the various agencies as a competent arbitrator."

I shook my head no to that route. I wanted to go into private practice and represent ordinary people in civil matters, including employment discrimination and land use.

I did not want to work for a union or a firm representing management only. I didn't want a real job.

"The other alternative is the academic route," Snow said. "That's the route I followed."

He explained he had never been an advocate for either side in labor relations, but had taught courses in contracts, labor law, and arbitration. He joined professional organizations, worked at the American Arbitration Association, and published scholarly articles on labor issues.

"Those articles," he said, "demonstrated I could balance both sides' positions in my writing. Since you have decided to conduct a private practice of civil law and you don't wish to work full-time for either unions or management, the academic route is an option you could consider."

I asked how I could begin. He suggested I ask some locally-based union and management advocates for permission to sit in on contract negotiation sessions to see how contracts are made. "Usually, such meetings are confidential and outsiders are excluded," he cautioned, "but academics can attend for educational purposes, as long as they agree to maintain the confidentiality of what they hear. The advocates like to find out who the new academic experts are." He thought for a moment, then continued, "You could then put together short workshops in labor law and collective bargaining and offer those as part-time adult-learning courses in state and community colleges, while pursuing your law practice. You would also write articles and speak at conferences on current issues in collective bargaining."

I asked Dean Snow if it would be okay for me to represent non-unionized individuals in employment discrimination matters before agencies like the EEOC or ERB while doing the workshops and speaking at conferences. I was concerned that such representation might make me appear biased in favor of workers and against management.

"Representing individuals would not likely be a problem," he responded, "as long as you never served as an advocate for any union-represented worker. That's what would interfere with your future acceptability as an impartial arbitrator."

I knew an arbitrator's reputation was built through word-of-mouth reports from one advocate to another within the profession and from reading the arbitrator's opinions and other writings. Usually those writings were based on actual cases the arbitrator had heard. So I asked Professor Snow how I could even start getting cases as an arbitrator, assuming I went through the steps he outlined. I had heard it was poor form, in spite of freedom of speech, to advertise oneself as a labor arbitrator or make cold calls.

He explained, "You'll have to convince the administrative agencies you are knowledgeable and experienced in labor relations law and are a good opinion-writer. Once your name is approved and on the rosters, it will be included on various lists of five or seven arbitrators when parties seek an arbitrator for a particular case. In the beginning, if you are selected, it means you were the least unacceptable to both parties. They are willing to take a chance and test you out. It's the most common way a new arbitrator gets an initial case."

I nodded. Since acceptability was far in the future, I knew I could work at it gradually. At least I might achieve being the least unacceptable on a list someday. It would be a start.

He went on, "Once you are selected for that first case, you'll have to continue demonstrating the highest ethical standards and practices, disclosing any facts and circumstances that might make you biased for or against either party. You'll recuse yourself if an actual conflict of interest exists when you are selected for a particular case or if one arises during the hearing. Most importantly, you must demonstrate a willingness to listen to both sides and consider all their arguments. You must explain thoroughly and credibly why the winning party has prevailed and the losing party has lost. If you appear biased at any stage of the process, the offended party will never choose you again. The message will get out that you are unfair and should not be trusted with further case selections. The grapevine between the advocates is as close as their telephones."

Listening to Dean Snow's explanation made me want to become an arbitrator more than ever. Life had already presented me with difficult challenges, and I had always been willing to face them and was usually able to overcome them. I knew I could be fair to both sides and would have no trouble following ethical rules. I promptly set a long-term goal of becoming an acceptable labor arbitrator, following the academic route. I felt empowered to accomplish the goal, in spite of my gender.

During my third year of law school, I took a Trial Practice course and participated in a Mock Trial. The case involved a railroad accident. My "client," a purported passenger, was severely injured and alleged her injuries resulted from the negligence of the train's engineer and an inadequate track-lighting system. A case of that nature required considerable research about railroad procedures and standards, legal and administrative rules applying to railroad management and the evidence required to prove the tort of negligence. It also required the ability to interview my client and her doctor on direct examination and to cross-examine the railroad's witnesses at trial.

As I prepared my case, I recalled Attorney Cotter's able representation of my family during the personal-injury trial we went through after our car accident. I worked hard to mimic Cotter's skill. At the end of my trial, the mock jury ruled in favor of my client, finding the railroad negligent.

Also during my third year, I accepted a clerkship at Blair & McDonald, a law firm in downtown Salem. I did research projects in land use matters, personal injury cases, employment disputes, criminal matters, and domestic relations issues. The clerkship gave me broad experience in actual law-office duties, such as depositions, settlement negotiations, and preparing documents for court. It gave me the opportunity to build a network of lawyers familiar with my legal skill who knew I intended to establish my own local law practice after passing the bar.

The lawyers at the firm gave me helpful advice on practical issues and were an ongoing source of guidance later, when I opened my solo practice office. However, I realized I could never really be a part of their network because I didn't play golf and I didn't like to go to taverns for an afternoon beer. Much of lawyer networking is achieved through those "male" activities, and I knew the men did not admit women to that world.

By the end of my third year, I was ready to take the Oregon bar examination. I first took an intensive bar review course that emphasized Oregon statutory law.

The bar exam was administered in Portland at the end of July. I invited Gene and the children to stay with me in my hotel, so I could relax with them between the test sessions, which required about nine hours each day for three days. Gene took Melanie and Rocky to the Portland Zoo, the Art Museum, the Japanese Garden, and Historic Pittock Mansion. Then each evening, they shared with me the events of their day. As I listened to them, I could free my mind of its intense concentration on legal theories and hypothetical legal problems and just enjoy dinner with my family. Then, when the grueling three days were over, we celebrated with a weekend at Timberline Lodge on Mount Hood, hiking on the mountain trails and swimming in the hotel pool.

The results of the bar exam did not become available for at least four weeks after the test. The wait was frustrating, but my fellow students and I tried to be patient. I had no idea whether I would pass or fail. The uncertainty was hard to bear. I knew twenty-five or thirty percent of test-takers failed to pass each year. Sometimes the most outstanding students were among those who failed. So I awaited the outcome of the exam with anxiety and fear of failure, recognizing I might have to take the test again a year later. Added to my frustration was knowing the test results would be posted on the entrance door of the Oregon Supreme Court Building. No notices would be mailed out. All of us applicants had to go to Salem in person on the day of the posting to learn our individual results.

My legs were shaking as I climbed the stairs and searched the list for my name and the word following it. There were some audible tears and angry words in the crowd around me as others saw their results—about a quarter of my classmates had failed. But that crucial word following my name was indeed: "PASSED."

I had succeeded in passing the bar on my first attempt. I was able to breathe and even cheer along with the other successful candidates.

I was proud to go home that day and announce to my family that I was now eligible to practice law in the great State of Oregon.

The president of Willamette University congratulates me upon earning the juris doctor degree (May 15, 1980).

"Don't Mess With Me—
My Mom's a Lawyer"

———⟨∞⟩———

"Oyez, oyez. All rise. The Supreme Court of the State of Oregon is now in session."

The chief clerk's voice boomed through the speakers. It was September 25, 1980. The Chief Justice of the Oregon Supreme Court would be swearing in all three hundred of us who had passed the Oregon State bar examination. I was proud to be included among the new admittees.

Our families, friends, and members of the press were seated in the balcony. The excited buzz of conversation in the crowd diminished to a hushed whisper as Oregon's distinguished judiciary made its grand entrance through the doors at the back of the room. We who were seated at the State representatives' desks quickly rose to our feet as the seven Supreme Court justices and ten Court of Appeals judges moved regally down the center aisle, their black robes swishing.

When they reached the dais, the jurists moved to their respective seats, standing silently before the assembly until the entire judiciary was in place. The clerk then made a solemn pronouncement: "The Swearing-In ceremony is about to begin. Please be seated." The judiciary all sat down as did the rest of us on the floor of the House and the visitors in the balcony.

I noted, of course, that only one member of the judiciary was a woman. Governor Atiyeh had appointed Judge Betty Roberts to the Court of Appeals three years earlier. *Just one female among all those judges*, I mused, *and there's only a smattering of women serving on the bench in our trial courts.* Then, looking around at the group of new admittees, I estimated that the men still outnumbered the women among my colleagues at least five to one. *Will I find my niche in this male-dominated profession?* With a sudden pang of anxiety and some deep-set anger as well, I wondered, *Will I be able to break the glass ceiling of this Good Ol' Boys Club? Can I ever succeed in my dream of practicing law, or is Doug right about my chances?*

But brother Doug had shown his support in his own way. Glancing up at the balcony, I made eye contact with Gene and our children sitting in the front row. I waved to them, and they waved back. Gene wanted the kids to have seats with good visibility, so he had ushered them in well before the ceremony began. *They're proud of me*, I thought. *I can see it in their smiling faces. They'll be glad to see me sworn in. They've been a big part of my journey. Finally, today, they know my dream is coming true.*

Melanie and Rocky had removed their jackets. *It must be hot up there in the balcony*, I thought. But then I could see the colorful T-shirts they were wearing. Doug had had them made especially for this event. Black letters on the front of each shirt spelled out, "Don't mess with me," and on the back, "My mom's a lawyer." Melanie's shirt was bright yellow and Rocky's was red. I smiled, thinking that the message would be visible to just about everyone in the chamber if the children were to stand up and turn around. *It was generous of Doug to get those T-shirts for the kids*, I thought. *He tried so hard to discourage me from going to law school in the first place. But I think he's pleased I've made it this far.*

In a more positive moment, I realized the ratio of men to women in the legal profession had been ten to one just a few years previously. I thought, *We women are finally making some inroads. But it's token recognition at best. I'll still be facing an uphill battle.*

My mind continued to wander, as the speakers rose to the microphone, one after another, to congratulate us for passing the bar exam and entering the legal profession.

I'm part of a new breed of women, I thought. *Some people may call me "overly ambitious." I'm so happy that Gene always supported my decision to be a working mom.*

The President of the Oregon State Bar droned on in his speech welcoming us to bar membership. Then other distinguished speakers approached the podium one-by-one and I began thinking about my future work.

I'll write wills and trusts for local people, I thought. *I'll handle probate cases and personal injury claims. I'll let other lawyers know I'm willing to handle employment discrimination claims and other work-related issues. I'll follow Carlton Snow's advice about teaching short courses. I'll write articles for legal publications. Eventually, I'll qualify as an arbitrator. I know I can do it.*

Suddenly, my thoughts were interrupted. The Chief Justice boomed out with instructions to all of us candidates, "Please rise when your name is called and remain standing until all names have been called and the oath of office has been administered."

It seemed an eternity before my name was read. When I heard "Sandra Lee Smith Gangle," I stood up with pride. Glancing up at the balcony, I saw that Melanie, Rocky and Gene were looking proudly down at me and had their thumbs raised.

After all the names had been announced, the Chief Justice asked us to "please repeat the words of the oath of office together." We then swore to uphold the Constitutions of the United States of America and the State of Oregon, and we promised to maintain the integrity of the legal profession. A roar of applause emanated from the gallery when we completed the oath. The message on the kids' T-shirts was now a reality. They could proudly remind their friends from now on, "Don't mess with me—my mom's a lawyer."

Rocky (7) and Melanie (9), wearing their "Don't mess with me" T-shirts, celebrate with me after my swearing-in ceremony.

Getting Started as a
Sole Practitioner

D oug called me a few days after my swearing-in ceremony and asked what I intended to do next. I told
him I was looking for office space to rent so I could launch
as a sole practitioner. His reaction, once again, surprised me.

"Sandra, I think you're making a mistake. You have no
idea how complicated and stressful the work will be in private practice." After taking a breath, he argued, "You're too
naïve, Sandra. The clients will walk all over you. The other
lawyers will tear you to shreds. Some judges will give you
a hard time as well—they don't like dealing with women in
the courtroom. It's a vicious world, believe me."

I tried to get in a response, but he just kept talking.

"You should look for a nine-to-five job as a corporate
attorney or legal counsel for a public agency. There are many
good options and you'll be well paid. If you really want to
be in private practice, apply for an associate position in a
local firm."

"Well, you opened your own office," I retorted, when I
finally had a chance to speak, "and you've been successful
at it, so I believe I can do it, too. You know I'm as smart as
you are. I know there are risks, and I don't expect everything
to be perfect."

He apparently did not have confidence in my ability

to deal with difficult people. He was trying to prevent me the heartache and stress. But I believed I could do what he had done.

"I had a nine-to-five job before I went to law school," I told my brother firmly. "My goal is different now. I want to be a 'real' lawyer and represent real people, especially women. I want to do what *you* have done—help ordinary clients solve legal problems—not some corporation or government agency. Also, I want more balance in my life. As a sole practitioner, I can have the freedom to spend time with my children after school."

Doug replied emphatically to that last comment, "Sandra, you're dreaming if you think you can make a go of practicing law and still have time to watch your kids play soccer. You're going to have to work sixty or seventy hours a week just to keep up with the responsibilities. Otherwise you won't make enough money to pay your rent and stay in business."

"I only need to make enough the first couple years to keep my business afloat," I told Doug. "Gene's income is enough for us to live on. After that I'm determined to increase my earnings each year, and in five years I'll earn as much as an assistant attorney general. If that doesn't happen, I'll close my office and get a job at DOJ. The kids will be teenagers and I'll be ready for a nine-to-five job. But for now, I want to be a sole practitioner. I believe I can do it."

"All right, I can see you've given this some thought," Doug said finally—then he did an about-face. "Since you're committed to giving private practice a try, I'll come down to Salem this weekend and teach you what you need to know to get started."

"What? Thank you!"

"Be prepared for an intense training session!" he warned. "You can't start practicing law until you learn the nuts and bolts. What you learned in law school was the law itself. You still need to learn how to practice law. They don't teach those skills in law school."

It suddenly occurred to me that Doug must have had a harder time getting started in his practice than he ever disclosed. Maybe he was still just trying to protect me. It wasn't that he doubted my competence; it was that he had been through a terrible experience himself. Maybe he was the one who had naively thought it would be easy, so he assumed I was doing the same thing.

Doug was as good as his word. He spent the entire weekend going over the basics of getting a business up and running. He showed me how to organize my file system, manage my trust account, maintain financial records, and set up billing procedures. He role-played client interviews so I would gather the necessary facts and know how to evaluate credibility.

"You'll need to cross-examine your own clients," he said. "They often leave out significant details, the ones they don't want you to hear." He quickly added, "And, they sometimes lie or exaggerate the truth. It's essential to learn the full story before you begin representing them."

Doug taught me how to write a demand letter to an adjuster in a personal injury case and how to negotiate with the opposing lawyer. "Some of those guys," he said, "especially the older, more experienced lawyers, will string you along. They'll sound sincere; they don't like women lawyers. They'll use clever tactics to intimidate you. They may make irrational demands and throw out low-ball offers to get you to settle quickly. It's all part of the game. You're used to dealing with teachers, who are reasonably polite and believe in fairness. Practicing law is a whole different kettle of fish. You're going to need a very thick skin to deal with those other lawyers."

Doug then gave me some real gems of advice. He told me it was essential to introduce myself to every judge in the courthouse. "Talk to their staffs as well," he added, "so they'll recognize your name when it appears on their dockets. The judicial assistants have the real power. They can be a big help to you, so treat them with respect." Going on, Doug said, "Memorize all the court rules, so you'll be sure to file your pleadings on time and appear in the right courtroom or judge's chamber for every hearing. Not only is it *very* embarrassing to be a no-show or a late-arrival, but it could become a serious case of malpractice if the judge throws out your case."

Doug pointed out that I should establish a network of experienced lawyer friends. "You'll need to learn the unwritten court rules and practices, as well as published ones." Seeing my apparent disbelief, he said, "Every court has quirky expectations that are not written down anywhere. Some friendly lawyers will be helpful in finding out what they are. They were all brand-new lawyers themselves once, so they'll be glad to help you. Just be sure you always do your own research first. Other lawyers won't want to give you information you can find in the statutes and case law on your own. They'll just help you with the practicalities of court procedures."

I appreciated Doug's help. The tips he was sharing with me would be of great value and would save me years of learning by trial and error. By the end of that long, intense weekend, my mind was swimming. I had been naïve and ignorant of the practicalities. I had not known what I didn't know and needed to learn. I would later admit to Doug that his whirlwind training session had probably prevented me from committing malpractice many times during my first year of being a lawyer.

My brother Doug enjoys a recent visit with me (2013).

Introducing myself to the judges and court staff would also help me find out what kinds of cases might be available on referral from the court. I did not want to handle indigent criminal defense cases, but I had heard attorneys could accept assignments to represent mentally ill persons being committed to the State hospital. That option appealed to me as I had always been a calm listener when dealing with mentally ill persons.

The following Monday morning, I began making the

rounds of the Marion County courthouse, introducing myself to the judges and assistants, as well as the court reporters and front desk clerks. I obtained filing fee schedules and learned the process for filing a case and accessing court files. I learned where the law library was and how it was organized. I arranged to meet some experienced lawyers in the community, especially those who practiced in the areas I intended to emphasize.

I found a respectable, yet affordable, office suite on the upper floor of the Marion and Polk Schools Credit Union, where Gene and I were members. The suite consisted of an inner office that would serve as my private law office and an outer secretarial office with waiting area. The inner office had an impressive floor-to-ceiling glass wall behind the desk that would allow the afternoon sunshine to stream past my shoulders onto the desk. When I turned around, I would look out on the surrounding buildings and trees in the neighborhood. A teak desk for each room, executive and secretarial chairs, client chairs, and a four-drawer file cabinet were all included in the monthly rental fee.

I applied for a two-year renewable lease and the manager tentatively approved it, but the board of directors at the credit union only agreed to a one-year lease. "We are expanding," they explained. "In a year or so, we might need that office space for our own staff, so we cannot promise any renewals. We'll reconsider renewing next year."

I took the risk. The location would be excellent for attracting clients. My sign would be placed near the main entrance, visible to thousands of credit union members. An elevator led to my office suite, and plenty of free on-site parking was available. Best of all, the rent was affordable.

Unlike many of my fellow law graduates, I had not become a lawyer to make a lot of money. I wanted to serve the legal needs of ordinary folk in the Salem community, while continuing to be an active and involved parent. I meant to create a sustainable business, however.

I was determined not to put my family at risk financially. Gene and I had been married for twelve years and we had always lived within our means. I had saved enough from my teaching income before beginning my legal studies to cover two years of law school tuition, so I had graduated with only a small student loan to pay back. I had no intention of plunging into greater debt now for expensive overhead.

Nevertheless, I realized I would have to take out a modest business loan to make some necessary purchases, including business cards, stationery and a two-line phone system, bar dues, insurance, type writer, copies—the list goes on. I obtained a loan for about three thousand dollars from the credit union to cover those expenses and promised to repay that within three years.

The worst part of the loan was the interest rate. Because of the 1980 recession, interest was charged at 22% per annum, so my monthly payment would be about $125. Added to my monthly rent, phone, answering service, and miscellaneous expenses like postage stamps, I believed I could break even if I earned at least seven hundred dollars a month, until I hired a secretary.

Finally, I was ready to open my door for business. I had no idea who my first clients would be or what types of cases I would deal with right away. I was open to working on any civil matter, but would emphasize land use and employment issues. I also intended to visit the court clerk about handling civil commitment clients at the Oregon State Hospital.

Doug's mentoring advice had been extremely helpful and empowering. Not only had he taught me what I needed to know, but I realized he had prevented me from falling into some traps that likely would have materialized otherwise. I was on my way.

My Groundbreaking Mentor

—◦⦿◦—

O ne of the experienced attorneys I hoped to cultivate a relationship with was a woman—Hattie Bratzel Kremen, in Salem.

When the receptionist buzzed me in for my appointment, I hardly had time to catch my breath before Hattie marched through her doorway and shook my hand. "Hello, Sandra—you're the new lawyer in town. It's a pleasure to meet you. Come right in. You don't have time to waste here in my waiting room."

In spite of her graciousness, I knew her time was more precious than mine. Hattie was a few inches shorter than I, but her straight back and broad shoulders made her look taller. Her piercing blue eyes looked straight into mine. I sensed immediately that I could trust her. I also knew she was a sole practitioner with a busy law practice. I was the newbie who wanted to gain her support as one of my mentors. I silently pledged to keep the interview as brief as possible, while being sure to achieve my one objective for the meeting.

Hattie appeared to be in her late sixties, nearly twice my age. She was determined and confident. She wore a dark green plaid wool suit with a crisp white blouse. The outfit was completed with mid-high leather pumps that looked old-fashioned. I had chosen to wear a loose-fitting pants suit and flat-heeled shoes, which were the current fashion for women. Hattie's attire looked conservative and out-of-date.

Hattie walked briskly ahead of me as we entered her office. She directed me to sit in one of her well-used client chairs, while she slid gracefully into her executive chair. Reaching for her glasses, which hung on a jeweled chain around her neck, she raised them onto her nose while studying my face. "Tell me about yourself," she said. "How can I help you?"

I could see why Hattie had acquired a reputation as a no-nonsense, down-to-business lawyer. In her first career as a court reporter, she had reported for an American judge at the Nuremberg War Tribunals because she met the unique qualification of fluency in German. Upon her return to the United States, she decided to go to law school and become a lawyer. That was a highly unconventional choice for a mature woman in the early 1950s.

Due to learning from the best trial lawyers in both Germany and America, Hattie was proficient at cross-examining witnesses and making persuasive arguments to judges and juries. She had earned a reputation for fearlessness and was called "a tiger in the courtroom." During my meeting with her, I felt awed and somewhat intimidated by her intense, outspoken approach. It seemed she could look deeply into my soul and see who I really was inside.

I began my interview a bit awkwardly, as if I were meeting a new neighbor. "I'm married to Gene Gangle and I have two children," I said. "I taught foreign languages before starting law school."

"I don't need to hear about your family and your past job," Hattie interrupted. "I want to know why you became a lawyer. Tell me what kind of law you intend to practice and why." She then added, while looking at my clothing, "By the way, young lady, you'll have to learn to dress properly if you want to succeed in Marion County Court. Most of our judges will consider you out-of-line if you wear trendy fashions like that pants suit. Women have to wear dark skirts and jackets to be taken seriously."

I understood at that moment that passing the bar had given me a new identity. My personal habits, even my wardrobe, might have to change. I might have to look and act like a man.

I sat up straighter in my chair and uncrossed my legs, to show Hattie I respected her opinion, then began answering her questions, using as professional a voice as I could muster. "I want to represent ordinary citizens in the local community with civil law problems. I plan to write wills, handle real estate transactions and personal injury cases, and file land use petitions and appeals. I've studied Oregon land-use law and I wrote a Law Review article about the fair housing goal, which was just published. I intend to take divorce cases for a while, but my goal is to concentrate on employment discrimination cases, as I'm passionate about fairness in the workplace for women and minorities." Then, taking a quick breath, I added my main objective for the meeting. "I would be pleased to accept referrals of any clients with whom you might have conflicts."

Hearing myself speak those words, I felt empowered. I saw myself as a lawyer making actual career plans, not an aspiring beginner. I wanted to build a professional relationship with this woman, to be her colleague. Then, reflecting on the wardrobe issue, I added, "I'll dig through my closets when I get home and find some appropriate courtroom clothes. I wasn't aware that women lawyers were expected to avoid looking like today's feminists."

Hattie laughed lightly at my comment, tossing her auburn hair against her soft leather chair. "Judges have a hard time dealing with us women as 'real lawyers,'" she said. "Keep in mind that the women in their world—their wives, legal assistants, court reporters—are subordinate to their authority. They expect women to be meek and girlish. They understand we are lawyers, but they are confused by that. They expect us to act like the women who had authority over them in the past—their mothers and schoolteachers. So for now, we have to dress like those women. But I do hope the situation will change, and we'll be accepted for who we really are."

Hattie then told me about some of the challenges she had endured as the sole female lawyer in Salem during the late 1950s and '60s. She had applied for associate positions in several local law firms, but they only offered secretarial positions. Eventually she opened her own law office because that was the only way she could practice law.

"Even then," she said, "sometimes, when I went to court, the judge would call me 'honey' or 'dear.' It wasn't unusual to be treated as if I did not belong in the courtroom at all." Straightening her shoulders and raising her chin a bit, she continued, "So, I decided to show them I really was a lawyer to be reckoned with. I ran for District Attorney of Marion County. I won that election, even though I didn't have the support of the local bar or the judiciary. I showed them I was a respectable, competent lawyer, in spite of their attitude. And I was reelected twice. I was this county's prosecutor for ten years."

Hattie's eyes twinkled. I could see she was pleased and

proud the voters had accepted her as a qualified prosecutor. I thought she must have been deeply hurt when the judges and lawyers had failed to treat her as an equal. So, she had taken an end-run around the legal community, going directly to the voters and being elected as District Attorney.

Hattie then changed the subject, returning to advising me. "You'll need some bread-and-butter work while you get your name out in the community for land use and employment cases," she said. "You're probably going to have to do some divorce and child custody work to pay your office overhead. I can probably refer a few divorce clients to you right away, as I have way too many of those people calling me every day. Sometimes I have a conflict and can't take the case. But there isn't much likelihood I'll refer clients in those other types of work."

I nodded. This made sense.

Then she gave me a valuable warning. "I hope you understand it's extremely difficult to find a provable case of employment discrimination. Some would-be plaintiffs do talk to me sometimes, but most are disgruntled employees who don't like to follow work rules. You'll spend a lot of time talking to them without ever getting the evidence you need to prove illegal discrimination. Be really careful about going forward with such cases, especially on a contingent-fee basis. The costs you'll incur and the time you'll waste will eat you alive."

I appreciated Hattie's advice and her offer to refer some divorce clients to me. I thanked her and said I would work diligently to represent any clients she might refer.

"I've studied the divorce statutes and case law," I explained, "and acquired intake forms and sample pleadings. I assisted Attorney Sam Blair in preparing for a bitter custody battle while I clerked in his office so I'm aware of the issues involving minor children. I think I can be effective at explaining to a client that the judge will insist on recognizing the children's best interests."

As I spoke those words, I remembered my parents' highly conflicted marital separation. Because of that memory, I had decided not to do divorce work for long. I told Hattie, "I would be honored to accept some clients in divorce cases for a while, but my eventual goal in domestic relations is to become a mediator. I studied mediation in law school and I look forward to serving in that capacity, especially in parenting matters."

I then told Hattie I was aware that provable employment-discrimination claims are rare, so I would be very cautious about taking such cases on contingent fee. "I plan to charge a minimal fee for an initial half-hour conference," I explained, "then an hourly fee for investigation. I won't commit to proceeding with their case unless I see evidence that the claim is credible and has merit. My long-term plan is to serve as a neutral arbitrator in employment-related disputes. I interned with a labor arbitrator in law school and I feel I will be effective in that role. I will need some litigation experience in that area before I can take on the neutral role, however."

Hattie nodded, saying, "It sounds as if you are making some wise decisions about your practice goals. That's good. I've seen a lot of lawyers come and go in private practice, because they failed to do their homework. Most have a hard time saying no to problem clients. They want to make enough money to support their families and keep up their golfing memberships at the country club. But they aren't careful about protecting themselves." Having reminded herself of the economic realities, she warned me, "Be sure you always get a written fee agreement up front, before you do anything for any client. It's also a good idea to serve on some non-profit boards and do some volunteer service. That's a good way to get client referrals."

I thanked Hattie for her advice. I had taken up about thirty minutes of her time and had seen the light blinking on her telephone at least three times, so I knew she had to return some calls. I stood up and prepared to leave, but Hattie motioned for me to sit down again, as she had thought of something to add.

"You mentioned you are interested in land use work," she said. "That's an area of law I don't know much about. I just remembered that a client of mine lives in an area of the city where many of the houses, including her own, have historic significance. She tells me the City has been granting conditional use permits to some owners for non-residential uses and many houses are being demolished and replaced by parking lots for a mega-church nearby. The neighborhood is changing dramatically, and her residential property value is being threatened. Could you do something to help her?"

This sounded perfect for me. "Yes, I might be able to help," I said. "It's possible the land use laws are being disregarded or misinterpreted. We might be able to appeal the permits that have been granted or object to new applications. The neighborhood association might be interested in supporting your client's objections as well. I should talk to your client right away. These cases need prompt attention."

Excitement was welling up in my cheeks. Hattie had identified just the type of case I was hoping to handle. I had volunteered to assist my neighborhood association with the appeal of a land-use decision while I was in law school, and the appeal had been successful. I felt competent to represent clients in an area of law that most lawyers were unfamiliar with. I also knew my name would probably get into the newspaper if I represented Hattie's client in a case against the City. The exposure could be helpful in generating new clients.

"Good," said Hattie. "I'll call my client this afternoon. Remember, she'll remain my client for all other purposes. I'm only referring her for this one issue." Seeing my immediate nod, she added, "I've enjoyed meeting you, Sandra, and I wish you all the best in your practice. You'll be hearing from me as possible referrals come along. Also, please know that you can call me any time if you have questions and need a little help from an experienced practitioner. I had a couple of mentors myself when I started, so I'll be glad to reward their courtesy by helping you. Just be sure you always do as much research as you can on your own before asking any other lawyer for help. We're all busy people. We don't want to hold your hand."

I shook Hattie's hand warmly and said good-bye. I had no way of knowing it at the time, but a year later she would hire me as her associate to handle her entire practice while she took a six-week vacation visiting Australia and New Zealand. The following year, she would engage me for another six-week stint while she toured China. Hattie would prove to be both a long-time mentor and friend.

My First Clients

⚬⚬⚬

W ithin a week of meeting Hattie Kremen, three potential clients called me. Hattie had referred two of
them. She told them I was a brand-new lawyer, but she had
confidence in my character and my ability to serve them.
They each called to schedule an appointment.

The first was a woman with whom Hattie had a conflict
of interest. Her husband was a long-time client of Hattie's
for business-related matters. The couple had been married
eighteen years and had two teenaged children, but the husband did not want to be married anymore. He had bought
himself a sports car and had moved to an expensive apartment. Since Hattie already had an attorney-client relationship with the husband (including confidential information
about his assets), she could not ethically represent the wife's
interests against him in what sounded like would soon be
a divorce situation.

The second call was from the client with the land use
issue Hattie had told me about. The woman reported that her
house was in a quiet neighborhood where she had resided
over forty years. She was angry that a rapidly expanding
church had been buying up houses, intending to demolish
them and build a huge parking area to accommodate its
growing congregation.

"I'm not a bigot," she said, referring to the fact that she

was not of their denomination. "But their goal of allowing more than twenty-five hundred people to attend the same mega-service every Sunday and social activities on Saturdays will be a serious imposition in this neighborhood. The traffic from a thousand cars will be horrendous. The demolition of those homes will change the character of this neighborhood dramatically." She believed a carnival atmosphere would occur every weekend and an asphalt-covered wasteland would surround her house. "I believe the City is violating our residential zoning ordinance by issuing permits to tear down those houses and build parking lots," she said. "I could end up living in the only house in the middle of a giant used car lot. They want to buy my house, too, but I've refused to sell. This just isn't fair. I hope you can help me."

The third call was from a Native American man who had been laid off from his civil service job with a State agency. One of the lawyers in my new network had referred the man to me. His manager had put an African American woman with less seniority at the agency into the man's position. The caller believed the agency's action violated state and federal anti-discrimination laws, but the agency was asserting that affirmative action requirements for black persons and women took precedence. He believed seniority counted and that he should be reinstated to his position with back pay.

I scheduled appointments with all three of the potential clients for the following week, when I planned to open my office.

I also drove to the courthouse and registered with the clerk to be added to the list of lawyers who would accept appointments to represent indigent mentally ill people in civil commitment cases at the State Hospital. I realized the civil commitment process would present some challenges, especially with respect to the short preparation time I would have before representing my clients in court. In spite of this, the small stipend I would receive would be helpful in meeting my monthly office expenses. Also, the work would be more interesting to me personally than representing criminal defendants. I signed the registration papers and thanked the clerk for explaining the process to me. I knew I would appreciate the steady work.

Having talked to three potential new clients and secured a contract for ongoing work, I felt assured at the end of my first week I would be able to make ends meet without risking any greater debt than I already had incurred. I was ready to begin.

Opening My Law Practice

—◦◦◦—

I officially opened my law practice on November 1, 1980. There was no grand opening celebration, no champagne, cake, or balloons. It was simply the day I began operating as a sole practitioner.

My new office had a sign on the door that read "Sandra Smith Gangle, Attorney at Law." I had an answering service that would lead potential clients to believe I had my own secretary. By the end of my first week, I had opened files for those three referrals and I had welcomed my first client for an in-person interview. I had also interviewed one new client about writing a will.

After meeting each client, I opened a file, deposited the retainer check into my client trust account, and began researching issues the client presented. Since I was acting as my own secretary, I typed all relevant documents and correspondence myself. Back in high school, I had followed the advice of my counselor and taken a typing course, so I was a rather fast typist. I also knew how to draft a persuasive business letter.

Every document had to be copied for my file and every court pleading required four copies. Also, Doug had advised me to send copies of every letter and pleading to the client.

"That's the best way to show your clients you are working hard for them," he had said.

My monthly copy cost was going to add up quickly, so I decided to use carbon paper in the typewriter as much as possible, especially for copies that would remain in my own office.

I interviewed the divorce client for more than an hour and gave her the information she needed about the legal process and what would happen over the following months. I explained the acceptable basis for divorce had changed a few years earlier to "irreconcilable differences [that had] caused the irremediable breakdown of the marriage."[5] I also explained that both parties would have to consider the best interests of the children in all issues of "co-parenting," a new legal concept that replaced former issues of custody and support. The two of them would be required to cooperate on parenting issues even after the divorce was finalized. What a huge improvement those new concepts were over the conflict-ridden process my parents had gone through thirty years earlier.

As best I recall, the couple eventually reached an amicable resolution out of court, after exchanging full information about their marital assets and liabilities and cooperating on parenting issues. The attorney to whom Hattie had referred my client's husband worked with his client and me to agree to a reasonable marital settlement agreement, including spousal support and child support and a fair property division, including a share of the husband's retirement fund for the wife.

My second new client was the state employee who believed he had been improperly laid off. After gathering the facts and researching the applicable civil service statutes and rules, I prepared an appeal petition for filing with the ERB, which conducted quasi-judicial hearings in employment disputes between public-sector employees and their agency employers. I requested a hearing to determine whether the client, a Native American man who was a member of a recognized tribe, had been unfairly passed over when the employing agency allowed an African American woman with less seniority to bump into the position from which he had been released. According to my argument, his minority status equaled that of the woman who had bumped into the position, so seniority was the controlling factor. He was the more senior worker. I asked the board to order his reinstatement and back pay based on statutory civil service rules.

The case was set for hearing in about sixty days. The Board ultimately determined the affirmative action rules applying to women and African Americans did not trump civil service rules. On the basis of my client's greater seniority with the agency, he was awarded reinstatement with full back pay for the period of his layoff. My client was also awarded attorney fees and did not have to pay me out of his own pocket. I was thrilled to learn the result. Not only was this a win that would help pay my office expenses for a while, but I knew it would lead to additional calls from clients and referrals from my network of lawyers.

The woman who wanted to contest the conditional use permits in her neighborhood was my third client. I interviewed her, then spent time at City Hall, reviewing the Planning Department's file and studying the relevant zoning ordinances to understand what had already transpired before deciding on the best strategy for representing her interests. I could see that my client's protest at this late stage in the process now had a political dimension. She and her neighbors had been notified of the church's request for conditional use permits a month earlier and had not bothered to respond. The church already owned sixteen lots, so they had no complaints. Also, the neighborhood association had not indicated any disagreement with the plan. Their collective silence had likely been read as consent to the planned use of the house lots. As a result, the church's application for demolition permits had been tentatively approved. I was concerned it might be too late to protest. I wished the client had begun her quest for neighborhood justice much sooner.

The church's congregation had already grown large, and its members were a powerful force in the community. The client's neighborhood was small, and most residents were old-timers who were uninvolved. Few, if any, attended that particular church. Some of the homes that the church did not already own appeared to be rentals. Others were unoccupied and in deteriorating condition. Once the church demolished the homes it had purchased, the neighborhood would likely deteriorate further.

The church was essentially eliminating long-standing housing stock that was sorely needed by low- and middle-income residents, in order to build parking lots that would only be used two days a week, mostly by wealthy members of their congregation who lived outside the neighborhood. As for the legality of the City's decision, I questioned whether the issuance of the permits met the intent and purpose of the law that allowed demolitions of existing residences, regardless of ownership. But that train had already left the station. The neighborhood was in decline, and my client was the only citizen who was objecting.

I knew from my law school course in land-use that, however difficult, I needed to enlist community support—and fast. I decided a critical first line of attack was to approach the neighborhood association chairman and request an immediate public meeting.

When I met with the chairman, I presented these facts: Housing stock within walking distance of an elementary school, a middle school, and a high school was being removed. A bus stop along the street allowed neighborhood residents to access other parts of the city, including the hospital, the library, and the downtown shopping area, without driving cars. Now people from elsewhere would be driving to the parking lots. Nobody would need the bus. Grassy lawns and mature trees in the yards and along the sidewalks were going to disappear.

The association had not considered the social impacts of the conditional permits. The chairman agreed the project demanded reconsideration, and he promised to arrange a meeting to gather support. I suggested he post colorful flyers as widely as possible, calling attention to the pending action impacts (rather than the purpose of the action, which was to enhance a religious organization), and invite everyone to attend an "urgent meeting to discuss protecting the livability of the child-friendly neighborhood." He agreed and promptly set the meeting for ten days later, publicizing it with words like, "Save our neighborhood homes. Protect our children's walkable, healthy, environment. Parking lots don't belong here."

I also applied to the presiding judge for an emergency court hearing to seek a temporary injunction against the proposed demolition of the residences. Because of court rules, which are based on due process, I was obliged to notify the city attorney and the church's legal counsel that I was requesting the hearing. I told them I would provide the date and time as soon as those were available.

I did not realize at the time that the press would be advised of the court hearing and the neighborhood association meeting. Reporters and photographers would attend both. Once I obtained the temporary injunction from the court, the *Statesman-Journal* newspaper published a front-page article on the story with my name and that of my client included in the text.

The temporary injunction eventually lapsed because my client could not afford to pay the cost of the required bond before the court would grant a permanent injunction. Meanwhile, however, the neighborhood association conducted a well-attended meeting. It was clear that the public who came to the meeting wanted to preserve the neighborhood housing stock. They were angry about the proposed expansion of parking lots. After the meeting, the church's attorney spoke to the neighborhood chairman and said his clients would agree to reduce the planned parking-lot expansion by one-half, adding that church leaders would make every effort to retain most of the trees and eight of the sixteen homes as rental properties. They also said the church would provide a weekend shuttle service from other areas of the city, so churchgoers could attend services without driving their vehicles and parking.

As a result of the church's commitment, my client was willing to withdraw her motion to reverse the issuance of permits on the remaining eight lots. She realized much of the neighborhood would be preserved for residential use. And, more importantly for my career, I had become publicly recognized as a rising strategist in land-use disputes.

In addition to performing legal work for those three early clients, I received my first appointment from the court clerk to represent an indigent client in a civil commitment case. I went to the mental hospital, read the client's case file, and interviewed the client, who was unable to answer my questions coherently. The file disclosed a diagnosis of schizophrenia and obsessive-compulsive disorder. She had been hospitalized for past violent incidents. A police officer had found her on the street hallucinating and pounding on vehicles. Concerned for her safety and the property damage she had caused, the officer asked for her name and address and the names of family members, but she gave no information. So, he brought her to the hospital. The physician on duty examined her and prescribed medication to allow her to rest comfortably. He recommended she remain in the hospital for stabilizing treatment. It appeared the elements of the civil commitment statute[6] had been met, and I was unable to propose any less restrictive environment than the mental hospital where treatment was available.

I prepared to appear at the court hearing the following morning for the principal purpose of rigorously cross-examining the police officer and doctor to ensure their testimony was credible and consistent with the information in the file. I expected the judge would order the client's commitment for up to 180 days. If so, the order would meet the statutory requirements.

Meanwhile, I wanted to be informed about events in the local legal community, so I filed an application to join the Marion County Bar Association. By the end of that first week in my new office, I received an unexpected response. Instead of welcoming me as a member of the Bar Association, the letter informed me I was now a member of the Bar Auxiliary, a social group consisting of the wives of Bar Association lawyers. But I had earned the same J.D. degree that they had, had passed the Oregon bar exam, and had been sworn in by the Chief Justice of the Supreme Court. I decided to (politely) introduce myself to the bar president as soon as possible and point out that I was his professional colleague, not some attorney's wife, and that I would be pleased to receive his official welcome as a member of the Bar Association.

When I followed up a week or so later, the president apologized for the "mistake" and blamed his staff for not realizing I was an attorney, since my name was Sandra. He promised I would promptly get an official letter confirming my bar association membership. He appeared to be very gracious, so I responded in kind. While we both were well aware that there had been no "mistake," I decided it was best to avoid a confrontation and just move on.

At the same time, I let him know I was going to be a force to reckon with in the future. I asked when the monthly board meetings were and said I would like to attend in order to stay informed about the board's discussions. He said I was welcome to attend anytime.

When I followed through over the next several months, I was always the only woman in the room. I had to put up with smoke being blown in my direction while the men across the table from me conducted the meeting. It was clear they did not like my being there. Since smoking was allowed at meetings during that time, I put up with the annoyance. Unfortunately, I could not blow smoke back at them as I had quit smoking several years earlier, when my daughter Melanie, then five years old, had come home from kindergarten and begged me to quit, as she had learned the smoking would cause lung cancer.

A year after I joined the Association, the position of board secretary came open. It had been difficult in the past to recruit applicants for the position, so the board routinely recruited someone to perform secretarial duties before meetings. When I ran for the position, however, the board solicited a recently admitted male attorney to run against me. It was the first time the position was ever contested. When ballots were counted, I was not surprised to learn my male opponent had won handily. It didn't really matter. I had made my point.

My Neighbor's
Heart Attack

A few months after my office opened, my next-door neighbor asked to come in for a consultation. I was aware, from conversations with his wife, that he had suffered a myocardial infarction while at his job as a penitentiary classroom teacher with the Department of Corrections and had spent some time in the hospital. I assumed he was at home recovering on sick leave, but I had not asked any questions.

When he arrived at my office, he was walking slowly and breathing heavily. His skin was pale. He sat down in front of my desk rather clumsily, so I gave him some water to drink and asked if he was feeling okay. He quietly answered yes. I thought he was going to tell me he wanted to write his last will and testament, but that was not why he was there.

"I've been getting the run-around from the managers of my department at work and I hope you might be able to help me," he said. "I know you are good at solving employment problems."

He explained he had used all his available sick leave while in the hospital. His boss was now saying he would be terminated if he did not go back to work right away. One year earlier, he had had his first heart attack and had used up his twenty-five years' worth of sick leave while recuperating. He had only managed to accumulate a few days of sick leave by the time this recent attack occurred.

"I just don't think this is fair," he said. "Both of my attacks happened when I was on the job doing heavy lifting. They told me I wasn't eligible for Workers Compensation coverage for either one. They say a heart attack is a personal medical problem that comes from a pre-existing medical condition. I have to use my available sick leave, and, when that's gone, I lose my job if I can't return to work."

I told him I would do some research and see if there was any way I could help him. He signed releases for me to gather his medical records from both heart attacks. I said I could not offer much hope, but if it looked as if we could reopen his case, I would file the paperwork and ask for a hearing before an administrative law judge. He understood this might be a long shot, but he had confidence I would help him if I could. I agreed that this really *was* a long-shot.

I also worried that I risked doing a lot of work for no fee. Under the applicable law, if a claimant's attorney failed to prove that the Workers Compensation agency had mistakenly denied a claim, the lawyer could not recover any fee from the client. However, if the lawyer prevailed and the client won a recovery based on the lawyer's representation, the client's attorney fees would be fully paid by the Department.

Upon doing some research, I learned that a heart attack occurring on the job was not necessarily non-work-related, as the client had been told, nor was it always the result of a pre-existing medical condition, under Oregon Workers Compensation law. His heart attack could be covered as a compensable work-related condition if the evidence showed, for instance, the attack had occurred immediately after a particularly stressful work-related incident that was not part of his regular job duties. If a second heart attack were to occur on the job later, also under stressful conditions, that could be considered either a new claim or an aggravation of the first event.

My client's first event had occurred after he was involved in a physical altercation with an inmate. He had held the inmate down while another employee went to get help. The second heart attack occurred just after my client carried a heavy IBM Selectric typewriter up three flights of stairs to a newly assigned office in a building with no elevator. Putting those facts in the context of the applicable legal principles, I accepted the case and promptly filed to both reopen the old claim and appeal the recently denied claim.

When I presented the evidence to the administrative law judge, I pointed out that my client was not a guard at the penitentiary—he was a classroom teacher of inmates. When he was attacked by an unruly inmate and then had to hold him down forcefully, my client was doing work well beyond the scope of his ordinary job duties. When his office location changed a year later, he was denied janitorial help in getting his typewriter up to the new office. He had no choice but to carry it up himself. Again, this was a task outside the ordinary requirements of his teaching assignment. I argued that both heart attacks had been caused by the physical stress from the unusual tasks he was required to perform on the job. They should not have been treated as medical conditions, but as work-related injuries.

A few weeks later, the administrative law judge ordered both claims to be reopened and accepted as work-related accidental injuries. The client would receive full recovery of his lost sick leave hours as well as compensation for any out-of-pocket medical costs he paid for either event. I recovered full attorney fees for both claims. I was relieved, joyful in fact, about the result. It meant new workers comp clients would be calling.

The following weekend my neighbors held a huge neighborhood barbecue in their backyard and celebrated the work I had done in saving my client's job and recovering his sick leave benefits. It was a great celebration.

THE AFTERMATH OF A
CHIROPRACTOR'S PARTY

⸺⸺

On a Friday afternoon in March, just four months after I opened my office and a few hours before leaving on a getaway weekend at the Oregon coast with Gene and the children, I received an urgent phone call from a classmate of mine at Willamette Law School, Kathryn Logan, who was now working as a lawyer in a legal aid office. She had just interviewed a young lady who was seeking help after being fired from her job as a massage therapist in a chiropractor's office.

"This gal needs a lawyer like you," my friend said, "because we don't do employment-related disputes at Legal Aid and I know you are handling those cases. Believe me, Sandra, this lady has quite a story to tell, and I hope you can talk to her right away—this afternoon."

I called my husband and said we would have to delay our departure time for the coast. The client arrived within a half hour.

The woman, whom I will call Mary to protect her privacy, had been fired from her job three weeks earlier and then was deemed ineligible for unemployment insurance coverage. Her employer, the chiropractor, contended she had committed serious misconduct by lying to a deputy sheriff about a work incident. But she told me it was the employer who was guilty of misconduct. Even though her employer had instructed her to lie, she had told the truth to the sheriff's deputy. She now was unable to get a new job because of the twisted lies her employer was telling about her.

I said I needed to hear her entire story, because it sounded complicated. Then she calmly told me the details while I took extensive notes. I was not ready for the sordid story I would hear.

Mary had worked in the chiropractic clinic for several years. When attending a Saturday-night celebration of her employer's move into a brand-new, ostentatious home (where the party was held), a lot of alcohol flowed. Her employer became visibly intoxicated early on, but she herself did not drink a drop. She referred to herself as a "teetotaler." All employees had been invited and encouraged to attend, so this was a work-related event. Other employees, including a young female receptionist, about nineteen years old, were in various stages of inebriation as the evening wore on.

Mary became concerned about the receptionist because she believed the young lady was naïve and not used to drinking so much. At one point the girl had left the living room and didn't return, so Mary went looking for her. As she walked through the billiard room downstairs to check the bathroom down there, she saw her boss on the floor behind the billiards table with his pants off. Then she saw he was on top of the receptionist, who appeared to be unconscious and naked. She called out to the girl, who revived enough to try to sit up, but then fell back under the chiropractor's weight and started crying. It was her belief, Mary said, that she had stumbled onto her boss in the act of raping the young employee. She was so shocked and horrified that she left the room and ran into the bathroom and cried.

The receptionist approached her a few minutes later and said, "I just called 9-1-1. He raped me."

Soon after, the chiropractor came to Mary and said, "If anyone asks you any questions, you didn't see anything."

She said she had responded, "I won't lie for you. I know the authorities are coming and I'll tell them what I saw."

He responded, "It was totally consensual."

When the deputy sheriff arrived and started investigating the receptionist's report, Mary told him what she had observed and heard in conversation. He wrote everything down in his report. She then left the party.

Mary did not know what the receptionist had done after talking to the deputy. However, the receptionist was not at work the following Monday and no one had seen her after the party. A rumor was circulating in the office that she had been given a big check and told to get out of town and not come back. Later that same day, the bookkeeper hand-delivered a notice of termination, instructing Mary to clean out her workstation, take her personal things, and go home. She had been fired for cause (grave misconduct on the job, warranting termination).

When Mary later applied for unemployment insurance and started looking for a new job, she discovered the investigator had believed the chiropractor's story and denied Mary's application. Mary was unable to get a new job because the chiropractor and his staff were telling other potential employers she was not a trustworthy person when they called for a reference. All Mary wanted was to clear her name and be able to get a new job.

"The market for my services is very small," she said. "I can only work in medical clinics, and they won't hire someone who was fired for being a liar. Nobody will believe me when I tell them I did not lie."

After I heard her story, I told Mary I thought she might have a claim for damages against the chiropractor and his business under a tort theory called wrongful discharge for a socially undesirable motive or purpose. The Oregon Supreme Court had acknowledged the theory a few years earlier, when it approved a jury award for an employee who had been fired for taking time off to serve on a jury.[7] The court held the employee-plaintiff had performed a duty of every citizen and the employer was obliged by law to preserve the at-will employee's job during the absence. When the employer violated that obligation, it committed a tort (a wrongful act or an infringement of a right leading to civil legal liability), and the employee was eligible for a damage award, including punitive damages. The same theory was later used successfully by an employee who proved she had been fired for filing a worker's compensation claim after suffering an injury on the job.[8]

The facts of Mary's case did not fit precisely with the prior cases; however, I thought it legitimately fell within the wrongful discharge theory. It appeared Mary had been terminated for doing what every citizen is expected to do when interviewed by a public safety officer during an investigation—tell the truth. She had refused to lie to protect her employer, who was implicated in the specific crime under investigation.

I told Mary I would review the sheriff's report. If it confirmed her story, I would take her case on a contingent-fee basis, meaning I would not charge a fee unless we settled for an acceptable amount of damages or obtained a jury award through a full trial. She agreed. I then joined my family, who were anxiously waiting to depart for the coast. (We had a lovely time there.)

Once back in the office, I read the sheriff's report and it confirmed Mary's story. In addition, it disclosed that the receptionist had declined to press charges against the chiropractor, then disappeared. I realized this matter would involve hard-fought litigation, with complicated pleadings and depositions and the need to deal with highly experienced big-city lawyers who would vigorously defend the chiropractor. We might not be able to locate the receptionist to support Mary's story. But I believed the case had merit, and I wanted to get it to trial.

My only trial experience was that mock trial in law school. My opposing lawyer had been an inexperienced student like myself. I needed an experienced litigator to serve as co-counsel. I called several local trial attorneys, including Hattie Kremen, but none were interested. Their typical response was something like this: "Sandra, even if you can get a judge to agree that your theory applies in this case, I don't see the likelihood of getting a jury in Marion County to believe your client. The facts are preposterous. Everybody loves chiropractors, and they'll just think the receptionist was leading him on. They'll see your client as a busybody who probably should have minded her own business." Or, they just said, "Sorry, I'm too busy to take this on"—which amounted to the same thing.

In spite of their responses, I persevered in my search. Eventually, I convinced a litigator from Portland who specialized in cases involving sex discrimination and sexual harassment to work with me on the case. He suggested we sue not only the chiropractor, but his solely owned corporation as well. The corporation was the client's employer, so we would argue the chiropractor had interfered with our client's employment contract to benefit himself, an action that was prohibited by law.[9] The more theories we had going for us, the better chance we would have of settling the case or getting a judgment from a jury.

Our efforts to reach a settlement proved unsuccessful, so we went forward with the trial. Judge McConville allowed our theory of wrongful discharge for a socially undesirable motive to proceed as the theory of the case. That was the first hurdle. He also approved the second theory, interference with contract. Then we managed to draw a good jury panel, half men and half women. When we presented our evidence, we demonstrated that Mary was a woman of integrity who had worked for a corporation that was owned and managed by a domineering and controlling chiropractor. Our client told the jury in simple terms what she had observed at the chiropractor's house. The deputy sheriff presented his report and acknowledged that the receptionist, the alleged victim, had declined to press charges, then became unreachable, so they had closed the case. The chiropractor denied everything.

The jury found that Mary had been fired for a socially undesirable motive, namely, to punish her for cooperating with an investigation of possible criminal misconduct involving the owner of the corporation she worked for. They found she told the truth about her observations regarding the chiropractor's conduct, even though no crime was ever prosecuted as a result. They awarded Mary two hundred and fifty thousand dollars in damages as the remedy.

The chiropractor's attorney promptly appealed to the Court of Appeals on the basis there had been no crime and, since the receptionist did not testify, there was no evidence supporting the jury's verdict. Our theory was based entirely on supposition and hearsay and had no merit as a basis for damages. Since Mary feared the chiropractor's appeal might be successful, she ultimately accepted a settlement amount of about a hundred thousand dollars.

In spite of the post-trial events, the original jury result resonated with the public because of the article that appeared in the *Statesman-Journal* immediately after the verdict was announced. My reputation as a knowledgeable lawyer in employment disputes was enhanced in the community and my caseload grew.

Another outcome of the case was less pleasant. My co-counsel and I disagreed as to how we would divide the contingent attorney fee. I presumed we were equal partners. He disagreed, saying his skill in trial work had led to our success, so he should get the lion's share of the fee, eighty percent. Hattie and Doug had each warned me, "Always get a written fee agreement," but I did not realize their advice would apply to partnerships with other lawyers. I had not asked my co-counsel to sign a fee-sharing agreement when we began working together as a team. In order to resolve the dispute, I retained my own attorney who negotiated a compromise settlement with my co-counsel. To avoid litigation, I agreed to the settlement whereby he received sixty percent of the fee and I kept forty percent. I learned an important lesson the hard way.

My Law Practice
Expands and Grows

M y early successes in land use and employment disputes led to a flurry of calls from potential clients.
I became known as "that new lady lawyer down at MaPS
Credit Union." I was cautious about accepting risky cases,
but the cases I accepted kept me busy. For the first three
years, I regularly processed one land use appeal and one
employment-discrimination matter at a time, while also
writing wills, drafting land sale contracts, and handling
probate estates for credit union members and other clients.
Also, the court clerk appointed me to represent at least two
civil commitment clients every month at the Oregon State
Hospital and I continued working a few hours every week
for Professor Snow.

I suffered a few losses. One was a tort case involving an
elderly client who slipped and fell in a department store and
suffered a serious hip injury. We argued the store's negligence in arranging a public demonstration of Atari games in
the main aisle had caused her to fall. It had attracted a large
group of teen-age customers, some of whom were drinking
soft drinks and were blocking the aisle while they watched
the demonstration. While making her way through the
crowd, my client slipped and fell on some sticky liquid that
had spilled on the floor. We alleged the store should have

arranged the demonstration in a less well-traveled part of the store and should have prohibited drinking and eating in the store, as was common practice in other stores. In the alternative, staff should have provided for safe passage by customers like herself, who were interested in shopping, not watching the demonstration. I had taken the case on a contingent-fee basis, but was unable to persuade the store's insurance adjuster to settle, so proceeded to trial. The jury agreed with the store that my client had a duty to be watchful and to protect herself while she was in the store. She should have walked to the side aisle when she noticed the crowd in the main aisle. In other words, her contributory negligence matched or exceeded any negligence on the part of the store, so she was not entitled to damages. I learned an important lesson. Slip-and-fall cases are risky, as juries expect injured plaintiffs to watch out and protect themselves from the negligence of others. I never accepted another such case.

There is no requirement that a lawyer agree to represent every client who calls. If a lawyer is busy with other clients, doesn't have the time or expertise to do the research to handle a new case, or has a conflict of interest with a potential client, there is a professional obligation to say "sorry." Sometimes a lawyer withdraws from representing a client while working on a case, such as when the client refuses to pay the attorney fee or demands that the attorney do something illegal or say something untruthful in court.

After my first six months I needed secretarial assistance. I hired Gail Kellum to assist me with secretarial, bookkeeping, and reception duties. Gail was thirty-seven years old— my own age—and she had recently graduated from a legal secretarial program for displaced homemakers (widows and divorced women who lack skills or work experience) at Chemeketa Community College. I paid Gail one half the going rate of pay for new secretaries; the government paid the other half. It was a great deal for a single mom like Gail, and it was good for me, as I was still a new lawyer and had a limited income. Gail worked half-time during the first few months, then became full-time. She was bright, honest, and reliable. She worked steadily for nearly three years. Every day, I counted my blessings to have such a trustworthy and competent employee and to be able to pay her a living wage with government assistance.

At about the time the chiropractor case was resolved, three clients who owned farm land adjoining a gravel mining operation in Linn County retained me to represent them in a land-use action. I knew the case would require a major time commitment, as appeals would likely be filed no matter how the County ruled. The mine's owners intended to operate a mill that would produce concrete-and-gravel siding panels for large commercial buildings. My clients contended the mill would not be a farm use of the property, but an industrial use. Such uses were generally prohibited by the applicable zoning, but the specific mill was not expressly referenced. I lost the argument at the county level, as the hearings officer viewed the new mill as a benefit to the county. It would bring new tax revenue into the county's coffers and would provide needed jobs.

I was more successful in my appeal the Oregon Land Use Board of Appeals. The Board agreed that noise and vibrations emanating from the new mill would be hazardous to the health of my clients' goats and pigs and would result in financial loss to their legitimate farm-based income. The Board reversed the County and required the mining business to operate only mining. If they wanted to manufacture concrete siding panels, they would have to build their mill on industrial-zoned land where there would be no conflicts with neighboring uses. We won.

In a Jackson County case, I represented a client who owned a hundred-acre cattle ranching operation on exclusive farm use land. My client's adjoining neighbor owned a twenty-acre parcel on which he sought to build a winery to process grapes, most of which would be imported from vineyards as far away as Canada. A tasting room would serve tourist groups. A large parking lot would accommodate buses and automobiles carrying the visitors. We contested the winery as an improper use of farmland. The County granted the neighbor's permit and we appealed.

The first appeal was to Land Use Board of Appeals. They upheld the County. We then appealed to the Oregon Court of Appeals and finally the Oregon Supreme Court. At each level we argued the proposed project was a commercial or industrial use. The only grapes that would be grown on the small parcel were intended for landscaping purposes. The noise and pollution from vehicles accessing the tasting room would harm my client's cattle. Noisy concerts and parties, such as wedding receptions, which would be hosted in the tasting room were inappropriate in farm neighborhoods. We failed to convince each appellate court that the winery and tasting room should be denied, however. The courts reasoned that wineries were traditionally located on grape-producing land, just as barns and irrigation equipment are located on farms for animal-raising and wheat storage. They declined to consider the proposed project as being different from typical vineyards on large acreages, with small wineries and incidental tasting rooms on the premises.[10]

In spite of losing the case, the ultimate result satisfied my client. The neighbor was unable to proceed with his winery after all because he lost the financial support of his investors during the lengthy appeal process. He had to file for bankruptcy because he could not afford to pay his attorney fees. Ironically, his investors had feared the courts would ultimately deny him the right to use his property for the winery and tasting room because of the excellent arguments I raised in opposition to his proposal. They had pulled out, leaving him to defend the litigation alone. Sadly, he suffered a mental breakdown and was hospitalized.

A few months later, the applicant filed a petition in U.S. Federal Court in Portland, charging me with intentional misuse of legal procedures and seeking fifteen million dollars in damages. He filed similar lawsuits against my client, the Jackson County Commissioners and the Land Use Board of Appeals, as well as the judges of the Oregon Court of Appeals, but not the Supreme Court Justices. Although the applicant had ultimately won his battle to achieve the right to pursue his winery plan, he used the legal machinery to express anger and revenge about losing his financial backing. All of us became defendants who had to retain separate attorneys in order to obtain the ultimate dismissals of his frivolous complaints. Justice is sometimes complicated.

In the employment-law arena, I successfully represented a sixty-year-old woman in an age-discrimination lawsuit in federal court after she was fired from her twenty-five-year-long position in a state agency. My client lost her regular source of income and accumulated retirement benefits as well. The agency claimed she had not been performing her job duties adequately. However, her annual reviews had always reported her work performance as satisfactory, sometimes good or excellent. She had received no prior warnings or suspensions during her twenty-five-year career.

I located a witness who had attended a management meeting and heard the woman's manager say, "We have to get rid of the old dead wood in this agency. It's time to bring in new blood." That was the smoking gun that made the case a probable winner, as a violation of the Age Discrimination in Employment Act of 1967 (ADEA). At the last minute before trial, the employer's attorney requested a settlement conference and the judge granted the request. During the meeting, the employer agreed to reinstate my client to her position with full back pay and recovery of her retirement fund as well as payment of my attorney fees and court costs. To obtain such a full result without going through a trial is always a joy to a lawyer!

In another employment case, I represented a tiny sixty-year-old Mexican-American woman, the only female member of a tree-planting crew for a large timber company. Her supervisor fired her immediately after she filed a worker's compensation claim based on a serious ankle sprain she had suffered on the job. The employer's representatives denied any improper reason for the termination, arguing the employee had neglected to follow proper safety procedures and caused her own injury. I argued that the client's termination was not only a violation of Worker's Compensation law, but a tortious violation, pursuant to the theory of wrongful termination for a socially undesirable purpose. In addition, I claimed my client was a victim of employment discrimination based on age, sex, national origin, and disability. The timber company promptly settled her case for a substantial sum after receiving my demand letter with a copy of my proposed court petition attached. I proudly told my client she now could afford to retire and buy a new house.

In 1983, the credit union that housed my office notified me it was expanding its operations and would not renew my lease for a fourth year. I quickly located a lovely ground-floor office one block from the Oregon State Capitol. Gail accepted a new job with the Oregon Department of Revenue, so I hired a new executive secretary, Andrea Whalen. I bought a state-of-the-art computer, an IBM-PC, Jr., to replace my office typewriter. I spent three years in my second location, then moved again in June 1986, this time to Lancaster Mall.

Attorney Albert Depenbrock had established his general law practice in Lancaster Mall about ten years earlier and needed a partner to assist in serving his growing clientele. Al selected me to be his full partner in the practice, sharing all income and expenses equally. I was the first woman attorney in Salem, Oregon, ever to become a full partner with a male attorney who was not her husband or her father.

Al and I organized the law firm as a professional corporation, Depenbrock and Gangle, P.C. We retained an associate lawyer, Mitzi Naucler, on contract. Al concentrated his practice on business law, bankruptcy, real estate, and criminal defense clients. I handled all the personal injury and probate work, while continuing to represent my land-use and employment-related clients. Mitzi represented the divorce and child-custody clients, and all three of us handled wills and general estate-planning cases. Because I was good at supervising staff and managing the firm's finances, I became managing partner. The arrangement worked well, and Al and I remained partners until 1996. We had a wonderfully respectful professional relationship that was truly unusual for the 1980s and '90s. Fortunately, more male lawyers have been willing to enter such partnerships in recent years, giving women lawyers better options for entering private practice.

In 1986, I learned through a newspaper article that the City of Keizer was seeking applicants for a hearing-officer position. Keizer had been incorporated as a city in 1982 and passed its own land-use ordinance. The city grew rapidly, adding residential subdivisions and shopping centers. Attorney Paul Lipscomb, for whom I had worked as a clerk at Blair & McDonald while in law school, was Keizer's first hearing officer. He recommended me to replace him when the governor appointed him to fill a judgeship in Marion Court Circuit Court. Paul said the position would be perfect for me because of my land-use expertise.

I was hired on a two-year contract, which was subsequently renewed twice. Over the six-year period, I conducted land-use hearings every two weeks and played a significant role in the approval of many new residential and commercial projects. I conducted the hearings according to the established protocol, swearing in witnesses who testified on behalf of the developer and any opponents, as well as the City staff person who reviewed the proposal. I gave ample time to all citizens who appeared and signed the register, then testified about their concerns and objections. Some of the hearings lasted well past eleven o'clock in the evening because I insisted that everyone who wanted to speak have that opportunity. In cases where a number of people testified in opposition and made suggestions for positive changes in the proposal, I routinely invited the applicant to respond to the citizens' suggestions. As a result, some applications that were problematic for citizens at the start of a hearing became acceptable to them by the end of the hearing. The applicant had listened to the opponents' concerns and was willing to modify the application.

At the end of my third contract term with Keizer, however, a problem arose in two successive subdivision applications. In each case the neighboring property-owners appeared in great numbers and presented credible evidence showing that the additional homes in the proposed subdivision would cause overcrowding at the local elementary and middle schools. The schools were already at or beyond full capacity due to the city's rapid growth. The school district was not planning to construct any new schools or enlarge the existing ones because voters had been turning down ballot measures that would fund such construction. When asked for input to each application, the school district had responded vaguely, "We will accommodate all students who enroll in our schools." The developer of each proposed subdivision estimated that "two new students" would enroll in the local schools from the eighty new homes that would be built.

I found that the developers' estimates lacked credibility. There was no way to prove the actual number of new students who would be enrolling, but it was more reasonable to accept the neighbors' estimate of forty in each subdivision than the developers' estimate of two. At least two new classrooms would be needed in the schools to avoid unreasonable class-size increases. A school bond for construction was clearly needed, but no such process was underway. There was a history of voter denial of tax measures in the city.

In addition to the city's own subdivision ordinance, the statewide land-use goals applied to my decisions. The goals required that adequate public services, such as water/sewer services, roads, and schools, be available to serve any proposed new residential subdivision. I found that the developers failed to prove the City could meet that requirement because of the school issue, so I denied the subdivisions.

The city leaders were clearly unhappy with my decisions. They failed to renew my contract for a fourth term. I felt frustrated and unappreciated, but proud to have done my job with integrity, in accordance with the law.

Meanwhile, the State Superintendent of Public Instruction contacted me about serving as a reviewing officer for cases involving claims of inadequate accommodation for the special needs of students with disabilities in public schools throughout Oregon in violation of Section 504 of the 1973 Rehabilitation Act. In each case, I conducted a hearing and received evidence about the student's specific physical or mental condition that required accommodation. I then determined what accommodation the school district needed to make in order to provide the child a free and appropriate public education. Some students needed an extended testing time or a different desk or a classroom change. In other cases an aide was needed to assist a child with a learning disability or a feeding tube. Sometimes new equipment or a ramp was needed to accommodate a wheelchair-using student. Occasionally, I ordered a district to pay tuition for a student to attend a private school because the district was unable to meet the student's needs. These cases were challenging, but rewarding because I was helping people who had no way to help themselves to benefit from public education.

In the mid-1980s, I added another new dispute-resolution procedure to my practice—mediation. Mediation is a process whereby parties in dispute agree to meet with an impartial person to discuss the issues in a civil manner. They listen to each other and work in good faith to find common ground and consider options that might lead to a mutually acceptable resolution. The mediator assists the parties in framing the issues, listens to their positions, reflects back what each has said, asks questions to help them understand each other's positions better, and helps them work together to reach agreement. The mediator is not a judge and has no power to impose a solution. The mediator is a facilitator. Although the ultimate goal is to resolve the matter, there is no guarantee the parties will reach agreement. Often, the parties do resolve their dispute. Other times there is no agreement, but the parties understand each other's position better, so they are less polarized.

Al Depenbrock and I were trained as mediators when a Willamette University law professor offered the training as a public service to local lawyers and social-service professionals. Al and I served as pro-bono mediators with a Salem program called Neighbor-to-Neighbor. We mediated a number of cases for citizens who had identified problems such as barking dogs, noisy late-night parties, or improperly parked recreational vehicles and trucks. As an alternative to police involvement, the City encouraged callers to schedule a mediation session with the party they believed was responsible for the alleged offensive behavior. Then the City would ask the responding party to participate willingly. Al and I found our involvement in the volunteer process immensely satisfying, as we were helping our own neighbors solve community problems in a non-confrontational way.

After I served as a volunteer mediator for a few months, the presiding judge asked me to serve as a paid mediator in some of his domestic relations cases, where issues of co-parenting were involved. This court-connected assignment, which was paid at a modest rate, evolved into service as a mediator of small claims cases in the Circuit Court.

Because Al and I were doing mediation work in addition to my labor arbitration and hearing officer assignments, we established a second professional corporation, Alternative Solutions, Inc., to distinguish our impartial conflict-resolving work from our ongoing law firm work representing individual clients. I handled most of the cases for the dispute-resolution firm, while Al handled most of the legal cases I previously handled in the law firm. We shared the net income from both businesses equally. Over a period of years, I served on the board of the Salem YWCA and as president of Salem City Club and Peace Plaza, Inc.. As a result of our public service, we earned the Marion County Pro-Bono Law Firm of the Year Award twice, in 1990 and 1994.

During the ten years between 1986 and 1996, the clientele and workload of both Depenbrock and Gangle, P.C. and Alternative Solutions, Inc. grew exponentially. Meanwhile, our outside professional involvements expanded in new and different directions. After serving as Keizer's land-use hearing officer for six years, then arbitrating cases involving students with disabilities and mediating court-connected disputes, I began traveling out of town more and more frequently for my labor arbitration hearings. During the same time, Al received a promotion to lieutenant colonel in the United States Air Force Reserves, so he frequently had to fly to Washington, D.C., for meetings at the Pentagon.

He was spending less time handling the daily legal work of the firm than was needed. Mitzi had been invited to serve as clinical professor at Willamette University Law School.

The changes in our practice meant our secretaries and recently-hired associates were becoming overworked and overstressed. Al and I realized it was time to make a change in the business organization itself. We set a target date for closing the office in June 1996 and began the process of dissolving our professional corporations and dividing the responsibility for preserving client records and files between us. It was a complicated project that required several months to accomplish, while winding down our existing client caseload at the same time. Then, on the target date, we and our associates amicably went our separate ways to conduct our respective businesses as sole practitioners.

I was proud of my new office on the third floor of the Pioneer Trust Bank building in downtown Salem because I could look out at Riverfront Park and the Carousel building whenever I stood in front of my large corner window. I remained in that office until 2001.

Throughout this time and beyond, between 1995 and 2005, Key Bridge Foundation, a Washington, D.C., non-profit, appointed me to mediate cases involving individuals with disabilities who filed claims with the U.S. Department of Justice (DOJ) alleging they had suffered discrimination in violation of the Americans with Disabilities Act (ADA). Key Bridge was the intermediary that referred parties to a competent mediator when they agreed to attempt to resolve their ADA dispute without litigation.

They referred cases to me that arose in Oregon public accommodations, including restaurants, hotels, shopping centers and hospitals, as well as in government agencies.

Some cases involved access issues, including the need for elevators, ramps, automatic doors and enlarged rest rooms or allowing persons with mental illness and persons with service animals to eat in restaurants. Others involved communication issues, such as the need for hiring interpreters for deaf clients during office visits. Still others involved personal care issues, such as walk-in showers and grab bars in hotel bathrooms. Most cases ultimately resulted in settlement because the business owners, when faced with the facts about a complainant's disability, realized the person was a customer who was seeking accommodation, not money damages. Businesses who thought they would have to pay damages usually agreed to hire architects and contractors to remodel their business properties or install equipment that was essential to meet the needs of their disabled customers or change a policy that had previously excluded a disabled person.

This was not the whole of my law practice story, of course. After leaving the partnership, I was appointed to several interesting projects, including a multi-party collaborative project for the Oregon Department of Transportation that lasted six months and a two-year project as mediator of insurance claims, carrying out the settlement of a large nationwide class-action lawsuit. However, my long-term career goal had always been to become a full-time labor arbitrator, and that became the ever-growing focus of my practice.

Becoming Madam Arbitrator

———∞∞∞———

The path to becoming an arbitrator wove in and out of my career as a lawyer.

Beginning in the early 1980s, I pursued Carlton Snow's advice about establishing credentials as an academic in labor relations. I designed one-day and three-day workshops in collective bargaining and labor law that were appropriate for adult learners, then presented the workshops on a quarterly basis at Portland State University, Western Oregon University, and Chemeketa Community College. The institutions scheduled my workshops over several years between 1981 and 1985. I took half-days off from my law practice to conduct them. I covered the history of unions in America, the adoption of the NLRA and public-sector collective bargaining statutes, as well as the history and function of arbitration as the dispute-resolution mechanism of choice in most collective bargaining agreements. I talked about issues typically included in labor contracts—wages, hours, insurance benefits, and promotions. I explained the significance of seniority as a job-security issue and the meaning of just cause as the ordinary standard in deciding discipline and discharge matters. I showed how the Civil Rights Act of 1964 impacted the prior history of employment discrimination based on race, color, sex, national origin, and religion.

My workshop approach reached hundreds of citizens interested in learning more about labor laws and employment practices. Attendees included union officers and stewards as well as managers and human resource officers from businesses and public agencies. I maintained an objective approach and strived to demonstrate I was not biased in favor of or against the interests of either labor or management but respected the rights and obligations of both. Even though I had a history of representing non-union workers against management in discrimination cases in my law practice, I showed I would be fair and impartial in deciding labor relations disputes arising under collective bargaining agreements.

One of the questions my students frequently asked was, "Isn't it true that arbitrators just 'split the baby' when they make a decision, rather than ruling in favor of one side or the other?" That question made me aware that many people misunderstand what arbitrators do and how we make decisions. Many people have extrapolated a belief from the Biblical story of King Solomon that we simply compromise in our awards in order to please both sides in the dispute. They confuse the word "arbitration" with "mediation," and conclude that each process is a way to split the difference between what each side demands.

As I explained to my students, not only is this belief incorrect about how arbitrators resolve disputes and how mediators assist parties to reach agreements to resolve disputes, it also reflects a fundamental misunderstanding of the King Solomon story.

King Solomon was a just king who was known to be a wise arbitrator of disputes. He was asked to decide a dispute between two women, each of whom claimed she was the mother of a baby who had survived when the other woman's child died of an unclear cause. It had been impossible for either woman to prove which child belonged to which mother. Each mother argued she should be awarded the surviving baby.

King Solomon listened to the women's arguments, then ordered his aide as follows: "Bring me my sword, and I will split the baby and give each mother one-half." One of the women immediately yelled, "No, please don't harm the baby. Give it to her," pointing to the other woman. King Solomon immediately understood that the woman making the sacrifice was the real parent, as she was acting out of love for the child. The other woman's motivation was jealousy. He put away his sword and gave the child to its rightful mother, the one who was willing to sacrifice her parental right in order to save the child's life. That was his true goal, to make a just decision.

An arbitrator is a private judge, who decides whether a party has violated the parties' collective bargaining agreement in some specific manner and, if so, awards an appropriate remedy to correct the offense. (You'll recall the "private law" concept, in which a contract acts as a law unto itself between the signatories.) A mediator does not make a decision at all. A mediator facilitates discussion between opponents and assists them in reaching their own agreement.

Like King Solomon, a labor arbitrator is a person who understands human nature and seeks the truth, then fashions a just and fair decision. Arbitrators do not merely "split the baby" in making their awards. (Note: Neither did King Solomon!)

In actual fact, extremely few of the awards we arbitrators

issue in labor cases reflect an equal division between the disputing parties. One of the parties generally prevails, and the other loses. Sometimes the arbitrator makes an adjustment in fashioning the award. For instance, a discharge may be reduced to a suspension or a reprimand, based on principled reasoning. The arbitrator might have considered the grievant's length of service and prior work history and determined the employer should have considered those factors in mitigation of the seriousness of the offense. The degree of egregiousness of the misconduct might be a factor that leads to modification. Also, the discipline that management issued to the particular grievant in the present case might be compared with the discipline, if any, that had been handed out in previous cases involving similar conduct by other workers or managers. In each case, the arbitrator's goal would be to maintain consistency and fairness. These are the same principles that judges follow in court proceedings, where they enforce public laws.

If a long-term employee always merited satisfactory evaluations and was never previously disciplined for misconduct, an arbitrator would likely find that termination for a first offense was excessively harsh, unless the misconduct involved something egregious like violence or theft. Similarly, if an employee's misconduct resulted from a misunderstanding of the employer's expectations that could be rectified through retraining and better supervision, suspension and retraining would be a more appropriate penalty than termination.

By 1985 I decided it was time to proceed further with pursuing my goal. I applied for acceptance on the roster of public-sector arbitrators at the Oregon Employment Relations Board. I submitted documentation about the courses I was teaching in labor and employment issues and the articles I had written and published in labor-relations journals, as well as reports on my previous internships with Carlton Snow and the ERB itself. Within a few weeks my name was added to the agency's list of approved arbitrators.

I was pleased to be selected to hear a couple of cases right away. One involved a teacher's aide who had been terminated for excessive absenteeism and the other involved a janitor found sleeping on the job. My recollection is that I upheld both terminations based on the applicable work rules and lack of mitigating circumstances.

I then applied for admission to the national rosters of labor arbitrators of the American Arbitration Association (AAA) and the Federal Mediation and Conciliation Service (FMCS) in Washington, D.C., and was included on both rosters for the Pacific Northwest region. I was the second woman from Washington and the first from Oregon to be included on those regional lists of over fifty arbitrators during the initial years.

As a prerequisite for admission to each roster, I promised I would no longer accept any labor or employment cases as an advocate for employees or management. So from 1985 onward I did not represent clients with employment discrimination claims in my law practice. Also, in accordance with the applicable rules of professional responsibility for arbitrators, I always disclosed to the parties who selected me any facts that might make me appear biased in favor of either side. For instance, I disclosed my husband's employment as a teacher and counselor, as well as my own teaching experience, when selected to hear any school-related dispute.

In the beginning years, I was not well-known in the labor-relations community. It was still true that twenty percent of the arbitrators decided eighty percent of the cases submitted. Stated differently, eighty percent of the listed arbitrators, who were usually newer and less well-known, like me, were in competition for just twenty percent of the cases. I knew the risk was high, therefore, that I would be selected infrequently, and perhaps never, because I had no track record as labor arbitrator. My history as an advocate for workers, as well as my gender, might make me appear biased in favor of unions. Unions, on the other hand, might wonder if I would bend over backwards in favor of management.

Advocates usually have little or no information about how a new arbitrator is likely to analyze evidence and interpret contract language in order to make a fair decision in their case. They tend to feel safer choosing an arbitrator with a track record over one who has not yet produced case opinions that are available for them to read. As a point of comparison, in court cases, the judge must follow *stare decisis*, a requirement that prior decisions in similar cases control the current decision. In arbitration, arbitrators usually rely on their own independent analysis in a particular matter. A body of arbitral precedent is available in *How Arbitration Works*, a compendium of decisions that is updated regularly by editors Elkouri and Elkouri, but those volumes do not have the universal power of *stare decisis*. They provide guidance only.

Each arbitration award is based on the unique facts developed in the evidentiary hearing and analyzed according to the parties' unique contract (private law), not external law, unless that law has been incorporated into the agreement through express reference. Various arbitrators often decide similar cases differently, based on their individual points of view. Parties try to select the arbitrator they believe is most likely to rule in their clients' favor. When they know an arbitrator well, they feel more comfortable choosing that arbitrator. They are likely to view a new arbitrator as a "wild card" and strike their name.

I understood those risks, but I was confident in my training and experience. Presenting the academic workshops, as well as my professional integrity as established in my early hearings, would become my main assets in building my practice. My goal was eventually to become one of that top twenty percent. I set my fee schedule commensurate with fees that new arbitrators were charging. The most well-known and frequently selected arbitrators were charging about double that amount. I gradually increased my fee, always staying in line with that of my colleagues. I never charged a lower amount than my male colleagues whose experience level was equal to mine were charging. I made a decision early on that it would be demeaning and self-deprecating to charge lower fees than men charged for similar services.

I never felt parties selected an arbitrator because of the fee they charged. They chose their arbitrator based on their assessment of which person on the list would listen most fairly to their evidence and would make the right decision based on the contract language. Often their choice was based on a negative analysis, such as, "Which arbitrator do I want to strike because I think I would probably lose my case with them?" I always recalled the advice I had received from Carlton Snow: "Keep in mind that each of the parties is likely to strike the name of any arbitrator who has ruled against them recently, so you can sometimes be selected simply because you are the only unknown person on the list and the least undesirable of the arbitrators they can choose for that case."

During my first year of arbitrating, I was interviewed by a reporter for the *Perspective* publication of the Labor Relations Press. I acknowledged that even though I was aware there is no job security in arbitration, I wanted to do the work because I believed I would be a fair decision-maker. I was willing to work hard at making the right decision in each case—I was building my reputation on that basis. In the article, published in November 1985, the reporter quoted my comments regarding the professional risks of becoming a labor arbitrator, as follows:

> The words of Shakespeare's Richard II that: "They well deserve to have/That know the strong'st and surest way to get" echo in Sandra Gangle's voice when she explains that arbitration is no easy business. "Work, work, work," this Oregon arbitrator says is the only possible way to achieve the professionalism as an arbitrator that she expects in herself. Risk-taking is intrinsic to this professionalism, she believes. "You have to make decisions even though sometimes those decisions are very harsh and can affect your future in the field. You have to be willing to face that reality and take that risk."

Quite unexpectedly, in the fall of 1985, a labor-relations representative of the United States Postal Service called to inform me that he and representatives of the Service's three employee unions—the National Association of Letter Carriers, the American Postal Workers, and the Mail Handlers Union—had just chosen me as one of the five arbitrators to decide all grievances in post office expedited cases[11] throughout the Pacific Northwest for the next six years of their labor contract.

There had been a major postal strike in the 1970s, and one of the issues had been gender imbalance in the workforce. I believe the parties decided to include a woman on their rotating panels of arbitrators in the various regions of the country, as well as the national panel, as a way of demonstrating gender fairness and good will. I was the lucky woman they chose for the Pacific Northwest roster. I was a sole practitioner lawyer teaching labor law courses and was successful in handling employment-discrimination matters, so I would likely understand the issues in their cases.

The letter I subsequently received explained I would probably handle two or three cases every month. The parties would divide my per-diem fee and travel expenses, but I would not receive payment for travel time. This was less than my regular compensation, but I accepted the appointment enthusiastically because I knew the regional reputation I would earn would ultimately be more valuable than dollars for travel time. Also, I eventually learned the frequent-flier miles from my constant plane travel would allow me and Gene to spend our summer vacations in wonderful mountainous places we enjoyed visiting.

I ultimately conducted over 250 cases involving postal employees and their managers. I became familiar with post office procedures and personnel matters throughout Washington, Oregon, Alaska, Idaho, and Montana. Except for one complicated case involving religious discrimination, all my postal cases involved disciplinary matters and contract-language interpretation. The essential problem I saw in discipline cases involved personality conflicts between managers, who were often older males with military background, and younger workers, often female and with high school training. The contract-interpretation cases arose from disagreement between the union and management as to how certain words or phrases applied to a particular set of facts. I had to use various principles of contract interpretation to resolve the misunderstanding or ambiguity. My skills of writing and linguistic analysis served me well in those cases.

The religious discrimination case was particularly challenging. It involved a mail handler assigned to a shift that included Saturday work. Mail handlers work in shifts, often three each day, sorting mail in the post office building. The grievant had recently converted to the Seventh Day Adventist religion after a lengthy education process and had been confirmed in an official ceremony. Once admitted to the Church, he had applied to the postal service for reassignment to a shift that did not require working on Saturdays, now his Sabbath Day. His supervisor soundly denied the request, so he filed a grievance. The basis of his grievance was that religious discrimination in employment was prohibited by Title VII of the Civil Right Act of 1964, and the law was incorporated by reference in the parties' collective bargaining agreement.

The postal service had denied the employee's request on several grounds. First, the employee had not requested religious accommodation upon initial hire, so they maintained his conversion was not a sincerely held belief. Second, even if his conversion were serious, it had taken place too late to allow him to change his regular work schedule, as schedules are set in stone once each year on the basis of seniority. Third, the service could not accommodate the employee because avoiding Saturday work would pose an undue hardship on the business of mail processing, as large amounts of mail are processed on Saturday for delivery on Monday. Therefore, a full contingent of workers is needed on every Saturday shift. Finally, the grievant had little seniority in his department, so there was no likelihood he could be assigned to a shift without Saturday work for several years.

The union and grievant brought in witnesses who were leaders of the Seventh Day Adventist Church who explained the seriousness of the Saturday Sabbath in their religious practice. They testified at length about the intense honesty and commitment the grievant had demonstrated when he went through his conversion and confirmation. The grievant and his wife also testified about the conversion. The grievant said he would be willing to take any shift, including swing or graveyard, on any combination of days, including Sundays, as long as he did not have to work on Saturdays.

Having reviewed all the evidence in the context of the collective bargaining agreement, I granted the grievance and ordered the postal service to reassign the grievant to a shift that did not include Saturday work. I held that seniority did not apply, as the Civil Rights Act of 1964, which was incorporated in the labor contract, required accommodation of the grievant's religious conviction.

After my postal service contract ended, I arbitrated hundreds of cases through the ordinary selection procedures of FMCS, AAA, and the employment relations boards of northwest states. The private industries whose representatives selected me as arbitrator included retail chain stores, lumber mills, food packers, hotels, and hospitals. Government agencies included school districts, public colleges, police departments, and prisons, as well as city, county, and state government agencies. I was selected in federal-sector cases involving the Department of Veterans Affairs, Department of Forestry, and Department of the Treasury. Among the unions that selected me were AFSCME, UFCW, Teamsters, SEIU, FOPPO, AFGE, and subsidiaries of the National Education Association in Oregon, Washington, and Alaska.

In the new branch of my career, I became known as "Madam Arbitrator." In the beginning, some parties called me "Your Honor" because they knew that "Mr. Arbitrator," the title they were accustomed to using with their male arbitrators, did not fit my gender. I reminded them I was not a judge, so the title "Your Honor" was not appropriate, and suggested "Madam Arbitrator" or "Ms. Arbitrator." They preferred the first of those titles.

My postal hearings always took place in the post office where the case arose. Most other hearings took place in law-office libraries or hotel conference rooms. Occasionally we assembled in a noisy place like a break room, where the clatter from lockers and soft-drink machines nearly drowned out the voices of the witnesses. When I conducted a hearing in a jail or a nuclear-energy facility, I had to go through security.

The room arrangement was always less formal than that of a courtroom, in that we sat around a large rectangular table or a group of tables arranged in a square or horseshoe pattern. I always sat in the center, beside the court reporter (if there was one). The union representative, grievant, and sometimes the local union president sat on one side of the table while the management representative sat on the opposite side with one or two spokespersons for the employer. The witness chair was placed wherever both parties' representatives, as well as the court reporter and I, could see and hear the witness. Sometimes that chair was on the fourth side of the table arrangement; other times it was beside me and the court reporter, Occasionally, the parties brought in a sheriff's deputy to sit through the hearing and remain vigilant while providing security, as they feared a grievant or witness might become unruly or violent.

Arbitration hearings are not normally open to the public. Occasionally, however, a party would ask my permission, as well as that of the opposing party, to allow a spouse, family member, or other person to attend to give moral support to a grievant or witness. If a reporter or other outsider wished to attend, the parties jointly decided whether or not to allow the observer to remain. I abided by their wishes.

Like all arbitrators, my life was subject to unforeseen schedule changes. Sometimes the parties reached a negotiated settlement a week or so before the hearing was scheduled to begin. In such cases, I would have sufficient time to cancel my travel arrangements and work on other matters on days I would have been traveling and conducting the hearing. Other times parties settled at the last minute, just before the hearing was to start or even after I had called the hearing to order. In some cases, they would ask me to grant a short delay upon beginning the hearing, so they could meet and confer, then they would come back and ask me to confirm their settlement later. They would tape-record the terms of their agreement, then ask me to memorialize the terms as an alternative to writing an opinion. When the parties' settlement efforts were unsuccessful, we would begin the hearing an hour or two later than originally planned.

In deciding every case, I abided by the arbitrator's essential duty, as announced by the United States Supreme Court in *Steelworkers v. Enterprise Wheel & Car Corp.*[12] The Court pronounced that duty as follows:

> When an arbitrator is commissioned to interpret and apply the collective bargaining agreement, he [writing at that time followed the grammatical rule of using "he" as default] is to bring his informed judgment to bear in order to reach a fair solution of a problem. This is especially true when it comes to formulating remedies. There the need is for flexibility in meeting a wide variety of situations. The draftsmen may never have thought of what specific remedy should be awarded to meet a particular contingency. Nevertheless, an arbitrator is confined to interpretation and application of the collective bargaining agreement; he does not sit to dispense his own brand of industrial justice. He may of course look for guidance from many sources, yet his award is legitimate only so long as it draws its essence from the collective bargaining agreement.

In some cases, the employer would file either a substantive or procedural objection to my jurisdiction, or authority over the matter, as the initial issue of the hearing. If so, that basic jurisdictional matter had to be resolved before I could proceed further. Even though the parties had mutually selected me as their arbitrator, I had no power to proceed until my jurisdiction was clearly ascertained.

A substantive objection to jurisdiction would be based on a contention that the subject matter of the grievance was not covered by the parties' collective-bargaining agreement. If, for example, a postal worker filed a grievance over the brand of mail truck or the color of the uniform that management provided for the worker's use, the employer's representative would properly object to subject-matter jurisdiction on the ground that there is nothing in the collective-bargaining contract that gives a worker the right to contest driving a particular brand of truck or wearing a particular uniform. Because of that lack of coverage in the contract, management retains the authority to decide what kind of trucks and uniforms are provided to employees. If, however, the employee were to grieve (object to) the supervisor's assignment to operate a particular truck because they reasonably believed the vehicle was unsafe and needed repair or replacement, the grievance might be arbitrable, as employee safety would likely be covered in the contract and I would have proper jurisdiction to hear and decide the matter. As for uniforms, a requirement that employees always wear a heavy down jacket might be an issue of health or safety in hot weather and might be arbitrable.

If either party to a grievance raised the issue of substantive arbitrability in one of my hearings, I usually pointed out that, pursuant to *Steelworkers v. Warrior & Gulf Navigation Co.*,[13] I could not proceed unless they obtained a court order authorizing me to proceed. The Supreme Court held in *Steelworkers* that only a court, not an arbitrator, can decide whether an issue is specifically covered in a particular collective bargaining agreement. However, in a later case, *John Wiley & Sons, Inc. v. Livingston*, the Court decided that the parties themselves could decide to give the arbitrator express authority to decide the issue as an alternative to going to court.[14] Usually, the parties in my cases would expressly authorize me to decide any substantive arbitrability issue pursuant to *John Wiley & Sons* rather than go to court, especially in cases where they had already agreed that the jurisdiction issue and the merits of the dispute were inextricably intertwined and it would save time if I decided the jurisdiction matter without conducting a second hearing on the same evidence.

On the other hand, when a procedural objection to jurisdiction was raised, it meant the employer was arguing that the union had not followed the required steps of the grievance procedure outlined in the collective-bargaining agreement before filing its request for arbitration, which implied the union had waived its right to arbitration. For example, the contract might require the union to file a grievance within fourteen days of the event being challenged. Management would then have a specific number of days to investigate and meet with the union steward to try to settle the dispute. If they were unable to reach agreement, the dispute would proceed to the next level, and another meeting would be scheduled within a required number of days, etc. If they were still unable to resolve the matter, the union could then request a list of arbitrators from one of the referring agencies to begin the arbitrator-selection process. Time limits are intended to keep the grievance moving expeditiously so that management, union, and grievant will not be disadvantaged by unresolved conflicts in the workplace.

There are a number of reasons that delays might not automatically cause the grievance to be dismissed, however. If the union had filed a grievance more than fourteen days after the event, it might argue that two of the days were Sundays and the meaning of "days" in the contract was actually "workdays," not "calendar days." Therefore, the filing had indeed been timely. In a similar fashion, the union might show that management had failed to respond to the grievance within the required time, so it should be granted by the arbitrator. Management might then respond by pointing out that one of the days had been a holiday and there was no union representative in the building on the day following the holiday. And so on.

My responsibility in all these instances would be to take evidence on the procedural steps and on the prior negotiations regarding the intent of the words included in the grievance-processing provision of the collective-bargaining agreement. The goal would be to determine whether the procedure had been executed as the parties had intended. In some cases, there may have been extenuating circumstances, such as serious illness or hospitalization of the grievant or a manager, or perhaps weather conditions. Under principles of fairness and equity, the arbitrator could then find that the procedural requirements had reasonably been met.

With the parties' permission on a procedural matter, I usually went forward with taking evidence on both it and the merits of the actual case, promising I would decide the procedural question before analyzing the case merits, as authorized by *John Wiley & Sons, supra*. This would save decision-making time. If I subsequently determined the union had in fact neglected to follow the required procedural steps without justification, I would be obliged to dismiss the grievance as untimely, meaning, "too late." If I were to find that management missed its required response timeline, I would be authorized to deny management the right to defend based on the procedural issue. However, in my experience, that never occurred.

An arbitrator's role is similar to that of a judge, but there are important differences. The structure of the arbitration hearing is essentially the same as typical trial procedure. Once any jurisdiction issue has been resolved, the arbitrator opens the hearing and explains the process for the parties and their witnesses. Each advocate presents an opening statement, which is not evidence but a thumbnail sketch of what the evidence will be. The evidence is then presented via testimony of witnesses. They are each sworn by the arbitrator to tell the truth, then questioned by the advocate who called them and cross-examined by the opposing advocate. If the arbitrator believes anything the witness says is unclear, the arbitrator can, and often does, ask clarifying questions.

It is essential that the arbitrator be fully informed as to the facts. Since credibility of witnesses must be determined, the arbitrator carefully observes the witness's eye movements and physical changes and watches for inconsistencies during all testimony. Documentary evidence is usually submitted. Occasionally the parties invite the arbitrator to tour the worksite to show the setting where the incident in dispute occurred. The party that bears the burden of proof in the case proceeds first, and the responding party goes forward after all the first party's evidence has been completed. The employer bears the burden of proof in a discharge or discipline case, even though the union is technically the plaintiff, because the employer must convince the arbitrator there was just cause for the action it took. The union, however, bears the burden of proof in a contract-interpretation case, because the union-plaintiff must persuade the arbitrator the employer violated the contract in some provable way.

After the initial questioning and cross-examination phase, the opening party has the opportunity to rebut the responding party's evidence before the advocates present closing arguments. In other words, management has the opportunity to rebut in discipline cases, the union in contract-interpretation matters. Sometimes the advocates present final arguments orally, but usually they mail written arguments to the arbitrator on an agreed date after doing some research to find case law supporting their factually based argument.

There is a broad policy on admissibility of evidence in arbitration hearings. Arbitration is a conflict-resolution process in which parties and witnesses get to "tell their story" in their own way. Sometimes a witness wishes to tell a story that goes beyond the relevant details of the specific dispute. In a court case, the rules of evidence would not allow such expansion because a jury, which is not made up of legal professionals, might be improperly influenced by the irrelevant or immaterial evidence. Those rules do not apply in arbitration, however, because the parties trust that the arbitrator, who has extensive experience in weighing evidence, will rely only on relevant and material information when deciding the matter and will ignore any irrelevant testimony. A party may raise an objection to any extraneous evidence an opposing witness offers, but the arbitrator will usually deny the motion (while noting the objection and its basis for the record) and admit the evidence "for what it's worth." Since labor relations grievances arise in the context of an ongoing relationship between the parties, the open-evidence policy enables the parties to clear the air of everything they may have on their minds, alleviating worker stress and irritation, while the arbitrator's focus will always remain on the specific issues in dispute as identified in the initial grievance demand.

The arbitrator does not begin to reach a decision until all the evidence has been presented and the parties have submitted final arguments, either orally or in writing. Whichever party begins the hearing usually offers testimony and evidence that appears to present an "open-and-shut" win for that party. The arbitrator must, however, keep an open mind throughout all stages of the hearing. Evidence builds gradually, bit by bit, and often the most critical facts are revealed near the very end. In reaching a decision, the arbitrator must give primary consideration to the parties' collective bargaining agreement since it is the law that applies to the case. The agreement controls their employment relationship and is the source of the arbitrator's authority.

The arbitrator notes which party bore the burden of proof (meaning they needed to successfully achieve proving their case to win) and whether the party bore that burden to the proper extent. Sometimes the burden of proof standard that must be met is a *preponderance*, meaning more than fifty percent. Occasionally it is higher, such as *clear and convincing*, meaning seventy-five or eighty percent. It is extremely rare that an arbitrator will impose a *beyond a reasonable doubt* standard, which is about ninety-nine percent. That standard is used in criminal court where a conviction could result in incarceration or jail time and loss of a litigant's freedom.

The highest penalty an arbitrator can impose in favor of the employer in a discipline case is termination of the grievant's employment, which is indeed serious, but not of the same magnitude as a prison sentence. Therefore, arbitrators usually apply a "clear and convincing" standard of proof, and rarely a "beyond a reasonable doubt" standard, in cases involving discipline or discharge.

When the grievant prevails in a discharge case, because management failed to prove just cause for termination, the only "penalty" the arbitrator can assess against the employer is an order reinstating the worker and paying lost wages and benefits or doing whatever else the arbitrator orders for fairness, such as reinstating the employee's seniority position.

If the grievant prevails in a contract interpretation matter, the remedy is usually more creative. It may apply retroactively to correct the damage that resulted from the misinterpretation, or it may only apply going forward, to prevent future mistaken application of the provision. No money damages are awarded in arbitration cases, only equitable remedies. Sometimes the remedy involves money, but only where the error needing correction was a loss of money.

In most cases, the parties must share equally in paying the arbitrator's fee and expenses. The individual grievant is not charged any portion of the fee. Occasionally, however, the parties include a "loser pays" provision in their contract and the arbitrator must honor that by ordering the losing party, union or management, to pay the entire fee. The arbitrator's order is enforceable in a court of law; however, the parties rarely refuse to comply with an arbitrator's award.

I never had the experience of needing to sue the parties for non-payment of my fee. Their remedy if they believed I had made an improper or unfounded decision would be to file a motion to vacate the award in court. Such motions were filed in several of my cases, but none ever resulted in vacation of my decision. The mere fact that my case selections continued to grow tended to demonstrate that the labor relations community considered me to be an acceptable arbitrator.

Some Interesting and Challenging Cases

⸺⸻⸺

I dealt with a wide variety of situations in my cases. No two workplaces are alike and workers and management are human beings of all stripes who make mistakes, misunderstand rules, complain, sometimes misjudge each other. My role was to learn about the specific work environment where each dispute arose, listen to the evidence about what had led up to the problem before me, then solve the problem in such a way that workplace harmony would be restored and efficient work production could continue. In many ways, I was a teacher as much as a judge.

A. DISCIPLINE AND DISCHARGE CASES

The fundamental issue I had to resolve in any case involving discipline or discharge of a worker was whether management had met the elements of just cause for the discipline or termination.

Early in my career, I followed the rationale of the "Seven Tests of Just Cause," as developed by Arbitrator Carroll R. Daugherty in *Grief Bros. Cooperage Corp.*[15] A "no" answer to any of the tests would lead to the conclusion the employer did not have just cause for imposing the discipline. The seven tests (which reference "Company" rather than the

211

more general term "Employer") were devised in the years before collective bargaining existed in the public sector (which includes the post office, the focus of my work at that time). However, the tests continued to be followed in public sector cases even after the first public-sector collective bargaining laws were passed, until recent years.

Here is a paraphrased summary of the Daugherty tests, which were more awkwardly worded in the original form:

1. Did the Company give the employee clear warning of the likely disciplinary consequences of the employee's conduct, orally or in writing, acknowledging that some offenses (such as violence, theft and intoxication) are so serious that no advance warning of discipline is necessary.

2. Was the Company's rule or order reasonably related to the orderly, efficient, and safe operation of the Company's business and the expected performance of the employee?

3. Did the Company, before administering discipline, make an effort to discover whether the employee did in fact violate or disobey a rule or order?

4. Was the Company's investigation conducted fairly and objectively?

5. Did the "judge" obtain substantial evidence or proof that the employee was guilty as charged?

6. In the past, has the Company applied its rules, orders, and penalties evenhandedly and without discrimination to all employees?

7. Was the degree of discipline that the Company administered reasonably related to the seriousness of the proven offense and the record of the employee's service with the Company?

After the year 2000, many arbitrators considered the seven Daugherty tests somewhat rigid, so a more flexible and streamlined test for just cause was developed. The new version referenced the employer as "Employer" and included "she" where "he" had previously referred to all employees. From that point on, I emphasized the following areas of inquiry in discipline and discharge cases, as outlined in the revised standard[16]:

1. Whether the Employer afforded the grievant fundamental due process rights, such as granting foreknowledge that his/her conduct would lead to discipline, conducting a fair investigation, and then treating the grievant fairly and consistently with similarly situated employees;

2. Whether the Employer produced adequate proof that the grievant did what he or she was accused of doing, that is, whether he or she committed the charged offense; and

3. Whether the penalty that the Employer imposed was reasonably related to the seriousness of the proven offense, the grievant's disciplinary record and any mitigating or aggravating circumstances.

Just Cause Example No. 1:
Dishonest Cashier

A private-sector case of mine in the early first decade of the 2000s involved a supermarket cashier who allegedly took eleven dollar-off coupons that her register had produced for customers, then improperly passed them to her husband to use for a gasoline purchase.

The evidence showed the store's cash registers occasionally printed coupons along with customers' cash-register printouts. The coupons in question authorized one dollar to be deducted from a gasoline purchase at the store's gas station. Register receipts showed the eleven coupons the cashier's husband had used for a gas purchase were all issued at the employee's register on a single day. These facts justified termination, according to the employer, because it appeared she had improperly taken possession of them for herself rather than passing them on to the customers.

The grievant and her union argued that customers other than the grievant's husband had obtained the coupons at the grievant's register but stated they did not intend to use them. Therefore they were "throw-aways." The grievant had properly kept these for herself, then later gave them to her spouse.

The employer argued it was absurd to contend that all eleven coupons were throw-aways as they were the only coupons produced at the grievant's register on the day in question. Also, during the investigation, the grievant had contended her mother-in-law had acquired the coupons during various shopping visits and had given them to her son, the grievant's husband. That argument was also absurd, said management, as the mother-in-law would have had to visit the grievant's register eleven times in one day to collect them all. In addition, a work rule prohibited cashiers from serving family members, including extended family.

Based on the evidence as a whole, which was clear and convincing, I found the employer had proven just cause for the employee's discharge, based on violations of work rules and dishonesty. The grievant improperly collected the coupons during her shift, then passed them on to her husband. The employee's deception was a major complicating factor, however, which helped me to come to the final finding that discharge was a proper remedy under the circumstances, in spite of the grievant's long tenure with the employer and the relatively small amount of money involved in the infraction.

Just Cause Example #2:
Alcohol-Impaired Grievant

A long-term produce clerk was discharged in the late 1980s for a first offense of coming to work smelling of alcohol, walking and talking slowly, and having red, watery eyes. His performance handling vegetables on his shift was no different than usual, however.

The supervisor who first noticed the symptoms acknowledged at the hearing that the grievant had not performed as if he were impaired. It was his odor and visible symptoms that alerted his supervisor to a potential problem. Blood-alcohol and urine tests proved he was under the influence to the extent he needed to be driven home.

The grievant admitted he had been drunk the preceding night after attending a party. He also admitted consuming one beer before coming to work in the morning. He said his conduct at the party was unusual, prompted by his concern over his wife's recent diagnosis with lupus.

I found that the employer's evidence proved just cause for discipline based on prohibited intoxication. On the basis of the mitigating circumstances of the stress caused by the wife's condition, however, and the grievant's candor during the investigation, as well as his long tenure and excellent performance history, I found that discharge was too severe a penalty. I ordered his reinstatement, but without back pay. I also set as a condition of reinstatement that, if the grievant came to work under the influence again, he could be summarily terminated. This is known as a "last chance" reinstatement remedy in arbitration.

Arbitrators created that remedy in the late 1980s when alcohol and drug use, both on and off the job, were affecting the ongoing employment of many in all employment settings. Discharges, required under many employers' rules, were resulting in disastrous financial losses in families as well as problems for employers in replacing employees, some with high skills and experience, on short notice. Judges were ordering diversion treatment in lieu of incarceration for criminal misconduct such as repeat DUIs. Employers agreed that good employees might benefit from a similar "second chance" at recovery before suffering the severe penalty of discharge.

Just Cause Example #3:
Abuse of Complaint Procedure

In a complicated public-sector case in 2012, a community-college employer discharged an instructor for failure to abide by express employment conditions regarding respectful conduct. The evidence showed the instructor had filed frequent complaints against his supervisors and co-workers

216

through the college's internal complaint procedure. His superiors, after investigation, determined the complaints were frivolous and baseless and constituted harassment.

The applicable contract language on which the employer relied in pursuing the termination, and on which the union relied as well in defending his complaints, was as follows:

PROMOTION AND MAINTENANCE OF A RESPECTFUL WORKPLACE

All employees shall be expected to interact with co-workers and the public in a professional, respectful manner. This includes refraining from any type of behavior, action, or language that could be reasonably perceived as hostile, discriminatory, intimidating, violent, or abusive. Harassment is defined as any verbal, visual, or physical behavior reasonably perceived by the receiver as unwelcome or offensive and refers in a demeaning way to a person's race, religion, color, sex, marital status, national origin, age, sexual orientation, disability, pregnancy, or family relationship; creates a hostile or adverse work or educational environment; and subjects employees or students to different terms or conditions based on the characteristics listed above. In the context of curriculum outcomes and subject matter of a course, harassment does not include exposure to or discussion of knowledge with which one disagrees.

An independent investigator, known to be fair and impartial, had determined 45 of the 47 complaints were meritless. She determined the grievant had engaged in an abusive pattern of harassment. Curiously, neither the union nor management offered any of the complaints in evidence, so I could not evaluate them independently. The union's main contention was that the grievant had the right to complain and should not have been fired for exercising it.

The grievant was warned that any further abuse of the complaint procedure would lead to discipline or discharge, but he continued to file complaints the employer deemed frivolous. Neither party showed me any of them, however, so I accepted management's conclusion.

Witnesses testified the grievant regularly interrupted speakers during department meetings, used obscenities at staff meetings (especially regarding female supervisors), and refused to cooperate with time limits placed on staff for courtesy and fairness to all who wished to speak. Other employees reported they felt intimidated when he followed them in the parking lot.

The grievant contended all his complaints had been proper whistle-blowing complaints. He emphatically denied using offensive or demeaning language referring to race, but did not deny using offensive comments about women. He contended the female investigator who found most of his complaints to be frivolous had conducted a witch hunt against him, and he claimed he was a victim of sex discrimination. He did not deny following other employees in the parking lot, nor give an explanation for such behavior.

I found, based on the evidence as a whole, that the employer proved just cause. I upheld the discharge in full.

Recalling that there had been a sheriff's deputy in the hearing at all times, I gave my husband a description of the grievant and told him to call the police if a man answering that description ever showed up at our door. Such are the fruits of this work, on occasion.

Just Cause Example #4:
"Zero Tolerance" and the "Red Light Exception"

After 2000, when the use of video equipment began to increase in frequency, I heard two successive cases involving discharges of bus drivers whose conduct was observed on tapes that supervisors had retrieved from buses and bus stops. The first such case arose in Colorado in 2008 and the second in California in 2010.

The Colorado bus driver was observed on tape using his personal cell phone while driving. He was Ethiopian and spoke in his native tongue on the phone, so the supervisor could not understand the brief conversation when watching the tape. Nevertheless, the supervisor concluded he had used his phone in violation of the bus company's "Zero Tolerance" work rule, which was incorporated by reference in the collective-bargaining agreement through an express requirement that drivers follow work rules (which included no cell phone use).

The Zero Tolerance rule referenced immediate termination as the appropriate penalty. Relying on the video, the supervisor issued an immediate letter of termination to the driver. The union grieved the discharge, but the case did not get to hearing for a full year, during which time the driver was unemployed and unable to obtain substitute employment.

The union presented evidence showing there was a "Red Light" exception to the Zero Tolerance rule. A driver's "brief emergency use of a cell phone" was authorized. The driver testified his wife had been ill during the night before his cell phone use occurred. She had promised to go to the doctor and then call her husband to tell him the nature of her medical issue. He said he had received a phone buzz notifying him of her call, then waited to call her back during a brief stop after he heard the buzz. His call to his wife lasted about one minute. The location of the call and the length of time it lasted were confirmed by the videotape.

Management argued that the Red Light exception was intended to apply only when the emergency concerned the bus, but the union argued the grievant had not been informed of that limitation. Management offered no proof showing the grievant ever received the explanation.

I found, under the circumstances, the grievant's use of the cell phone was not just cause for termination. The grievant reasonably believed it was authorized by the Red Light exception. Further, the driver showed responsibility in using the phone only after the bus stopped moving. Finally, the supervisor failed in their duty to conduct a fair investigation before determining that the grievant's use of the cell phone had violated the Zero Tolerance policy and justified instant termination without further investigation. For those reasons, I granted the grievance, reinstated the driver with full seniority and back pay, and ordered the employer to fulfill its duty to investigate in all future discipline cases.

Just Cause Example #5:
Video Cameras Miss Important Details

In the California case, the bus driver had been verbally confronted by a passenger as he exited the bus and a physical encounter then ensued between the two men. The entire episode was caught on two successive video cameras, one on the bus, the other outside at the bus stop. The supervisor who watched the videos discharged the driver for violent conduct initiated by the driver.

Management showed the videos at the hearing and stated the case was simple. The driver had left his seat after the passenger appeared to speak to him, then followed the passenger off the bus in violation of his duty. Then the driver appeared to attack the passenger outside.

The union responded by stating the case was more complicated than it appeared. The passenger had initially boarded the bus carrying a liter-sized glass jar with an unknown liquid inside. The driver told the passenger liquids were prohibited on the bus, so the jar should be secured in the passenger's backpack. The passenger refused to comply. When the bus reached the end of the line, the passenger requested a transfer, which was required in order to reach a more distant destination on the same bus. The driver said there was a charge for the transfer and handed him a transit manual. The passenger said he didn't have any money and needed to get to the further location right away. Still aware the passenger was carrying an unknown (and potentially dangerous) substance in a jar, the driver gave him a courtesy transfer and continued on the route.

When the bus eventually arrived at the passenger's intended stop, the passenger assaulted the driver verbally, saying "F—you" as he was departing, then threw a heavy object onto the driver's lap. The driver, thinking the object was the bottle of liquid, testified that he was afraid and followed the passenger out the door, yelling, "Get that bottle off my bus." The driver said the passenger then turned and jabbed him in the ribs, knocking him to the ground. Because of its camera angle, the video did not show the jab. It only showed the driver grabbing the passenger's legs, then pulling him down. The two men then rolled behind a bench and were out of sight in the video from that point on. Neither the video on the bus or the one outdoors had a voice recording, so none of the conversations could be heard on tape. Also, the view of the conflict outside the bus was unclear as other passengers and a large trash can were in the area and blocked the camera's line of sight. The driver testified further that he was surprised to learn, when he went back on the bus, that the heavy item the passenger had thrown at him was the transit manual, not the glass jar.

I found the driver's testimony credible. The passenger did not appear, so there was no testimony contradicting the driver's story. Even though the driver should probably have seen that the object the passenger threw as he exited the bus was the transit manual, not a glass jar, his decision to exit the bus was not entirely prohibited. Managers had previously told drivers they could fight back if they were assaulted while they were in their seats. In view of that finding, as well as the driver's testimony that the passenger had initiated the physical confrontation outside the bus, I reinstated the driver. Due to his poor judgment, however, in assuming the passenger was dangerous and that the bottle might contain a dangerous substance, I found there was just cause for some disciplinary action and reduced the discharge to a six-month suspension with no loss of seniority. Evidence showed drivers had been trained to ask questions and avoid reaching improper conclusions about passengers' behaviors.

Just Cause Example #6:
The Teacher-Coach Loses His Extra Job

The grievant in this 201 case was a long-tenured high school teacher who had held an extra-duty assignment as football coach. He was well-respected in the community and often led his team to victory at state tournaments.

In two successive summers he volunteered to chaperone team members when they attended a school-sponsored training camp in a different state. During the second summer program, one of the team members brought along a pair of boxing gloves to use with teammates for fun during evening social times in the gym. The grievant, who supervised these social events, neglected to impose any rules on the boxing and did not insist on use of head protection by any of the participants. Suddenly, while he was watching the boys box, one boy fell and struck his head on the floor, suffering a concussion.

The grievant brought the boy to a hospital where he underwent emergency treatment. Upon his return to the high school in the fall, however, the teacher-coach was greeted with a notice of termination for alleged failure to protect his students from conditions harmful to health and safety during the summer event. He filed a grievance, and the union proceeded to arbitration.

The applicable collective bargaining agreement contained the following language:

> A teacher, including a teacher who has acquired tenure rights, may be dismissed at any time only for the following causes:...

- Substantial noncompliance with the school laws of the state, the regulations or bylaws of the department, the bylaws of the district, or the written rules of the superintendent...

In fulfilling obligations to students, an educator shall make reasonable effort to protect students from conditions harmful to learning or to health and safety.

The district's opening case seemed to show the grievant had clearly violated the applicable contract language. He had failed to protect students by allowing them to engage in boxing without providing any training or requiring head protection.

The union produced additional facts in its case that mitigated the coach's negligence. First, the summer event had not been a regular part of grievant's teaching role. It was a volunteer event conducted outside of school hours and after the daily training period was finished during the camp. Also, the coach did not initiate the boxing; a student did, when football players were engaged in a more social evening play activity.

Nevertheless, I agreed that, as an educator-coach, he was contractually bound to make "reasonable effort" to protect his students from harm at all times to the best of his ability. The coaches at this school had studied and discussed concussions at length during the prior year. On balance, I reinstated the grievant to his regular teaching position, but without back pay, and removed him from service in any extra-duty coaching assignments for one year due to his lapse of judgment in failing to require safety precautions during the extra-curricular activity.

I later learned the school district had refused to follow my award. The union went to court to seek enforcement of the award, but the grievant accepted a settlement from the district, saying he did not feel comfortable going back where he was not wanted. It is unclear whether he retained his retirement benefits as part of the settlement.

B. CONTRACT-INTERPRETATION CASES

Besides discharge and discipline cases, arbitrators often are asked to interpret unclear or ambiguous language in the collective bargaining agreement. In such cases, a dispute has arisen over the meaning of certain words or phrases or about how the language should be applied under the particular facts that gave rise to the grievance. The arbitrator's duty is to resolve the issue.

If the words or phrases in dispute are plain and clear and convey a distinct meaning, the arbitrator is obliged to apply them according to that plain meaning. Usually, however, the dispute has arisen because the words are ambiguous and each party assigns a different meaning to them. In those cases, the arbitrator's first duty is to consider the agreement as an integrated whole. The particular words or phrases in dispute must be considered in the context of the four corners[17] of the agreement, including any appendices, supplemental letters of understanding, or other documents incorporated by express reference in the contract document.

The evidence resolving a dispute over the meaning of contract language often involves negotiation history, that is, the discussion that took place during the bargaining sessions where the parties made offers and counteroffers before they eventually agreed to the language in the contract. The arbitrator considers what the negotiators' notes show regarding the parties' discussion, as those notes sometimes show the parties' intent in choosing particular words and phrases.

These cases require careful analysis, as the ultimate decision is a determination of whether the parties had a meeting of the minds at the time of the agreement. If they did not have a meeting of the minds, the arbitrator must craft an award based on a reasonable interpretation of the language they chose in the context of the agreement as a whole.

Most language disputes arise when the language applies to a particular situation, but one or both parties did not foresee the situation, so they did not think they were providing for that particular situation. It becomes clear there was no meeting of the minds regarding how the applicable language should apply under the circumstances. In those situations, the arbitrator usually makes a decision based on a reasonable assessment as to what the parties would have agreed upon if they had predicted that the unusual set of facts would arise. The arbitrator must be careful, however, to avoid legislating new language or assigning a meaning that goes beyond the ordinary meaning of the words or phrases. It is a delicate exercise that can entail looking at industry practice and public policy as well as using a dictionary and relying on common sense.

Contract-Interpretation Example #1:
Airport Redesign Causes Shuttle Changes

An interesting private-sector case involving language-interpretation arose in the context of the unanticipated redesign and reconstruction of a big-city airport in 2010.

Major design changes occurred in the network of roads in and around the airport terminals and surrounding private hotels. Those changes affected the normal access and egress for hotel shuttles carrying passengers and hotel guests between hotels and terminals.

Two of the affected hotels were owned by a single chain but were operated separately. One was unionized, the other was not. The hotels had always run separate shuttle services to and from the airport for guests. The shuttle service at the unionized hotel ran on an "on-demand" basis, and members of the bell staff served as drivers. Bell staff frequently received gratuities for the personal service. The other hotel ran shuttle service on a regular schedule, using multi-occupant vans driven by contracted drivers.

Management at the two hotels decided to collaborate on shuttle trips for expediency in using the new roadways. The vehicles and drivers at the non-union hotel would henceforth transport the guests of both hotels to and from the airport, using regularly scheduled trips. Management at the unionized hotel did not negotiate with the union before agreeing to the change.

Upon being notified of the change, bell staff promptly filed a grievance, calling it an unacceptable subcontract of bargaining-unit work. The union relied on the following language in their collective bargaining agreement with the unionized hotel in pursuing the grievance:

Subcontracting.

a. The Hotel may continue to subcontract the present gift shop and hood cleaning functions.

b. Except as provided in (a) above, the Hotel will not subcontract any bargaining unit work, absent mutual agreement of the parties.

c. Nothing contained herein shall prevent the Employer from continuing to use outside contractors or vendors where their use is necessitated by the absence of employees with sufficient expertise who are covered by this Agreement or when specialized equipment/tools is required (e.g., HVAC repair). In addition, the Employer may continue to use outside contractors or vendors to perform bargaining unit work where the work is sporadic, but the Union reserves the right to claim the work when it is performed on a regular basis (e.g., the use of a sushi chef for an occasional function is sporadic, while the use of a sushi chef to staff a daily sushi station in the restaurant would not be).

I determined the contract language was clear and unambiguous. If indeed the evidence showed the transfer of shuttle service was a subcontract, it violated the contract.

Hotel management argued strenuously that no "subcontract" had occurred, however. They believed the previous courtesy service was simply a non-essential item in the bell staff's job description. Driving was a "sporadic" duty that management had simply abandoned. Those employees were still performing their essential duties. None were laid off.

The union, however, pointed out that each bell staff member had lost the opportunity to earn about twenty dollars per day in gratuities. That benefit had made the "courtesy" service an essential duty, which arose at least once every day for each bellman on duty. The service now was subcontracted to outside drivers, not abandoned. Hotel guests still were able to arrange shuttle service through the bell staff; bell staff simply could not provide the service. As a result, they were suffering a significant change in their compensation that had not been negotiated.

After hearing all the evidence, I found the unilateral administrative change had indeed caused the transfer of a job duty, previously performed daily by bargaining-unit bell staff, to the employees of another hotel. Although convenient to both hotels because of the route changes around the airport, the change constituted a prohibited subcontract of duties previously assigned to bell staff and created a compensation loss. I granted the grievance and ordered the hotel to restore its courtesy shuttle service and reimburse the bell staff the sum of twenty dollars per day for each day they had been deprived of tips they would otherwise have earned.

Contract-Interpretation Example #2:
Double Homicide Causes Police Holiday Overtime

A public-sector contract-interpretation case arose in 2007 in the police department of a small coastal city. No officers had ever before been required to work overtime on a holiday, so the parties had not anticipated a need to determine what specific rate of pay would apply to overtime on a holiday. There was no contract provision covering holiday overtime pay.

It so happened that a double homicide occurred on a Sunday night during Memorial Day weekend. There had never previously been a murder case in that city, let alone a case involving two victims. This circumstance led to the grievance I was selected to hear and decide.

Two police investigators had worked many hours beyond their regular holiday assignments to handle the unusual investigative responsibilities. Specifically, they were each on duty 24 hours straight from 8 a.m. Sunday morning to 8 a.m. Monday morning. The contractual dispute arose over the rate of pay the city used to compensate those officers for their extraordinary overtime work, which entailed sixteen hours for each of them.

The evidence showed the city had paid the affected officers at the contractual holiday rate, double-time-and-one-half, for all the hours they had worked on the weekend. The officers grieved on the basis that the rate, when applied to the sixteen overtime hours was "absurd." They argued that an overtime bonus amount, an additional one-half the "regular holiday rate," should have been included to compensate each of them for the sixteen extra hours they had worked, because of the homicide, after their eight-hour shift had ended on the holiday.

The collective bargaining agreement contained a provision within its four corners that is quite common in agreements but is rarely applicable to specific grievances. It provided as follows:

GRIEVANCE AND ARBITRATION PROCEDURES:
Decision. The arbitrator shall have no authority to amend, modify, ignore, add to, or subtract from

the provisions of this Agreement and shall hold a hearing so that both parties may present their respective cases.

Clearly, when the parties negotiated their agreement. they did not anticipate a situation like a double homicide on a holiday weekend. In fact, they had apparently not anticipated that an officer would ever work overtime on a holiday, as the need had never occurred.

Although I empathized with the grievants' argument that they had performed extraordinary service without extra compensation, I was unable to grant their grievance. If I were to do what the union asked me to do, which was to create a special overtime rate for holiday overtime work, I would be amending, modifying, or adding to the terms of the agreement. Yet, the parties had expressly denied me such an option in the language of their contract.

The union's only remedy would be to discuss a holiday overtime rate with management as a possible addition to their labor contract the next time contract negotiations took place. The new rate would be effective for future events; it would not be retroactive.

Contract-Interpretation Example # 3:
Pay Scale Changes Lead to Unforeseen Problems

A complicated dispute came before me in 2013 after a large community college and its staff union agreed to coordinate the pay scales for two separate programs it had offered over a long period of time.

Both programs offered classes in English as a Second Language (ESL). One was part of the regular course schedule throughout the fall, winter, and spring terms, while the other was offered only in summer. The design of the summer program initially was different from that of the school-year program because its students were mostly foreign students with specific needs for English language improvement. Because of the differences in course content, the pay scale for instructors in the summer program was different from the pay scale for teachers in the traditional course. Over the years, however, the summer program enrollment had changed and all ESL programs had become substantially equal. Since many of the teachers were accepting appointments to teach in both programs, they were paid at different pay rates for the two programs.

What led to the dispute before me was that the union had negotiated a new pay scale for all ESL instructors, intending to equalize the pay scale in all programs. The union assumed, in making the change, that no employee would be paid less than previously and that most, if not all of them would be paid more. Also, the union assumed that any new hires, regardless of their level of education and experience, would be paid no more than current employees with similar qualifications.

After the agreement was reached and ratified, however, some instructors realized their previous pay rate had actually been higher than their new pay rate, so they had suffered a wage reduction. On the other hand, some new hires with similar qualifications would earn more than current employees were earning. The instructors who were impacted negatively filed a grievance, and the union, contending there had been a "mutual mistake" in the final agreement, proceeded to arbitration.

After conducting a lengthy hearing in which many witnesses testified, I took the matter under advisement. I found no evidence that the union had ever communicated to the college's bargaining representatives its goal to ensure that no employee would earn less than previously and no new hire would be paid more than a current employee with similar qualifications was paid. The negotiation process had been fair and without any subterfuge. All pay records of union members had been available to the union bargaining team for its review while it debated proposals for changes in the pay scale. The union had agreed to the new proposal and the contract had been duly adopted by and ratified by both parties.

In addition, the parties had expressly prohibited the arbitrator from making any equitable changes, such as those the union requested in the grievance, based on the alleged "mistake" that had occurred. Unfortunately, the union simply had failed to calculate how the new pay scale would apply to each of its bargaining-unit members. Although I felt sorry for the teachers who had been adversely affected by the union's mistake during bargaining, it was not within my role as arbitrator to make any correction, as I would be adding or changing language that the parties agreed upon in bargaining.

Every arbitration case is new and different from every other case. Although cases sometimes follow a familiar pattern, the particular facts and issues in each case are unique and require careful analysis. Unlike a judge in a court case, who may write a brief decision as short as one page, an arbitrator usually writes a comprehensive *Opin-*

ion and Award in which all the evidence is summarized and the rationale for why one party has prevailed and the other party has lost is carefully developed. The particular elements that every arbitration award includes are:

- Introduction of the Parties
- Statement of the Issue in Dispute
- Relevant Provisions of the Collective Bargaining Agreement
- Summary of the Facts
- Positions of the Parties
- Analysis and Decision of the Arbitrator
- Award

My decisions usually ran between fifteen and twenty pages. Often, however, they exceeded thirty pages and the longest was nearly sixty pages long.

One of the main duties of the arbitrator is to educate the parties on what their labor contract means and where the losing party went wrong in interpreting the language incorrectly. The arbitrator strives to assist the parties, who are often represented by labor-relations advocates who are not lawyers, to go forward with a correct understanding of their contract and its application, so they will avoid future violations.

The arbitrator can never give legal advice to either party. In cases like the ESL teachers' pay inequity case, for example, the teachers whose pay resulted from the union's failure to compute every teacher's new pay scale before agreeing to the contract language may have had a potential claim for negligence against their union, but as the arbitrator, I had no right to suggest it. Similarly, in the police overtime case, an arbitrator would be reluctant to suggest that the parties should try to negotiate, in this example, a provision in the subsequent agreement that would change the pay scale in such a way as to repair the damage that had resulted to some employees from the language the union had agreed upon. This is outside the scope of an arbitrator's work.

I always knew that my role was only to decide whether the parties had violated their established agreement. If the contract itself was flawed, it was not my job to suggest changes to it. Although I sometimes felt helpless when I issued an opinion in which I felt I had been unable to establish a fully just result, I believe overall that the arbitration system brings fairness and closure to many situations that would otherwise incur lengthy litigation or remain unresolved.

Balancing Parenthood with Professional Life

⊸⊱

For the first fifteen years that I served as arbitrator, I continued to be an advocate in my civil law practice, regularly handling land-use, real estate, probate, and personal injury matters for individual clients. My professional duty was to represent the individual interests of my client against the opposing party.

When I worked as an arbitrator, however, I did not represent either party. I was the impartial judge in their conflict. My loyalty was to the collective bargaining agreement—to the negotiated contract—of the parties who had mutually selected me, to listen to their evidence and reach a fair result in their dispute.

In other words, I had to put on one hat in my law practice cases and a different hat in my arbitration cases. When I was in the office or in court with a civil-law client, I put on my "advocate's hat" and was loyal to a person. When I was in an arbitration hearing, I wore my "arbitrator's hat" and was impartial. When I wrote pleadings or demand letters as a lawyer, my goal was to persuade that my position was the correct one. When I wrote arbitration opinions, my goal was to explain and apply the private law that the parties had agreed upon in their collective bargaining agreement.

Interestingly, I found that being a mother to two young children provided good practical training and experience for playing my dual role as a professional dispute-resolver. As a mother, I had to discipline each of my children when they misbehaved and I had to defend them against outside dangers, including bullies. At other times, however, I had to listen to both children and administer fair and just advice when they were engaged in a dispute with each other according to the "collective bargaining" rules of our home. Sometimes I had to administer appropriate discipline when I determined one of them created the conflict and harmed the other in some way. One thing I emphasized constantly, however, both in my legal and arbitration work and at home, was that truth-telling is the main factor in achieving justice.

I knew I had chosen to lead a complicated life. It was not easy to practice law and arbitration while being a fully-involved mother of two. Each role required commitment, loyalty, and attention to detail. My brother Doug had said it would be impossible for me to do both. Hattie Kremen and most other women lawyers I knew when I first launched my practice chose not to have children. But I was committed to making it all work. I knew Gene was standing behind me every step of the way.

Gene was my rock. He provided the stability and trust I needed. He was a full teammate in the parenting role as well. I could not have been successful in my law and arbitration practice if I thought my children were suffering because I was not at home and Gene was uninvolved in their lives. Gene could not have been a good high school counselor if he thought his children were suffering either. I believe we were better marriage partners and better parents because we used both our brains and our professional training to do the important work of our careers while always staying involved with the children—letting them know we loved and valued them and were there to protect them.

In the beginning of my law career, it wasn't difficult to do my share of parenting. I only had two or three clients at a time, so I could take time off every day to be at home with Melanie and Rocky after school. Both were enrolled at Queen of Peace Elementary School, Melanie in third grade and Rocky in first grade, when I opened my office. I could drop them off in the morning and be back at home by the time they arrived home in the afternoon. I could attend their after-school activities, supervise their piano practicing, take care of Lily (the family cat), and fix dinner. Gene was teaching driver's education at the high school after school every day, so he didn't get home until six o'clock. We usually had dinner together. On Friday nights we all went out for Fisherman's Chowder or Italian food at a local restaurant.

During spring and summer vacations, Gene and I traded blocks of time when we each stayed at home for a half-day or even a full day with the children. There were many options for activities. Gene liked to take them to the library, and he played games with them on the Atari system and the Commodore-64 computer at home. He took them to see every Star Wars movie. Once every summer he took them for a full-day trip in his big yellow rubber raft, floating down the Willamette River and letting them just be relaxed together.

I often took them to the neighborhood park and the skating rink, where I would rent skates for myself as well as for them. On rainy days we planned creative activities at home. I helped the children plant a garden in our backyard in the summer so they could pick green beans and carrots and asparagus for me when harvesting time arrived. We had a succession of pets, beginning with a pair of lovebirds (that turned out to be sick), then a parakeet (who was noisy), then a gerbil (who bit Melanie's finger), and finally, a wonderful cat we named Lily, who remained our family pet for eighteen years.

One summer, Gene decided to build a playhouse on stilts in the back yard and enlisted the help of both children in designing and constructing it. They were six and eight and were thrilled at the idea of having a private place outdoors where they could read or just talk without having parents nearby. Gene bought them each a carpenter's apron and specially-sized hammers, so they could help him put the structure together. It even had a deck, a window, and a short staircase that led up to the entrance door.

When the children were still in primary grades, we hired a responsible high school senior named Ramona, who lived near us, to serve as "mother's helper." Ramona would arrive as soon as the city bus dropped the children off after school, and she would then supervise piano practice, help with homework, and play board games. If she had extra time, she would put a load of laundry in the washing machine and help the kids pick up their toys before I arrived home to fix dinner.

My mother retired from her job with the Eugene School District in the summer of 1981. Beginning in the fall, she came to Salem and stayed with us for a week or so at a time. Melanie was ten and Rocky was eight by then, so they enjoyed spending time with Nana. She would take them to Woodmansee Park and entertain them with stories about "life in the good old days in Brockton," even though she and I both knew those days had not been as good as she represented them to be. Mom sometimes came with the four of us on hikes together in the forests. Once a year we all hiked together on a special five-mile round-trip trail to Pamelia Lake in Central Oregon. We also rented an A-frame cottage at the coast several weekends every year, especially during the winter when we could watch storms roll in over the ocean and build a fire in the fireplace after dark. Our favorite unit at Alpine Chalets in Otter Rock had three bedrooms and a large open family kitchen, so our whole family, including my mother and Uncle Fran, could get together for summer visits, making popcorn and putting jigsaw puzzles together.

Mom, Uncle Fran, Melanie and Rocky at Otter Rock Beach (1978)

Things became more complicated as my practice grew and mother's helper Ramona graduated and married her sweetheart. The children told me not to hire someone new as Ramona was "irreplaceable," and I agreed with them. Melanie was twelve by then and a sixth-grade student so she could babysit for other families. I knew she could be responsible for Rocky at home after school. He was ten and had lots of hobbies by then. Melanie could call me at the office if any problems arose.

Also, we had moved to a larger house closer to Queen of Peace School, so the children could walk home with their neighborhood friends. I trusted them to do their homework and practice piano for thirty minutes each on their own; they were not allowed to have other children come into the house without my permission. I felt this was a good way to build their independence while keeping the line of communication open.

This didn't entirely insulate our family from adolescent shenanigans. One that I learned about many years later was Melanie and Rocky had renamed a certain piece on the piano "Thirty Minutes"—so that, when I asked if they had both "practiced thirty minutes" on any particular day, they could truthfully answer yes. Kids will be kids.

Melanie was an excellent writer. She had a wonderful imagination and wrote stories and poems galore. A singer, she played Dorothy in *The Wiz*, a musical based on *The Wizard of Oz*. A good runner, she was a key member of her class's relay team at the annual Jaycees' Relay, a city-wide event. An excellent swimmer, she rose through all training levels, even becoming a life-saving expert. Eventually she became a scuba-diver and, as a young adult, earned a pilot's license and flew a Piper Cub airplane.

Rocky's hobbies focused initially on magic shows and, later, children's theater programs. My mother bought Rocky a set of juggling balls and a book of magic tricks, and he worked hard at becoming a juggling magician. He wrote jokes and skits, which he put on for other children. Since he knew I had my own business cards, he asked me to design cards identifying his "business" as "Rocco Ganglini the Great, Magician." He handed those out to families we knew who might hire him to entertain at birthday parties for their children.

Gene was always the glue that held me together. When I was busy, I often felt as if I were coming apart at the seams. He and I spent rejuvenating time together whenever the children were off on some summer event like camp. One time, we took a rafting trip together on the Deschutes River in Central Oregon. Eight people were on the raft, and the tour guide gave us instructions before we began the excursion on what to do if we fell out of the boat. We were not provided with head protection, however, as is the practice today.

Later, when we were well on our way and at the roughest spot on the river, where the rapids were throwing us around at Level IV, I suddenly felt my feet pull out from my shoes under my seat and my whole body was thrown out into the water, head-first, by centrifugal force. Remembering the guide's instructions, I worked hard to keep my body going in the same direction as the boat, to prevent being drawn under the boat and to keep my head above water—but I had the passing thought I was a goner. Then, suddenly, I saw Gene lying down flat across the boat, his arms reaching out towards me. I was able to grab one of his hands, then the other. With a burst of strength, he pulled me back into the boat.

Gene (back corner of the raft) and me (middle, behind the lead person) just prior to our emergency on the Deschutes River (August, 1986)

I have always enjoyed traveling to new and unfamiliar places, so I was pleased that my caseload often included hearings in states outside my home State of Oregon. I heard cases in Alaska, Idaho, Colorado, and Utah; as well as many cases in the Seattle, Spokane, and the Olympic Peninsula areas of Washington. I usually scheduled an extra day so I could spend some time visiting places of interest in a new location.

My first Alaska-based hearing was scheduled in the summer, so I rented a car and spent an extra day out on the Kenai Peninsula, enjoying the beautiful Portage Glacier. The glacier glistened against the mountainside in bright sunshine, with tinges of blue showing in its cracks and around its edges. The long daylight hours of the Arctic permitted me to continue driving until after midnight, then I had to close the heavy dark curtains in my hotel room in order to sleep. In December of that same year I had a multi-day hearing in Anchorage, when the temperature was close to zero and daylight hours were only from nine to three each day. In the darkness of early-morning, I was crossing a downtown street that was covered in ice to get to my hearing when a bitter wind suddenly blew against my leather briefcase and pushed me across to the other side as if I were a sailboat on a lake. Arbitration was a somewhat unpredictable and occasionally dangerous profession.

When I had hearings in Seattle and Tacoma, I usually chose to take the train to and from Portland, rather than wait at the airport for a shuttle flight to Sea-Tac Airport then rent a car. The time was about equal for both travel modes, but the train ride was scenic and relaxing and allowed me to do some work while I was en route. I could sometimes stop overnight and visit my brother Doug and his wife Pam on the return trip.

Once, when I had a hearing in Salt Lake City, I invited my mother to go along with me. We rented a car and toured the area. While I was conducting the hearing, Mom attended the visitors' program at the Mormon Temple and learned a great deal about the history of the city and the leaders of the Mormon religion. Another time, when I had a hearing in Spokane, Mom came with me and spent time with her brother and sister-in-law while I was busy. When I had two hearings scheduled in northwest Washington state on a Friday and the following Monday, I took a weekend cruise to Victoria, British Columbia, rather than return to Salem on Friday evening and then turn around and go back north on Sunday. I saw a pod of Orca whales playing in Friday Harbor as I ate my dinner on the ship. Then on Saturday, I went to Butchart Gardens and the British Columbia Museum in Victoria before returning to Washington on Sunday. All wonderful memories.

Melanie and Rocky always enjoyed hearing my stories when I returned from my trips. I sometimes took pictures to share with them and occasionally brought back souvenirs I knew they would enjoy. I would communicate with them via Skype whenever I was out of town, so I would stay informed of what was going on in their school lives and extra-curricular activities and empathize with their struggles. They told me they were proud of me as the parent who went off on business trips to other states. For most of their friends, it was the dad who visited new places and brought back interesting stories. Meanwhile, they appreciated the complicated role Gene had in their lives. Whenever I was gone on travel for one of my cases, he was the parent who cooked for them, supervised their homework and activities, and listened to their stories about problems at school. In fact they occasionally teased him by calling him "Mr. Mom."

PUBLIC POLICY VS. PUBLIC OPINION

⸺⟨᙭᙭᙭⟩⸺

A lthough each labor grievance arises in a particular employment setting and must be decided within the context of the contract between union and management and the evidence presented at a factual hearing, the arbitrator must sometimes deal with opinions expressed by the wider community on the issues involved in the dispute. Those opinions are of two kinds: public policy, as expressed by external law, and public opinion, which is often based on emotional conclusions reached by individuals, including journalists, who have limited facts available to them. Such issues arise most often in public-sector cases involving police and teachers.

One of my most interesting cases of this nature involved a discharge grievance filed by a nurse in a mental institution.

The hospital alleged the nurse had abused a patient and there was just cause to fire her. The nurse's supervisor testified in the arbitration that she had arrived at the patient's room soon after a violent encounter had begun. She observed the nurse placing a pillow over the patient's face multiple times while the patient was acting out violently. The supervisor immediately concluded the nurse's action was intentional elder abuse and that it put the patient at risk of asphyxiation and death. She did not report the incident to the authorities as an incident of elder abuse, which would ordinarily have been required by law when a nurse observed an action she believed was intentional abuse. Instead, the supervisor immediately discharged the nurse.

The union's chief witness was the grievant herself, who did not deny she placed a pillow over the patient's face. She testified she used the pillow only as a protective measure in self-defense, to prevent the patient's spit from reaching her face. The patient was thrashing about and spitting at the nurse, and she had no other way to protect herself. Her use of the pillow was sporadic over a few minutes, and the pillow never touched the patient's face for longer than a couple of seconds, if at all. The nurse admitted her conduct was intentional but contended she had used the pillow only in an attempt to calm the patient and catch spit. The patient was never in any danger of suffocation.

After reviewing the evidence, I determined both witnesses were credible. While the grievant should have called for help from a colleague when the patient began acting out, there was no express work rule on how she should handle the situation. She had no training on dealing with violent patients, nor had she been warned that use of a pillow would be called elder abuse. Her decision to use the pillow was a defensive tactic only.

I found no evidence the nurse intended to harm the patient, nor had any apparent harm occurred to the patient. I ordered reinstatement of the nurse, with a brief suspension as a penalty. I also required that management provide training to the grievant and others like her on defensive techniques they should use in any similar future incidents. Finally, I required that protective face masks be provided to nurses, either to carry in their pockets or to have readily available in all patients' rooms.

The employer promptly filed a motion with the local County Circuit Court, seeking to vacate my award on the basis I had exceeded my authority by second-guessing the supervisor's judgment that the conduct was abusive. The employer's opinion represented the public's views on what conduct was so improper that a nurse should lose her job and her livelihood, regardless of the facts and circumstances that precipitated the conduct.

The court rejected the employer's analysis, however, and upheld my decision, based on the authority the parties had given to me as their arbitrator pursuant to the just cause provision in their collective bargaining agreement. The court relied on my finding that the grievant's use of a pillow was a defensive mechanism and did not constitute intentional abuse under the circumstances. Also, if the supervisor had believed the nurse's conduct was abusive, she should have reported the conduct to the authorities as the law required.

As a follow-up to that case, I did extensive research on the issue of violence in residential-care facilities. I discovered patient abuse was a common allegation. I wrote an article on my research for the Montana Arbitrators' Quarterly publication and subsequently spoke on the issue at a Federal Mediation and Conciliation Service Conference in Seattle. The article was entitled, "Patient Abuse Cases: Violence in Residential Care Facilities."[18] Following publication, I heard many care facilities were developing clear and specific policies and procedures to deal with violent and uncooperative patients and improving staff training. New equipment was available for lifting heavy patients in and out of bed, and managers in many facilities were providing back braces, face masks, gloves and hairnets for nurses and orderlies in order to protect their bodies, faces, and hair from being harmed when working with hostile patients.

Later, I researched the role of public policy in other situations where an arbitrator had reinstated a discharged employee even though the employer insisted the grievant's misconduct required discharge on "public policy" grounds because of its egregiousness. In one Oregon case a teacher's aide had pled guilty to a misdemeanor charge of shoplifting and had shown remorse and an intent to make amends, but she was not prosecuted or convicted of any crime. The employer contended any person guilty of shoplifting was a bad role model for children and discharged her.

After a full hearing on the issue of just cause pursuant to the parties' collective bargaining agreement, however, the arbitrator determined the aide's act of shoplifting did not meet the just cause requirement and reinstated her with a lesser penalty. The employer contended the reinstatement violated public opinion, which the employer called "public policy." The arbitrator relied on Oregon statutes which listed 46 specific crimes that would cause a teacher to be removed from a classroom, but shoplifting (Theft II) was not one of them. Therefore, even if the teacher's aide had actually been prosecuted and convicted of the misdemeanor charge, public policy as expressed in the criminal statutes would not require the discharge to be upheld.[19]

After the district filed a motion to vacate that arbitrator's award, the Oregon Court of Appeals held that an arbitrator's reinstatement of an employee would only be overturned if the award itself violated some "clear statement of public policy, as found in statutes or judicial decisions." Since shoplifting was not one of the 46 crimes listed in the criminal statutes that would justify removal of a teacher, the arbitrator's award of reinstatement did not violate public policy. So, there was no basis to grant the motion to vacate.[20]

In my article about the aide's shoplifting case, I emphasized there is an important difference between the "public policy" of arbitration, which is based on statutes and judicial opinions,[21] and "public opinion," which is based on conclusions about justice that community members often draw when they learn about misconduct through the media but do not know the law or the full story that an arbitrator learns in the context of a hearing. I cited as an example a case in which an employee had been fired for a first offense of failing a drug test. The arbitrator reinstated the employee because of a provision in the parties' labor agreement that required referral of any employee failing such a test to the Employee Assistance Program or counseling after a first offense. If the drug-affected employee had been a commercial truck driver whose license was taken pursuant to an applicable state statute, the arbitrator's decision granting reinstatement might have been reversed, as the award would have violated the public policy of the motor vehicle statutes.

My article was published in the annual Proceedings of the University of Oregon Labor and Education Center Publication, entitled "Public Opinion vs. Public Policy: ERB and the Courts are Gradually Eliminating Confusion Over the Meaning of 'Public Policy' in ORS 243.706."[22]

In the 1990s, the issue of child abuse through "grooming" was constantly in the news. One of my cases involved an issue of potential grooming by a school custodian who was observed several times talking with fifth-grade girls during their lunch period and distributing candy to them. The custodian's supervisor first warned him to stop, then later observed him interacting with the students again.

When confronted, he argued that the girls had initiated the contact by asking for more of his jokes. The supervisor reassigned the custodian to an evening shift as discipline, but the union grieved the reassignment as being excessive; a written reprimand would ordinarily have been appropriate after a warning. In that case, I upheld the reassignment as I agreed there was a grave risk to the District if the custodian remained near the girls. Maybe I was influenced by public opinion, but I also relied on my maternal instinct.

In the final years of my arbitration career, I was selected to hear several cases involving police officers who were disciplined for alleged use of excessive force in arrests. In each of those matters, the officer's supervisor had not observed the event, but was influenced by the arrestee's accusations against the officer as well as written reports filed by observing witnesses who stated they believed the officer's behavior was "excessive" or "abusive." Each of those cases had led to outbursts of public opinion against the local police. In each case, however, the full evidence, which included cross-examination of the reporting witnesses and sometimes a video of the scene, convinced me the officer had followed proper protocols and legal standards during the arrest. Therefore, I granted both the grievances and reversed the disciplinary actions.

In the course of my career, I joined a number of professional labor-relations organizations, including Montana Arbitrators Association, Society of Professionals in Dispute Resolution (SPIDR), and Labor and Employment Research Association (LERA). I was frequently invited to speak at their conferences and workshops on topics from my recent cases and other research. As a follow-up, I sometimes wrote an article for publication in the organization's professional journal. Advocates appreciated hearing arbitrators' comments about labor-relations issues they had encountered in their own cases. Not only did such events help advocates broaden their advocacy skills, but they provided an opportunity to observe and evaluate the arbitrators whose names appeared on arbitrator lists.

After noticing that the participation of women and men in leadership roles was unequal in the labor relations profession, I prepared a conference presentation on that topic. I was often the only woman in the room, besides an occasional female grievant or witness. Not only was a woman arbitrator a rarity but there were extremely few women advocates representing workers and management as well. When I attended my first labor law conference in Seattle in 1986, over four hundred men attended but only a handful of women. Although more than twenty years had passed since the Civil Rights Act of 1964, the labor-relations community still had not evolved as the law intended. I did some research on actual statistics and presented my results at a National Conference on Peacemaking and Conflict Resolution in 1993. Subsequent to the presentation, my research was published in an article entitled "Gender and Power in the Workplace."[23] Among the statistics from a 1992 study that I cited in the article were the following:

1. Thirty-nine percent of unionized workers in the private sector were women, but only nine percent of union leaders and six percent of national union presidents were female.

2. Forty-one percent of executive, administerial, and managerial employees in the private sector

were women, but only eleven percent of high-ranking managers and three percent of top-level administrators were women.

3. Ten percent of labor arbitrators on FMCS and AAA national rosters were female.

In other words, twenty-eight years after the civil rights legislation passed, the gender balance of labor-relations leadership still did not reflect the makeup of the American workforce even though the workforce itself had slowly become more gender balanced. The postal service was hiring significant numbers of women as letter carriers, postal clerks, and mail handlers, but few of them were earning promotions to management roles. The wages being paid to women professionals were significantly lower than wages paid to their male colleagues, just as the wages of women workers were still less than seventy percent of wages being paid to males for comparable work. There was still a long way to go to establish gender equality in employment.

I also spoke on a panel and wrote an article on the use and abuse of alcohol and drugs, which had frequently been an issue in my discipline and discharge cases. The article was entitled "Alcohol and Drug-Related Issues in Public Sector Arbitration Cases: 1982–86."[24] The article analyzed issues such as: (1) addiction as a mitigating factor to a charge on drunkenness on the job; (2) drug and chemical testing; (3) fair and adequate investigation; (4) strict conditions on reinstatement; and (3) last-chance agreements.

In the 1990s, employers generally had no tolerance for misconduct related to substance use. I saw long-term employees lose their jobs due to substance addiction that was treatable or a single episode of intoxication that had shocked management and led to immediate discharge. Also, I found that management sometimes treated ordinary employees differently from management-level staff when they noted signs of intoxication at work. This was patently unfair.

Alcohol was a legal beverage for all adults. Marijuana, though illegal at that time, was becoming more widely used in social situations for people of all economic levels. It seemed to me that employees should be given reasonable opportunities to correct their behavior before being discharged for a lapse of sobriety. One solution I found was a "last-chance agreement," by which an employer could suspend, rather than fire, an employee, on the condition the employee pursue counseling or rehabilitation. Any further event related to substance use would be cause for immediate discharge. Another solution was to implement a reasonable policy for alcohol and drug-testing that would apply equally to all employees, including managers. I found through my research that other arbitrators agreed with my compassionate approach.

Another interesting role I played as arbitrator was deciding public-sector cases involving fees that unions were authorized to charge employees who opted out of union membership on First Amendment grounds. By law, these employees received the benefits of the union's collective-bargaining work because their jobs were included in the applicable bargaining unit. So, although they did not pay dues for membership, they were required to pay reasonable fees for the union's services in bargaining and conflict-resolution. The United States Supreme Court had required that impartial arbitrators who were knowledgeable of labor-relations activities conduct audits in order to ensure the unions charged reasonable fees to those opting-out in a series of decisions beginning with *Abood v. Detroit Board of Education.*[25]

On five different occasions, the American Arbitration Association appointed me to decide such cases, which were known as "chargeable-fees cases." In each of those cases, I was required to review time records and financial documentation that showed how the union spent its member dues and the chargeable fees from non-members.

My duty was, first of all, to determine whether the timesheets of the union's business agents and staff properly separated union-only services from bargaining-unit work. By law, bargaining and dispute-resolution services had to be compensated by members and employees who opted-out alike. The time the union spent in political or ideological activity and social meetings that benefited union members only could not be charged to non-members.

Secondly, I had to determine whether the fees the union charged to bargaining-unit individuals who opted out of union membership fairly reflected their share of the bargaining and dispute-resolution activities.

Two of my chargeable-fees cases involved the Washington State Education Association and its local affiliates. Two others involved the Alaska State Education Association and its local affiliates. The fifth involved a faculty union of the State of California's higher education system. These were complicated cases, in which I brought home multiple boxes of documents to analyze in conjunction with the testimony of the union's business leaders and accountants. I also gave serious consideration to statements by persons who had opted out of union membership but felt the fees the union charged them were excessive. I believed the process was a fair way of compensating the union for the duties of representation they were legally required to perform for bargaining-unit members who chose not to join the union. Reasonable chargeable-fees prevented those who opted-out from being free-riders.

Unfortunately, *Abood* and its progeny were overturned in 2018 by the Supreme Court's decision in *Janus v. AFSC-ME*.[26] As a result, chargeable-fees are no longer permitted of public employees who opt out of union membership. I will discuss issue this further in a later chapter of this book.

I also handled a number of public-sector cases in which the parties were unable to reach a final agreement on one or more terms in their collective bargaining process. Known as "interest arbitration matters," most such cases involved employees in public-safety units, such as police, fire, or prison guards, who do not have a right to strike as a bargaining strategy. As an alternative, the applicable state statutes provide for arbitration to determine the issues remaining in dispute when the union and management reach an impasse.

A number of parties involving police officers called on me to take evidence in interest arbitration matters. In each case, I decided whether the offer of the union or that of management was the more reasonable when compared with the wages, hours, and conditions of employment recently agreed upon in similar bargaining units elsewhere. The offer I chose would then be incorporated in the party's final contract.

My continued acceptability for such cases reflected the parties' trust in my integrity, impartiality, and reasonable decision-making. Clearly, it is an honor to be an arbitrator whose name continues to be selected by employers and unions, including those who have never chosen the arbitrator previously. Selection is confirmation of having achieved a reputation for integrity and fair decision-making—or at least, as my mentor Carlton Snow told me, a reputation as the least undesirable person on the list. Selection as an interest arbitrator is a particular honor because it shows the parties trust the arbitrator to decide what would reasonably have been negotiated by the parties themselves if they had not reached impasse.

My Published Cases

A n arbitrator's reputation is built through publication of their thoughts and analysis regarding legal issues connected with everyday workplace problems. Often, after speaking at a conference of labor-relations advocates or publishing an article in a professional journal, I would receive a flurry of case selections during the following year where the subject matter of the cases was related to the subject of my recent research.

A similar result would come after an opinion of mine was included in *Labor Arbitration Reports*, the national reporter series that publishes selected labor-relations opinions. Unlike court opinions, which are nearly always available as public records, arbitration awards are usually private documents. Occasionally, however, the parties permit an opinion to be published in the reporter series. The case might involve an issue that is becoming common in workplaces and parties are struggling with it, or it may simply offer a fresh look at an old issue.

Over my first two decades of deciding grievances, six of my opinions were published in their entirety in that distinguished resource. I will summarize some of them here.

The first two involved alleged ambiguity of words or phrases in a labor agreement. In each of those cases a grievance had been filed over the application of certain language, and one of the parties alleged there had not been a meeting of the minds. My responsibility was to determine whether there had been a mutual understanding, and if not, whether the mistake had resulted from subterfuge or simple mistake by one party or both parties.

One of the cases, *United Grocers, Inc. and Teamsters Local 162*,[27] involved a latent ambiguity that had resulted in an unanticipated wage decrease for some employees. The parties had agreed in bargaining to increase the deductions that management could take from all employees' paychecks for insurance premiums, based on an agreed formula. Unfortunately, the employees who worked less than forty hours a month were not eligible for insurance, but the wage reduction formula applied to their checks anyway. I had no authority to change the formula or to add language to the contract that would erase the inequity, as the contract was clear and unambiguous and there was no evidence of subterfuge by the employer.

The other ambiguity case, *Down River Forest Products, Inc. and Graphic Communications Union District Council 2*,[28] involved an alleged missing contract term. The parties' final integrated contract expressly provided that certain red-circled wage rates and cash-bonus payments would be paid to employees. There was no reference, however, to a general wage increase, although the union contended in its grievance that the parties had agreed upon such an increase verbally during negotiations. I determined, based on testimony and documentary evidence, that the union's chief negotiator had agreed to the specific language that ultimately appeared in the contract at 4:00 a.m. on the final day of negotiations. There was no evidence that the parties had discussed a general wage increase during that early-morning bargaining session. Therefore, I determined that the contract was clear and unambiguous. Also, the typed version had subsequently been ratified, thereby memorializing the terms of the parties' final agreement. I had no authority to add the alleged missing term.

My third published opinion, *Department of Veterans Affairs (White City, Ore.) and American Federation of Government Employees, Local 1089,*[29] involved same-sex sexual harassment on the job, an issue that had been discussed in a recent United States Supreme Court opinion.[30] In my case, a bully-like male employee harassed a younger male worker in the kitchen of the mental hospital where they both worked, asking him if he wanted a "blow-job." The younger man, who was usually quiet and timid, was offended by the words. He had previously complained to his supervisor about the co-worker's insults, which contained sexual innuendos, and he had told the co-worker to stop using such language. This time the supervisor suspended the perpetrator. At the arbitration hearing the grievant argued he had only been joking, engaging in typical locker-room shop talk between males. I determined, however, that the young man had perceived the words as an unwelcome invitation to a sex act and under the circumstances the words had constituted unacceptable sexual harassment, not simply a joke or shop talk. Therefore, I denied the older man's grievance and upheld the suspension.

My fourth published opinion, *Valley Communications Center and Valley Communications Center Employees Assn.,*[31] involved management's implementation of a dress code without consulting the union for input. The case involved employees of a 9-1-1 center where the work was extremely stressful and fatiguing. They had an established policy of allowing casual clothes, such as printed sweatshirts, athletic pants, or shorts and baseball caps, along with taking naps in sleeping bags on the floor and eating food at their workstations. Management had always tolerated the behaviors.

When a new facility was constructed, however, it included a glass wall that allowed the public to view the employees at work. Management suddenly announced that "beach-like clothing" was no longer allowed, naps could only be taken on couches in a separate room, and food was strictly limited to the break room. The employer had not consulted with the union about the new rules, and the employees were upset. Some said they could not afford to buy new clothes and they needed food for energy while they dealt with emergency calls.

I upheld the union's grievance over the sudden draconian rule-change, based on the fact that management had issued arbitrary work rules that changed longtime practices of acceptable conduct without negotiating the impacts on the employees and considering acceptable alternatives. To save time, I also issued some reasonable provisions in my order that, in the course of the hearing, representatives of both parties said they would accept. For instance, I upheld the restrictions against wearing sweatshirts carrying political and social messages and sleeping at one's desk, but I allowed limited snacking at one's station, to relieve the stress of dealing with emergencies.

After each of these publications came out, I received cases involving similar subject matters, as the new parties had an idea of what my analysis would be like in their cases and they could predict how I would likely rule. It is fair to say that every arbitration case I heard was new and different from every other case, however. Cases sometimes followed a familiar pattern, but the particular facts and issues in each case were always unique and required careful analysis.

Although the specific labor contract was the governing law for each case, I always considered the human issues involved. I knew every worker's second home is the workplace and many of the problems that arise can be cured by considering the humanity of the situation that led to the grievance. For that reason, arbitration is not an automatic process.

WE ADJUST, WE ADAPT. . .

Our family faced a sudden crisis when Melanie turned fifteen. She became physically weak and terribly fatigued with what turned out to be rheumatoid arthritis, a terrible, disabling condition.

We aggressively pursued all available treatment options and negotiated with her high school for accommodations. Sadly, she could no longer play softball or throw the discus or javelin on the track team. She could only walk short distances, so she needed an electric scooter to get from math to American History located at separate ends of her huge high school building. She needed extra time to write exam papers because of her painful arthritic hands.

Her sudden disability caused me to face a terrible dilemma. Should I take a leave of absence from my arbitration work and stay home? Should I trust that her doctors were doing all they could to alleviate her pain, and were we providing adequate assistance? Would I be able to do more if I were at home all the time?

Gene and my mother both advised that I continue with my work. Mom helped out as much as she could, but her own health was deteriorating at that time. Gene no longer was teaching drivers ed because the school district had abandoned the program and young people were retaining private teachers instead. He was at home every afternoon during the week, so I decided, reluctantly, to continue with my regular arbitration work.

Thankfully, Melanie was able to graduate on time and live a more-or-less normal life from that time forward. She even worked as a part-time receptionist in my law office for a while, then worked in a health food store full-time during the summer before she went off to college.

My mother spent twenty-six happy years in Eugene, Oregon. She was proud of her fifteen-year career at the Eugene School District, from which she retired at age sixty-two. She then traveled to Russia and Hawaii on her own and spent two weeks in the British Isles with Melanie in the summer of 1987.

Mom celebrates her 70th birthday in Hawaii (April, 1989).

Mom had some health issues after retiring. She underwent bi-lateral mastectomies for breast cancer, then began to experience balance problems and issues with eyesight. Eventually she fell and broke a hip and became unable to get around without help. She moved to our Salem home in January 1992 and, unfortunately, suffered a stroke and passed away about two weeks later.

During those last weeks, Mom was able to talk to Rocky and Melanie by phone from her deathbed. (They were both college students, Rocky at Oberlin College in Ohio and Melanie at University of Durham in England.) Doug, Pam, and Gene were all beside me at Mom's bedside.

Mom had been welcomed back to the Catholic Church by Sister Joan Jett, a progressive nun and pastoral assistant at our parish church. Sister Joan prayed with Mom, counseled her, and was compassionate in listening to Mom's concerns about gender bias in the Church and her sadness at having been told she was excommunicated for refusing to accept my father's irrational marriage demands forty years earlier. Sister Joan brought peace, joy, and reconciliation along with daily communion to Mom during her final illness.

Uncle Fran, who was always Mom's closest sibling and an important person in all of our lives, officiated at her solemn funeral Mass, which was held in Queen of Peace Church, our parish in Salem. Her brother Rob and his wife Ann and two of their adult children, Buzz and Patti, traveled from Spokane, Washington, for the service. Doug and his wife Pam and their daughter Tracy, who had visited Mom in her final days, came down from Seattle again for the funeral. Cousin Bruce, whom Doug and I had long considered our "little brother," came from Portland with his wife Doreen and their teen sons Tom and Sam.

Mom's early life had involved much turmoil and depression, but her older years had been more pleasant and calm. I felt blessed that she had come to Oregon with me in 1966 and then was able to thrive with a good job and a loving family around her, including grandchildren, for the next twenty-six years.

Three years after Mom's death, Uncle Fran passed away. I represented the family in attending his funeral at the Viatorian Priests' Residence in Evanston, Illinois. A convocation was in progress that eighty priests from throughout the United States were attending, so they all participated, in addition to several of my uncle's colleagues from Loyola University and some former students. He received wonderful tributes for his wisdom and spiritual guidance to all of them. I felt honored to be able to attend and share my own personal memories.

Meanwhile, as I traveled throughout the Pacific Northwest conducting labor arbitration hearings, the children benefited in several ways. I always told them about the city where my most recent hearing had been held. I showed them photos of the mountains in Montana and Alaska and the features of Seattle, including Pike's Market and the Space Needle. Without getting into the specifics of the hearing I had just conducted, I talked about the problems that could arise in workplaces in general and how they could be prevented or resolved. I explained how I would work to make a fair judgment in the case I had just heard, by deliberating all the facts and evidence and reviewing the collective bargaining agreement and any applicable law before reaching my conclusion. I believe, in those ways, I prepared them for their own adult roles in the working world while empowering them to be critical thinkers and reasonable leaders in their own future lives.

BEGINNING IN THE EARLY 1990S, CLIMBING STAIRS gradually became a struggle for me. I began limping for no apparent reason. My legs seemed to become inexplicably deformed, my knees bumping into each other strangely and my feet separating more and more from each other, thereby causing me to waddle like a duck. Around the same time, I noticed the tissues around my hips swelling and my jeans and skirts did not fit anymore. My balance was becoming a problem, and I became fatigued when I walked even a short distance.

By the end of the decade, I was experiencing ever increasing pain if walking or squatting as well as when sitting down or getting back up. I thought I was not getting enough physical exercise and was growing old at an early age, so I put up with the problem for several years. Eventually, however, I realized the pain and stiffness were much more serious than I had allowed myself to admit. I needed to determine the causation and hopefully, get appropriate medical treatment.

An orthopedic specialist informed me I was suffering from serious bone-on-bone osteoarthritis due to a congenital, but previously-undiagnosed condition: hip dysplasia. I told him I had always been a klutz in physical activities and sports, but I was a good walker and hiker and was never aware I had a birth defect.

The orthopedist said I was a candidate for total hip replacements and would probably need knee replacements as well. Then, shaking his head, he cautioned that I was "too young" to begin any of those procedures at my age, which was fifty-six at the time of the consultation. "You'll just have to take Advil for a few years," he added, "until the pain gets so severe you can't take it anymore. Hopefully, by then you'll be old enough that the joint replacements will last long enough that they won't need to be replaced a second time."

While Gene and I were disappointed with the advice, we decided to deal with it. We sold our two-story house and moved to a one-story condominium with a walk-in shower, as my mobility had become seriously impacted, and I seemed to be aging quickly. I decided to wind down my law practice and pursue only arbitration work from that time on, working out of my home office and using public transportation and taxis for hearing travel. I was not ready to retire. I just needed to simplify my complicated and physically demanding life.

Gene retired from his teaching position with the Salem School District in 1998. We decided we should begin enjoying some early retirement travels. When we were first married, we had talked about seeing as much of the world as possible and enjoy meeting people of different cultures. Now was the time.

Our itinerary over the next several years took us around the globe, including the Route of the Maya, The British Isles, Egypt, Israel, several river cruises in Europe and Russia, India, and Costa Rica.

Gene and I enjoy visiting the Taj Mahal in India (2011)

Our first trip was to South Korea to visit our son Rocky, who was teaching English as a Second Language at a private school in Daegu. Using bus and train travel to limit my need to walk, Rocky took us to visit Buddhist temples and monasteries and showed us the wonderful scenery of Korea and introduced us to Korean food. We then went on to China, where we toured Beijng and Xian and met Chinese people who were still adjusting to their new openness to the world.

Another trip was to Australia and New Zealand, where we met some of the kindest and most hospitable people on earth. We snorkeled on the Great Barrier Reef, drove along the Great Ocean Road and talked to Aborigines in Australia. We visited Auckland and Rotorua in New Zealand and attended a Maori festival.

Later, we traveled to Scandinavia: a week each in Denmark, Norway, and Sweden. On that trip, we stayed mostly in student quarters in local *folkhochschule*s, which resemble American community colleges.

We also traveled to Portugal and Spain, where we visited fishing villages, castles, cathedrals, and Roman ruins, all along the route beginning at Cascais and Lisbon on Portugal's Atlantic coast and continuing through Madrid and Toledo in central Spain and eventually arriving in Barcelona. During that trip, I had to use a cane and Gene had to assist me to the point of carrying me up and down many of the flights of stairs in the old stone buildings we visited.

On a later trip to Belgium, we had the wonderful opportunity of visiting our dear friend Ed Haasl, the priest who had officiated at our wedding. About thirty-three years had passed since that day, and we had a lot to talk about. Ed had left the priesthood within a few years after our wedding, when he was studying Sacred Theology at the University of

Louvain. He met and married a lovely woman there, Margot, and they had raised two sons and one daughter.

After returning from that 2002 trip, I decided to seek a second opinion as to whether it was time to begin my joint replacements. The orthopedist at Oregon Health and Sciences University confirmed I was ready and promptly scheduled the first surgery.

Before the first joint surgery could take place, however, another more immediate medical issue was discovered. My annual mammograms disclosed a tumor in my left breast. After a biopsy confirmed the diagnosis of cancer, the doctors scheduled a full mastectomy surgery and a subsequent three-month series of chemotherapy treatments. I wasn't surprised at the diagnosis. My mother had had double mastectomies at age sixty-two and my grandmother in her mid-sixties. I bought myself a blond wig because I had always wanted to know if blonds have more fun. I subsequently learned that old adage was true. I seemed to get more attention than I ever received as a brunette.

I notified the case administrators at FMCS, AAA, and the various state Employment Relations Boards that I was undergoing a series of complicated medical procedures and would need to take a temporary leave from my arbitration practice. Finally, about two months after the cancer surgery and chemotherapy were completed, my doctors cleared the way for me to return to the hospital for my first hip replacement surgery and subsequent physical therapy.

When I turned sixty on January 11, 2003, my family threw a big birthday party celebration for me at Illahe Hills Country Club. Sixty people came and others sent cards and letters. I was still wearing my blond wig, as my hair was barely beginning to grow back, and I was using a walker due to the hip surgery. I think many of the party guests were concerned I might be dying, as the prognosis regarding my cancer treatment was still uncertain.

Rocky served as the cheerful emcee for the party and told funny stories about me. Melanie read a lovely poem she had written for the event and took lots of pictures of the guests for a scrapbook she intended to make. Doug, Cousin Bruce, and their families all came. My former law partners, Al Depenbrock and Mitzi Naucler, came with their spouses. Our parish priest, Father George Wolfe, gave the opening prayer. Some of the people I routinely served with on the Parish Peace and Justice Commission showed up, as did my friends from the League of Women Voters, Salem Peace Plaza, Inc. and Salem City Club.

Unfortunately, Professor Snow, Hattie Kremen, Sam Blair, Ron McDonald and ERB Chairman Cleveland had already passed away, as had my dear mother and my Uncle Fran. Gene's sister Rose, who had been such an inspiration to me in my dream to become a lawyer, had also passed away due to heart disease, back in 1986 when she was a 36-year-old senior at Lewis and Clark Law School. My birthday party turned out to be quite an emotional event for me, as I was fearful I might be joining these loved ones soon myself, knowing many women who go through breast cancer fail to survive more than a few years.

In April 2004, I underwent my second hip replacement surgery. While I was recovering in the hospital, Gene suffered a heart attack and was admitted to the same hospital. Doctors inserted two stents in one of his arteries. Although I was shocked to learn of his unexpected crisis, I was pleased and surprised a day later to learn he was up and walking. We both recovered at home together, after spending a few days with Melanie in Portland. I then had my right knee replaced in December of the same year.

By January 2005, I was a new person. I was somewhat exhausted from all the surgeries over the eighteen-month period since my cancer surgery, but my mobility had improved and I was still cancer-free. I opted to delay my second knee replacement because I was anxious to resume my arbitration practice and Gene and I were ready to resume our travels. We chose Athens, Greece, as our initial destination, and flew there in March 2005 because I wanted to climb the Acropolis and celebrate my improved physical condition at that historic location. When I reached the Temple of Athena on top of the Acropolis, I told Gene that I felt as if I had just run my own personal marathon and deserved an Olympic medal.

My watercolor painting of the Acropolis
memorializing my climbing event.

After this refreshing time of self-care and recovery, it was time to pick up the plow again. I took the necessary steps to reestablish my eligibility to accept cases.

I realized I could go back to my professional work and operate out of my home office. I was still an active member of the Oregon State Bar, but I decided to limit my practice to labor arbitration and mediation from then on. I had established an excellent reputation among the lawyers representing unions and management in collective bargaining disputes, so it did not take long before they began to choose me once again to arbitrate their cases. I soon began receiving notices of selection from throughout the Pacific Northwest and some cases in California as well. I was very busy with arbitration case appointments for the next twelve years.

My caseload of labor arbitration matters increased steadily, with assignments throughout the Pacific Northwest and in California. I also was appointed to arbitrate a federal sector case in Dallas, Texas, which resulted in two rounds of hearings, followed by an appeal to the Federal Labor Relations Authority. It took five years for the appellate authority to decide the appeal, but ultimately, the Authority upheld my Opinion and Award entirely.

The California cases were especially interesting because many involved police officers. In one of them, a detective allegedly failed to investigate an excessive force charge against a fellow officer, but the evidence did not show he had been directed to do the investigation. In another case, an officer whose partner had accepted a bribe was discharged for failure to report the partner's crime, but there was no evidence the grievant had known anything about the bribe. These were emotionally charged cases because management and the union were both concerned about ongoing public scrutiny of police officer ethics. In each of those cases, I granted the officer's grievance, overturning the disciplinary action that had been issued, based on the lack of just cause.

During the years between 2005 and 2011, our family grew. Rocky married Margaret Young, a poet, and in 2006 they had a son whom they named Quentin. Melanie married Jim Dewey, a history teacher, and in 2011 they adopted Maria immediately after her birth.

Family celebration of Maria's adoption.
Rocky, Margaret and Quentin (left front); Melanie, Jim and
Maria (right front); Gene and me (behind), Christmas 2011

Rocky and Quentin (2016)

Maria and me (2017)

In 2014, my annual mammogram revealed a lump in my right breast that a biopsy showed was cancer. I promptly underwent a second mastectomy surgery. Fortunately, I did not need to undergo chemotherapy or radiation after the surgery, so I could return to work quickly. Three years later, in 2017, I had my second knee replacement surgery. My arthritic knee had begun acting up very badly since going to Disneyland with Melanie, Jim, and Maria the prior year, so I knew it was time for my fourth joint replacement surgery. Fourteen years had passed since the other knee and both hips were replaced. While I was recuperating from the knee surgery, Gene underwent a quadruple bypass surgery.

In the fall of 2017 Gene and I sold our house in Salem and moved to one we had already purchased in Camas, Washington, just a half mile away from Melanie and her family. I reluctantly made the decision to retire at that time.

I was 74 years old.

I wrote this book to inspire you, the reader, to pursue your dreams, especially if those dreams relate to achieving a career that seems impossible due to employment discrimination, either explicit or implicit, or financial insufficiency. Even if you have experienced difficulties in life that have made your dreams seem impossible to overcome at present, there may be opportunities in the future when one might not expect to encounter them.

That was the way my career took shape. I call it "the zigzag route." I do not regret any of the decisions I made along the way to achieving my ultimate dream, because I always used my talents to contribute to matters of peaceful communication and problem-solving. I am proud of the work I did serving as an instructor of French and English as a Second Language and being a mother to Melanie and Rocky Gangle. However, I never ignored my dream of becoming a woman attorney doing work that I had admired in Attorney Cotter, the lawyer from my childhood.

Although I had to accept that a judgeship was not feasible for me, I followed the advice of my law school mentor Professor Snow and achieved a similar career, as an impartial labor arbitrator. Patience, determination, hard work, and trust in myself and others who supported me made it possible to achieve a meaningful career as Madame Arbitrator.

Transformation in 21st Century Workplaces

﹏﹏﹏

"Unions, by and large, are democratic organizations with freely chosen leaders and policies determined by the membership. They concern themselves with individual dignity not only in their aims but in their method. We have no better example of what is worthy of emulation abroad than the workings of a good union."

—Robert F. Kennedy

M y arbitration case selections grew steadily over my thirty-three year career, even more rapidly in the years following my two-year hiatus for health issues than in previous years. At the same time, a dramatic downward trajectory was occurring in union involvement, particularly in private sector workplaces. Fewer and fewer of my cases originated in industrial union settings. The majority came from public-sector sources, including teachers, police, prison guards, probation officers, and other government personnel. The downturn in private sector cases was even greater outside my own region.

The official statistics on union representation in industry and government support my observations. According to the Bureau of Labor Statistics (BLS), as reported in the

Washington Post on January 19, 2018, only 11.9 percent of American workers were in jobs covered by union contracts in the public, private, and federal sectors combined in 2017. By contrast, however, one-third of American workers were in unions in the 1950s. Since public employees had no right to bargain collectively until 1959 (when the Wisconsin State legislature was the first to authorize it), all of those mid-century union workers were employed in private-sector jobs.[32]

The numbers of public-sector unions grew quickly after 1959. The federal government authorized unionization for federal workers pursuant to President Kennedy's executive order no. 10988 in 1962. Forty-four states then adopted public-sector collective-bargaining statutes during the 1970s and '80s. Most were in the northeastern, central, and western regions of the country. Ultimately, in 2017, 38 percent of public-sector employees in these states were represented by unions.[33] Unionized public-sector workers therefore constituted more than one-third of the 11.9 percent of America's overall workforce that was represented by unions in 2017. The downturn in private-sector unionization had indeed been dramatic over the half-century time period when public sector unions were growing

That downturn causes me grave concern. I strongly believe unions have been beneficial to society as a whole during my lifetime—not just the workers represented in collective bargaining, but their families and, by extension, their communities. Unions have traditionally bargained successfully for fair wages, so middle-class Americans have been able to buy homes and send their children to college. Their wage levels tended to lead to increases for non-union workers in their communities as a result of competition. The overall compensation of those non-union workers was usually about ten percent less than the union-won pay schemes for similar work, however. There also tended to be fewer strikes in communities with union workplaces.

My husband Gene was in the teachers' union throughout his career, so the children and I enjoyed health care benefits as his dependents. We always owned our home. Lower-wage employees were able to live decently in apartments and rental homes, while mid-level employees like my mother (a skilled clerical employee) could afford to buy a small house. Many had employer-paid health care and vacations.

I am saddened to see unions disappear. Nearly ninety percent of workers in America are now unrepresented in bargaining. They are powerless to negotiate with their employers for favorable wages, hours, and terms and conditions of employment. I believe the current stagnation of workers' wages and insurance benefits and the ever-widening gap between their compensation packages and the schemes their managers enjoy, which often include stock options and other hidden benefits, is directly traceable to the loss of contractual protections unions used to negotiate for workers through collective bargaining.

Sadly, the workers who produce the wealth of those business executives and shareholders have to work longer hours today than ever before, yet they bring home fewer wages and benefits for their labor. Even more sadly, they lack the fairness protections through dispute-resolution procedures that are included in typical collective-bargaining agreements. When they have a grievance, their recourse is to complain to the employer's human resources officer, not an impartial decision-maker. Most workers cannot afford to buy even a modest home or condo today. Many are becoming homeless because they cannot afford to rent an apartment. They have little or no savings for their children's future education or family emergencies. They have no plans to retire because they fear their Social Security payments will not provide a livable income.

When unions were representing private-sector workers, business owners and investors were more accountable to their workers than they are today. Collective bargaining provided a forum for dialog in which owners and their representatives had to communicate their financial interests in response to the employees' demands. The parties strived to reach mutual agreement after addressing each other's legitimate needs and concerns.

The negotiation process is by its nature adversarial in collective bargaining. But the parties actually sit together and communicate in a civil manner with each other, listening and taking notes as they explain their respective interests. The union's bargaining team usually consists of actual workers from the various departments, rather than a hired negotiator. The management team faces the employees as real people and hears their stories, as well as their demands. Sometimes the negotiation sessions last until the middle of the night. The workers describe human needs for better wages, hours, and working conditions. Management negotiators are forced to explain why they can or cannot meet those demands and what they can reasonably offer in response. Through bargaining, a mutually acceptable resolution is usually reached and written down in contract form. Mutually beneficial relationships based on trust are often formed and become effective at preventing worker unrest during the contract term. The most effective results occur when the representatives of both parties are respectful and honest with each other. It is only when the relationship breaks down that confrontations occur and sometimes lead to strikes.

None of that relationship building is possible in an employment setting where management offers a "take it or leave it" wage package and employees are aware that managers are paid disproportionate salaries and that shareholders are making huge profits. Even the wage increases that are offered to workers are significantly lower than increases that are offered to higher-earners today. As a result, the wage gap has been increasing steadily and dramatically while unionization has been decreasing. According to a 2015 study by the Hay Group, a consultancy, the average wage increase that workers earning less than $100,000 per year received in 2015 was 4.7 percent, while those earning $100,000 to $200,000 obtained a 7.4 percent increase and those who received over $250,000 got a whopping 13.8 percent increase, nearly triple that of the average wage-earner.[34] This ever-growing disparity between the earnings of workers and high-earning managers has not only led to the loss of middle-class living, but it has led to distrust and polarization among people who work together every day.

There has been a tendency to blame foreign competition and outsourcing of American jobs to Mexico and Asia for the losses that have occurred in blue-collar industrial workplaces.[35] A number of other factors have contributed to the downturn, however. Technology and robotics have often substituted mechanized processes for duties that were previously performed by humans in the factories.[36] Also, many large commercial employers, who once hired blue-collar union-represented employees to serve as drivers, janitors, food preparers, warehouse staff, security guards, and other low-skilled workers, began in the 1980s to sub-contract those jobs to non-unionized employers right here in American cities, as a cost-saving maneuver.[37] Not only were the wages paid to such subcontracted employees lower than they had previously earned, but their insurance and retirement benefits had disappeared and the job security they once enjoyed was no more. Even in the public-sector, privatization or subcontracting of many jobs has led to union losses and the resulting insecurity and dip in wages for low-skilled employees.[38]

One writer claims the downturn actually began as early as the 1970s when high inflation and interest rate increases caused the value of the dollar to increase and U.S. exports to decrease, thereby decimating the production opportuni-ties of the manufacturing sector. Unemployment skyrock-eted among blue-collar workers, as 21.2 percent of them experienced involuntary job loss between 1981 and 1983.[39] Other writers point to the trend toward hiring permanent replacements for union workers during strikes, which began when President Reagan fired the air traffic controllers and dissolved their union in 1981.[40]

Another contributing factor for the decline in union membership is a procedure known as "employment arbitra-tion." The process, which is not the same as labor arbitration, involves a requirement by many non-unionized employers that their workers sign a pre-dispute agreement to arbitrate any and all workplace disputes that might arise in the course of their employment as a condition of their initial hire. The clauses they sign, which may seem innocuous and even beneficial, pack a powerful punch because they prevent the employees from going to court if there is a dispute that might otherwise give them a legal right to a trial. Sometimes the employee is notified of the procedure in a booklet that is presented at the time of hire and the employee does not even read it. There is no negotiation of its provisions. Pursuant to the deceptive "agreement," the employee "promises" to submit any claims of employment-related violations to arbitrators who have been pre-selected by the employer or the employer's chosen representative, at a hearing that will be arranged unilaterally by the employer and will be conducted according to procedural rules that are either pre-determined or non-existent. Usually the employee has little, if any, opportunity to present witnesses or to gather documentary evidence that is in the possession of the employer.[41]

At first blush, the process appears to mirror labor arbitration, while avoiding the involvement of unions and payment of dues. Many employees believe the deceptive agreement is the same as a collective bargaining agreement. So, if a union attempts to organize such a workplace, it often runs into opposition from the workers because they mistakenly believe they do not need a union to protect their employment rights. Even some labor arbitrators believe naively that employment arbitration is a positive new practice option for them and that it is similar to their work in arbitrating grievances pursuant to labor contracts, so they agree to participate in the process. Those beliefs are mythical, however. Since there is no collective agreement to serve as the applicable private law, all the arbitrator can do is enforce what the employer has imposed unilaterally regarding work rules and policies, including issues such as promotions, layoffs, transfers, and so many other issues. Just cause may not apply as the standard in discipline and discharge cases.

Employment arbitration was approved by the United States Supreme Court in *Gilmer v. Interstate/Johnson Lane Corp.*[42] The *Gilmer* Court allowed employers to enforce their unilaterally established arbitration provisions in their employment manuals and brochures, even though the employees had provided no input to the terms. In spite of the employees' ignorance as to the specifics of what they had "accepted," the Supreme Court held that individual employees were bound to abide by the "agreements" and pursue whatever complaints they might have by filing a claim in the process the employer had designed. Such complaints might include allegations of discrimination based upon race, sex, age, and other protected classifications, as well as work disputes regarding wages, hours, and terms and conditions of employment. They will no longer have the right to file such claims with the Equal Employment Opportunity Commission (EEOC) or the right to file a lawsuit in federal or state court as well.

In 2018, the Supreme Court also expanded its analysis of the scope of employment arbitration, when it ruled in *Epic Systems Corp v. Lewis,*[43] that employment agreements requiring arbitration of *all* employment issues, including wage and hour claims, and contain express class-action waivers are enforceable. As a result of this case, an employee who alleges that their wages are in violation of federal wage-and-hour law and that other similarly-situated employees are likely affected in the same way cannot enlist the support of those other employees in pursuing a class action. Any other employees who might be in a similar situation would have to pursue their own claims in separate arbitrations. This is unfair, because every other employee would then have to hire their own lawyer at significant expense in order to get the same result the first employee might achieve in the employer-arranged arbitration. Lawyers are reluctant to represent individual employees in wage claims because they are time-consuming and not lucrative to process for one employee at a time. Each employee would likely have to self-represent, while the employer would always have well-paid legal representation available at the so-called "hearing."

A third legal change in 2019, which dealt with class-action waivers, is even more draconian than *Epic Systems*. The Supreme Court ruled in *Lamps Plus, Inc. v. Varela*[44] that, even if the employment agreement's arbitration require-ment is ambiguous and does not expressly include a class-action waiver, the employee who wishes to assert a class action will be precluded from doing so. The only time a class action is permissible, according to the Court's analysis, is where the employer has expressed clear and affirmative consent to participate in a class-action arbitration. There is no likelihood whatsoever, in my mind, that any employer would ever give such consent.

Because of my concerns about employment arbitration, I chose not to accept any case opportunities that came my way under the employment arbitration process. I always chose to work in the traditional labor-relations context only, where a collective-bargaining agreement included a union-negotiated grievance procedure with arbitration as the final step. When the parties appeared before me at a hearing, they each were competently represented by an attorney or a labor-relations professional. No worker had to hire their own attorney. As the arbitrator, I was mutually selected by the employer and the union to serve as their impartial arbi-trator, and both parties agreed to share equally in my fees and expenses. I was equally loyal to both parties to reach a just and fair result, with the labor contract controlling my decision as the law of the case. I did not expect to be hired again by either party for another case.

Although some non-unionized employers might reference the American Arbitration Association rules or the rules of some other private arbitration provider in the employment agreement that the employee signs, none of those rules carry the exact requirements of the ethical Code that applies to labor arbitrator. This is a matter of special concern for me.

I have always abided by the ethical protections that the *1985 Code of Professional Responsibility for Labor-Management Disputes (Code)* contains. I routinely disclosed to the parties, before accepting any particular appointment, all current or past managerial, representational, or consultative relationships I may have had with the union or the employer involved. I disclosed any pertinent pecuniary interest, such as stock or bond ownership, and any family interest in the union or employer, as well as any circumstance that might reasonably raise a question as to my impartiality in deciding the case. Pursuant to the Code, my disclosure requirement was ongoing. It applied, for instance, if someone I knew personally appeared as the representative of a party or happened to be called as a witness in the course of the hearing. It applied if I happened to sit next to one of the parties' representatives on a plane that took me to the hearing and I became engaged in a conversation with that person. Finally, I refrained from keeping a tally of how many of my cases resulted in union wins and how many were employer victories. My rationale was that an arbitrator who tries to balance the numbers may decide a case in a particular way in order to maintain numerical balance, rather than treating the case on its own merits.

Under some employment arbitration agreements, the employee is required to pay their share of the fees and expenses of the arbitrator, which is bad enough—that can be burdensome for the employee. Worse, however, is that in most cases, the employer alone pays the arbitrator and the arbitrator might be a person the employer calls upon frequently. The desire to obtain repeat appointments can interfere with an arbitrator's objectivity in deciding any particular case. It can lead to an appearance, and possibly the actual fact, of preference for the employer's position in the case.

Another recent change (discussed earlier) that has adversely affected public-sector arbitration is that fees public-sector unions were previously permitted to charge non-members for providing bargaining and dispute-resolution services to them were declared illegal by the United States Supreme Court.[45] As a result, arbitrators will no longer be deciding cases like those I decided in Washington, Alaska, and California because chargeable fees will no longer be an issue. More importantly, however, the case jeopardizes the ability of public-sector unions to continue representing all the employees in a particular unit, since some of those employees are not contributing their share of the costs of representation. I fear that the new law could be the death-knell to public-sector collective bargaining for this reason.

I also have serious concerns about the changes that have been occurring in the wages and benefits that employees are able to earn in non-union jobs today. A report by the Bureau of Labor Statistics showed that the inequity between the average weekly compensation of union-represented and non-union workers for comparable jobs in 2018 ($1,051 vs. $860) was the direct result of the presence or absence of union bargaining power.[46] When combined with the value of insurance benefits and enhanced working conditions that unions would have been able to achieve for their members, the resulting difference in overall compensation packages was probably more substantial than that seen in the comparable wage structure alone.

Many non-union workers now have to bundle together two or three part-time jobs in order to earn enough to pay rent, utilities, and transportation expenses, let alone food or sending their children to college. Such workers cannot afford quality child care for their young children, so they depend on relatives and friends on an ad hoc basis or they leave the children at home with an older sibling. Most of such workers lack employer-paid health care, so they avoid going to the doctor when they are sick, often going to work when they should be at home because they lack paid sick leave. If they have student loan debt, the interest on unpaid balance continues to accrue onto the amount they already owe when they are unemployed. Perhaps most seriously, they have no savings for unforeseen emergencies and no retirement benefits.

Many young people say they are content with pursuing the gig culture today, meaning they feel fortunate to patch together several consecutive or simultaneous short-term assignments in music, writing, technical support jobs, personal services, or research, rather than have a routine 9 to 5 job. A large number of people now serve as part-time drivers for Uber and Lyft, using their own private vehicles as taxis. These trends have offered creative options and stimulated independence and flexibility in employment. But I wonder what the long term holds for people who simply live from project to project or month to month, without any plan for future security and no back-up resources to cover the slow periods when no gigs are available or when they or their loved ones are sick.

Meanwhile, technology continues to produce new tools to improve and simplify work procedures, but often the technology causes further cutbacks in job availability. The mechanization of work that used to be accomplished by human beings has led to layoffs.

I believe we need to find ways to bring unions back into American workplaces. Unions need to adapt to the needs of modern workplaces. They need to organize workers who have previously been unrepresented. In some sectors, such as home care workers and part-time college instructors, as well as some workers who previously were treated as subcontractors rather than as employees, unions are making great strides toward improving the wages and working conditions of the people they represent. Legislation might be needed to allow some additional groups, such as agricultural workers and transportation workers, many of whom are excluded from the NLRA, to organize in unions. Congress is more likely to pay attention if constituents demand appropriate changes in collective-bargaining laws to allow unions to regain the legitimate power they have lost. The voters need to demand such change to reduce homelessness and wage inequality and, most importantly, to rebuild the middle class.

> *"True individual freedom cannot exist without economic security and independence. People who are hungry and out of a job are the stuff of which dictatorships are made."*
>
> —Franklin D. Roosevelt

Epilogue

"There is no true peace without fairness, truth, justice, and solidarity"

—POPE JOHN PAUL II

My life story has involved a series of struggles, but no progress is possible without a struggle. My persistent goal was to achieve peace and justice, not only in my own family but in my community and the world of work. It was as much a calling as religious service might be to some people. I knew I had to make things right—for my mother, for the women of my generation who suffered employment discrimination and unequal earning capacity, and for those in my community who were treated unfairly through abuses of power as well as racism and sexism.

I decided as an eight-year-old, upon observing that lawyers and judges were all male, to become a lawyer and a judge. When the timing was not right to pursue my dream of studying law, I studied foreign languages. I thought I could be a translator at the United Nations or a diplomat with the U.S. State Department, but there were obstacles to women serving in either of those occupations. So, I became a middle school teacher, then a college instructor of French and English as a Second Language. Finally, at age thirty-four, with a husband and two children in tow, I was able to enter law school, as a direct result of a major change in federal law, Title VII of the Civil Rights Act of 1964. Once at law school, I learned about labor and employment laws and decided that my true calling was to serve in a quasi-judicial capacity as a labor arbitrator.

I did not achieve my goal without a lot of support from many people. My fourth-grade teacher and a YWCA music instructor saved me from the loneliness and depression I had suffered as a result of the "broken-home" syndrome I had been living with. Those women gave me hope and confidence in myself. The organizations that had faith in me by providing scholarship assistance and the funding I received from the National Defense Education Act made my college education and professional advancement as a foreign language teacher possible. Even though I worked steadily at every available employment opportunity along the way, I could never have finished college and graduate school or mastered native French fluency on my own earnings.

Once in law school, I benefited from the tremendous guidance and assistance I received from my mentors, Professor Snow at Willamette University Law School, the hearings officers at the Oregon Employment Relations Board, the lawyers for whom I clerked at Blair & McDonald, and Hattie Bratzel Kremen, the first woman to serve as District Attorney in Marion County, Oregon, and a successful practicing lawyer. Then, after establishing my own solo practice with the help of my brother Douglas Smith, I benefited from the trust of Attorney Albert Depenbrock, who had the courage to accept me as a full partner in his law firm, and the United States Postal Service and its three labor unions, who selected me as the first woman to serve on their Pacific Northwest Panel of Arbitrators. I fully believe that, without the trust and support of all these people and organizations, I could never have achieved my calling to serve the cause of peace, justice, and solidarity that Pope John Paul II spoke about in his eloquent quotation.

The power of the individual can be a good thing, but it is a myth to say it is all we need in order to succeed in life. Individualism has been celebrated to such a degree that we have lost the ability to see its shortcomings. The downturn in the power of labor unions is forcing workers to go back to struggling as individuals, without the support of a community of workers like themselves or the ability to negotiate collectively and achieve fair compensation and benefits. Without dispute-resolution procedures in place that have been negotiated fairly between employers and employees, and enforced by impartial arbitrators who maintain high ethical standards, there is no justice in the workplace. Meanwhile, corporations can use their power in unethical ways that reduce their workers to the level of poor beggars.

It is my hope that the pendulum will swing in the opposite direction in future years. Through renewed union organizing and improved public awareness of the benefits of collective bargaining, I believe the tide can change. Wage inequities can be reduced and employment security and fairness can be restored.

I believe that the rule of law is of prime importance to maintain the civil rights of all Americans. It is absolutely essential we vote for legislators who value human rights and support legislation for the common good, to benefit all members of the population fairly and equitably. We must choose judges and labor arbitrators who are independent and follow the rule of law, while maintaining the highest integrity.

I am proud to have been Madam Arbitrator.

Acknowledgments

⎯⎯⎯ ✦ ⎯⎯⎯

It took fifteen years to write this book. I began in 2004, after undergoing mastectomy surgery and chemotherapy, then three successive joint replacement surgeries. Unsure of the outcome, I felt compelled to let my children know more about my early life and the reasons I decided to go to law school when they were young. After completing my first twelve chapters, I thought my work was done. My health had improved, and I was resuming my arbitration practice.

Ten years later, I underwent my second mastectomy and the fourth joint replacement surgery. Reluctantly, I decided it was time to wind down the practice and set a retirement date. Then, during a visit with my son's family in Massachusetts, my daughter-in-law, Margaret Young, invited me to attend her writing group and bring along a couple chapters of my "book" to discuss. The participants liked what they heard. They enthusiastically persuaded me to finish my book and publish it. Fortunately, I had saved copies of my published opinions and research papers and was able to reconstruct my professional career and produce the final twenty or so chapters.

I am grateful for the excellent medical care that made it possible for me to finish the manuscript. I owe my life to breast cancer surgeons, Debbie Eisenhut, MD, and Eric Laro, MD, and oncologist Charles Petrunin, MD. I owe my recovered mobility to orthopedic surgeons Ted Vigeland, MD, Malcolm Snider, MD, and Alan Newman, MD.

My long-time friends Cynthia Wall, Andrea Whalen, Rosemary Fulgaro, Carol Hoagland, Maureen Flemmer, and Joyce Crisi, encouraged me to keep writing. My friend Tom Kerns, of the Yachats Academy of Arts and Sciences, and my colleagues in the League of Women Voters, including Jan Markee, Sally Hollemon, Diana Bodtker, Cindy Burgess, and Jean Sherbeck, invited me to give PowerPoint presentations on my zigzag route to becoming a labor arbitrator, which helped form the framework for many chapters of the book.

I especially want to thank the hundreds of labor-relations practitioners representing a multitude of unions and employers throughout the Pacific Northwest, who trusted my judgment and selected me as the arbitrator who would listen to and decide their clients' disputes. It was an honor and a privilege to serve them all.

I am grateful to my editor, Laura Matthews, and my publishing team at Luminare Press, including Patricia Marshall and Kim Harper-Kennedy, for their patience and skill in putting together the final manuscript and guiding me through the modern publication world. And I have appreciated the kindness and respect shown by the Hon. Robert D. Durham, arbitrator Ross Runkel, Attorney Mitzi Naucler, Prof. Brian Jones, and Prof. James Nafziger, who read and made thoughtful comments on my manuscript.

And most of all, I thank my husband, Gene Gangle, and my children, Melanie and Rocky, for their patience and understanding as I spent countless hours over the past months sitting at my computer in my home office working on the book, when they would have preferred I was spending grandparenting time with Maria and Quentin.

Endnotes

1   See *Roe v. Wade*, 410 U.S. 113 (1973).

2   See *Engel v. Vitale*, 370 U.S. 421 (1962).

3   See *Brown vs. Board of Education*, 347 U.S. 483 (1953).

4   Gangle, Sandra, "LCDC Goal 10: Oregon's Solution to Exclusionary Zoning," *Willamette Law Review*, Vol. 16, No. 3 (1980).

5   See, e.g., Oregon Revised Statutes, Chapter 107, 1980 version.

6   See Oregon Revised Statutes, Chapter 426, 1980 version.

7   See *Nees v. Hocks*, 272 Or 210, 536 P.2d 512, (1975).

8   See *Brown v. Transcon Lines*, 284 Or. 597, 588 P.2d 1087 (1978).

9   See *Swanson v. Van Duyn Choc. Shops*, 282 Or. 491, 493, 579 P.2d 239 (1978).

10   See *Craven v. Jackson County*, 308 Or 281, 779 P.2d 1011 (1989).

11   Expedited cases involved letters of reprimand and suspensions as well as contract interpretation issues involving leave requests, assignments, and other questions affecting one post office only. In those cases, a decision was required within thirty days of the event that gave rise to the filing of the grievance. A panel of national arbitrators decided all discharge cases as well as contract issues that affected the nationwide workforce.

12   See *Steelworkers v. Enterprise Wheel & Car Corp*, 363 U.S. 593 (1960).

13   See *Steelworkers v. Warrior & Gulf Navigation Co*, 363 U.S

574 (1960).

14   See *John Wiley & Sons, Inc. v. Livingston*, 376 U.S. 543 (1964).

15   See *Grief Bros. Cooperage Corp.*, 42 LA 555 (1966).

16   See Lankford, Levak, et al., "Did He Do It?: Employer Handbook 'Just Cause' Meets the Collective Bargaining Agreement," *U. of OR LERC Monograph* No. 17 (2003), 17, at 23.

17   The term "four corners" refers to the corners of a document page and, by extension, the four corners of the entire document. Basically, it implies that the only legally binding contract provisions are within the pages of the document. If evidence exists that indicates the contract includes provisions outside of the four corners, it cannot be used in court or arbitration, as it would add to or contradict the terms of the written contract.

18   Gangle, "Patient Abuse Cases: Violence in Residential Care Facilities," *Arbitration Quarterly of the Northwest*, Vol. XIII, No. 2 (1992).

19   See *Salem-Keizer Association of Classified Employees and Salem-Keizer School District*, 19 PECBR 349 (2001).

20   See *Salem-Keizer School District and Salem-Keizeer Association of Classified Employees*, 186 Or App 19 (2003).

21   See ORS 243.706 (1), which provides in pertinent part as follows: "243.706 (1)... [A]ny arbitration award that orders the reinstatement of a public employee or otherwise relieves the public employee of responsibility for misconduct shall comply with public policy requirements as clearly defined in statutes or judicial decisions including... policies respecting... serious criminal misconduct, related to work."

22   Gangle, "Public Opinion vs. Public Policy: ERB and the Courts are Gradually Eliminating Confusion Over the Meaning of 'Public Policy' in ORS 243.706," *U of OR LERC Monograph* No. 17 (2003), at 75.

23   Gangle, "Gender and Power in the Workplace," *Arbitration Quarterly of the Northwest*, Vol. XIII, No. 4 (1993).

24   Gangle, "Alcohol and Drug-Related Issues in Public Sector Arbitration Cases: 1982–86," *Labor Education and Research Center Monograph Series*, Issue No. 5 (University of Oregon, 1986), p.1.

25   See *Abood v. Detroit Board of Education*, 431 U.S. 209 (1977); See also *Chicago Teachers Union v. Hudson*, 475 U.S. 292 (1986).

26   See *Janus v. AFSCME*, 585 U.S. ___ , 138 S. Ct. 2448 (2018).

27   See *United Grocers, Inc. and Teamsters Local 162*, 92 LA 566 (Arb. Gangle, 1989).

28   See *Down River Forest Products, Inc. and Graphic Communications Union District Council 2*, Local 388M, 94 LA 141 (Arb. Gangle, 1989).

29   See *Department of Veterans Affairs (White City, Ore.) and American Federation of Government Employees, Local 1089*, 113 LA 961, Arb. Gangle (1999).

30   See *Oncale v. Sundowner Offshore Services*, 523 U.S. 75 (1998).

31   See *Valley Communications Center and Valley Communications Center Employees Assn.*, 119 LA 1767, Arb. Gangle (2004).

32   Christopher Ingraham, "Union Membership Remained Steady in 2017. The Trend May Not Hold," *The Washington Post*, January 19, 2018.

33   Priscilla Murolo, "Five Lessons from the History of Public Sector Unions," *Labor Notes*, June 11, 2018.

34   Stephen Miller, "Confront Pay Disparity Between Management and Workers," SHRM.org, April 1, 2015.

35   Christopher Ingraham, Note 32, supra.

36   Mike Moffat, "The Decline of Union Power," *Thought Co.*, February 28, 2019.

37   Charles R. Perry, "Outsourcing and Union Power," *Journal of Labor Research*, Vol 18, Issue 4 (December 1997).

38   Andy Kim, "The Pros and Cons of Privatizing Government Functions," *Management and Labor*, December, 2010.

39   Dwyer Gunn, "What Caused the Decline of Unions in America," *Pacific Standard*, April 24, 2018.

40   Perry, "Outsourcing and Union Power," Note 37, supra.

41   Stone and Colvin, "The Arbitration Epidemic," *Economic Policy Institute*, December 7, 2015.

42   See *Gilmer v. Interstate/Johnson Lane Corp.*, 500 U.S. 20 (1991).

43   See *Epic Systems Corp v. Lewis,* 584 U.S. — ,138 S. Ct. 1612 (2018).

44   See *Lamps Plus, Inc. v. Varela*, U.S. Sup. Ct. No. 17-988 (Slip Opinion, April 24, 2019).

45   See *Janus v. AFSCME*, Note 26, supra.

46   "Economic News Release," *Bureau of Labor Statistics*, January 18, 2019.

About the Author

SANDRA SMITH GANGLE EARNED HER BA AT THE COL-
lege of New Rochelle (1964), her MA at the University of
Oregon (1968), and her JD at Willamette University College
of Law (1980). She taught French and English as a Second
Language in Massachusetts and in Oregon. She was admitted to the Oregon State Bar in 1980, then practiced law as a
sole practitioner (1980-86) and as partner with Depenbrock
& Gangle, P.C. (1986-96).

Beginning in 1985, Attorney Gangle was admitted to the
labor arbitrator rosters of the Federal Mediation & Conciliation Service, American Arbitration Association, and States
of Oregon, Washington, Montana, Alaska, and California.
She conducted hundreds of cases as a labor arbitrator, published articles in professional journals and spoke at labor-
relations conferences throughout the Pacific Northwest.

Arbitrator Gangle was declared a Woman of Distinction
by the Salem YWCA (1986), was elected President of Peace
Plaza, Inc. (1995), President of Salem City Club (1998) and
the Marion-Polk League of Women Voters (2004). She
received an Emeritus Arbitrator Award from the Oregon
Chapter of Labor and Employment Relations Association
(2018) and an Ursula Laurus Award from College of New
Rochelle (2019).

Arbitrator Gangle retired in 2017 and moved to Camas,
Washington. She currently serves as leader of a Great Deci-

sions Foreign Policy Discussion Group at Camas Public Library and is active as a watercolor artist and member of Yachats Arts Guild in Oregon. She is married to Eugene M. Gangle and has two adult children, Melanie and Rocco, and two grandchildren.

Made in the USA
Monee, IL
14 November 2020

47693375R10174